LATIN AMERICAN WOMEN WRITERS: YESTERDAY AND TODAY

Yvette E. Miller and Charles M. Tatum,
Editors

With an Introduction by Yvette E. Miller.

Selected Proceedings from the Conference on Women Writers from Latin America, March 15-16, 1975, sponsored by the LATIN AMERICAN LITERARY REVIEW, Carnegie-Mellon University, Pittsburgh, PA., 15213.
This project was supported in part by the National Endowment for the Arts, a federal agency, Washington D.C.

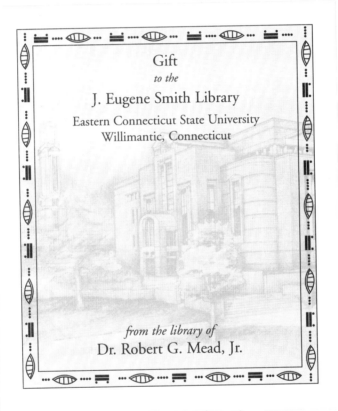

WOMEN POETS

Introduction

by

YVETTE E. MILLER

Carnegie-Mellon University

The United Nations declared 1975 International Women's Year and the *Latin American Literary Review* joined in its celebration by holding a Conference on Women Writers from Latin America during March 15-16 at Carnegie-Mellon University. To our knowledge, this was the first congress of Latin American women writers in the Western Hemisphere. Its announcement was welcomed with great enthusiasm. After many months of intense planning, my collaborator, Professor José Varela-Ibarra, formerly of Carnegie-Mellon University, and I were greatly gratified to see the distinguished and large community of scholars and artists who had come to participate in the event. At the conclusion of the Conference, our guest women authors and participants moved to establish a Center of Inter-American Women Writers. The primary purposes were to promote women writers and their works, primarily in the United States, where they have been heretofore virtually unknown. Since the *Latin American Literary Review* has been a pioneer in the advancement of women writers, I had the honor of being elected president of the newly-formed center. It was proposed that a Second International Conference be held at San José State University for the year 1976, a motion which was greeted with wholehearted approval. It was also established that a program of annual Latin American women writers' conferences should take place henceforth. This program has already been put into effect with the Conference at San José in 1976 and with plans for a convention at the University of Ottawa in 1978 and in Caracas, Venezuela, in 1979.

Among the distinguished guests at the Conference at Carnegie-Mellon University were the women novelists Ofelia Machado Bonet from Uruguay, Carlota O'Neill, novelist and playwright from Mexico, and Mercedes Valdivieso, novelist from Chile. The women poets were represented by Teresinha Pereira from Brazil, Iris Zavala from Puerto Rico, and Silvia Barros, Maya Islas, Mireya Robles, Olga Casanova Sánchez, and Gladys Zaldívar, from Cuba.

At the inaugural session of the Conference, Carlota O'Neill spoke about "The Latin American Woman Confronting the Problems of our Contemporary Society." Ofelia Machado Bonet chose as her topic "The Movement of Feminine Vindication." At a poetry session, the women poets read from their works, their readings being immediately followed by English translations. Selections from those readings are published in the present anthology in bilingual form. Throughout the two days, papers were read by critics on works of Latin American women writers, encompassing prose fiction, poetry and drama. At the closing of the Conference, Mercedes Valdivieso agreed to give an impromptu analysis of two of her novels. The meeting also featured a stimulating panel discussion about the problems of women writers today, which included the participation of authors and critics.

In following the format of the Conference, I will refer briefly to the talks given by Carlota O'Neill, Ofelia Machado Bonet and Mercedes Valdivieso, which followed the interesting opening remarks made by Provost Arnold Weber from Carnegie-Mellon University at the inaugural session. Carlota O'Neill's presentation focused on the need to enlighten the subjugated Latin American woman as to her rights and on the position she deserves in society; an endeavor that should be undertaken by educated women and extended to benefit the greater majority of women whose education is denied or neglected. Ofelia Machado Bonet spoke about discrimination against women in the economic, political and governmental areas, and proposed a series of recommendations which the *Latin American Literary Review* published in its issue No. 6, as follows:

1) to designate a panel to study the status of women on the Continent, and to establish Inter-American programs of concerted action; the panel would present the results of its findings to the *Latin American Literay Review* no later than one year from the date of the Conference;

2) to express the hope that in the year 1975, proclaimed as International Women's Year, women would be awarded Nobel Prizes for Literature and Peace, and that the scientific efforts of other women in all fields might be considered for the awarding of the corresponding prizes;

3) to encourage women from universities, scientific and educational institutions all over the world, as well as the appropriate authorities, to nominate women candidates for 1975;

4) to encourage the governments of Latin America to designate qualified women to occupy meaningful posts in the orientation and direction of culture and education, such as Representatives of International Organizations. as officials of Secretariats of State. Education, and Culture, or of Directive Councils of Education, and any other appropriate institution;

5) to express the hope that governments will name women to international posts designed to avoid armed conflicts and, in particular, to Secretariats of Foreign Affairs;

6) to encourage writers, without attempting to dictate standards upon creativity, to try to rectify, in their works, the false image of women, which does not coincide with historical and contemporary realities, and impairs the integration of women into the proper development of the culture of our times and from political and socio-economic activities.

These recommendations were included in the agenda of the Center of Inter-American Women Writers to be put into effect by a special committee which is now headed by Dr. Martha Paley Francescato from the University of Illinois at Urbana, and by Dr. Beth Miller from the University of Southern California at Los Angeles. Mercedes Valdivieso spoke about her novels *Breakthrough* [*La brecha*] and *The Nights and One Day* [*Las noches y un día*]. As the author explained, *Breakthrough* deals with divorce among the Chilean upper-middle classes, and with the discrimination and repression to which women were subjected twenty years ago in Chilean society. The book dared discuss openly the anguish, terror, and rejection of maternity as the protagonist feels trapped and utterly frustrated in her hopes for a possible emancipation through marriage. She then rebels against the lack of freedom in matrimony. When the novel appeared, it was hailed by the feminine readers as a "breakthrough" for the woman's position but it was also subjected to bitter attacks by the Catholic faction of the Chilean press. The novelist remarked that the attack was primarily aimed at the book's ideology, as it did not contain any erotic scenes or related images.

In *The Nights and One Day* the chronological time has been broken. The plot unfolds within an internal fictional time framed by the events of a presidential election. It is a novel of three characters, one woman and two men. An emancipated woman contemplates the drama her country is living as it is reflected upon her. It is Chile in the presidential election of 1964 and the defeat of Allende by Frei. It is not a political book — Mercedes Valdivieso remarked — but painfully lucid. The husband appears only on the scene when he is seen through the eyes of the spouse. What is unraveling on a personal level is a relationship that does not respect the rules of a unilaterally established faithfulness. A love relationship that the protagonist accepts and has permitted to exist and whose termination she will accept later, in a society that does not merit her respect.

The session concluded with an open forum where the women writers and the critics discussed the achievements and purposes of the Conference and the projects for the future. Here, the creation of the Center of Inter-American Women Writers materialized. The functions of the Center would include several activities, but one of the most important would be the annual congresses, such as the one organized by the *Latin American Literary Review* at Carnegie-Mellon University, to continue focusing attention on women writers.

The essays included in this volume were selected for a representative anthology from the papers read at the Conference. They vary from general topics of interest in the field to studies concentrated on one or two Latin American women authors. Beth Miller studies the representation of female versus male poets in anthologies published in Mexico. In her essay, "A Random Survey of the Ratio of Female Poets to Male in Anthologies: Less than Tokenism as a Mexican Tradition," the author concludes that there is an "obvious discrimination against women writers in Mexican anthologies and in Mexico generally" and furthermore, she points out the overall "sexist discrimination in literature on the part of critics, editors, historians, and anthologists."

Martin Taylor, in his study "Women Intellectuals in Chilean Society" focuses his analysis on education, politics, and literature, vis-à-vis the Chilean woman in a historical perspective. He concludes his paper with a strong critical note which mentions two women writers who were victmized by the system, Gabriela Mistral and Marta Brunet.

John C. Miller's article "Clorinda Matto de Turner and Mercedes Cabello de Carbonera: Societal Criticism and Morality," studies the works of two 19th century Peruvian novelists who mirror national social problems, providing a "positivistic sociological commentary on Peruvian institutions. Clorinda Matto de Turner devotes her attention to the position of the Indian and of the woman while Mercedes Cabello de Carbonera directs her attack against an urban middle-class structure based on hypocrisy and political corruption."

Harold E. Hinds focused his analysis on another 19th century woman writer in his article, "Life and Early Literary Career of the 19th Century Colombian Writer Soledad Acosta de Samper." He analyzes the life and literary career of the most prolific and prominent figure of the century, giving a wide and interesting overview of the writer's literary production that covers essays on *costumbrismo*, literary criticism, travel columns, the status of women, biographies, histories and historical novels.

Ronnie Gordon Stillman's study entitled "Teresa de la Parra, Venezuelan Novelist and Feminist," centers on the author's novel *Ifigenia* which she finds has been neglected by critics. She states that the novel "is the work of Teresa de la Parra, feminist, and it is a valuable contribution to the cultural anthropology of Spanish America. The partially autobiographical tableau allows us to abstract truths about the upper class Spanish American woman, especially in the first twenty-five years of this century." The critic concludes her article on a strong note of solidarity along the following lines: "This novelist and feminist, and extraordinary phenomenon in the Venezuela of the 1920's and the 1930's, integrated her art in the spirit of reform in the hope that women would no longer be sacrificed to that ferocious deity of male supremacy-society-family-honor, as was the protagonist of *Ifigenia*."

Charles Tatum, in his essay entitled "Elena Poniatowska, *Hasta no verte, Jesús mío*, A View of Post-Revolutionary Mexico" analyzes the author's views of the picaresque mode in this panoramic model of modern Mexico from 1910 to the present. The critic finds that the reappearing theme in *Hasta no verte, Jesús mío* is the inferior status of the Mexican working-class woman. He states that "while Poniatowska does not present a well-defined feminist position in her novel, she does not create in her *pícara* a combative, aggressive figure who is unwilling to conform to the constraints and expectations of her society. Jesusa exhibits qualities and attitudes which run contrary to those of the passive female character who fills the pages of contemporary Mexican literature. As a *Lazarina*, who has been forced, because of the social circumstances of her life, into a defensive stance vis-à-vis employers, her husband, her family, etc., it is natural that this stance also manifests itself in her attitude toward men, marriage, the mistreatment of fellow females, and her role as a *soldadera* [camp-follower]"

Ester Azzario studies the works of two Argentinian novelists in her article, "María Angélica Bosco and Beatriz Guido: An Approach to Two Argentinian Novelists between 1960 and 1970." She focuses her study on four novels written by María Angélica Bosco within the decade of the sixties: *La Casa del Angel* [*The House of the Angel*], *La muerte baja en el ascensor* [*Death is Coming Down in the Elevator*], *La trampa* [*The Trap*], *El comedor de diario* [*Everyday Dining-Room*], *¿Dónde está el cordero?* [*Where is the Lamb?*], and *La Negra Vélez y su Angel* [*Blackie Vélez and her Angel*]. The most prevalent topic is the attitude of the upper middle class of Buenos Aires towards life and love, and its solutions to loneliness and lack of communication.

The critic selects three novels by Beatriz Guido which envision Argentinian society from different points of view. In *La mano en la trampa* [*The Hand in the Trap*] it is the violent reaction of youth who rebel against repression, even if it leads to self-destruction: "Repression and violence are the two extremes which determine the drama within the traditional provincial middle class family which lives its memories of past generations and shuts its eyes to reality." The other two novels analyzed, *El incendio y las vísperas* [*The Fire and the Days Before*] and *Escándalos y soledades* [*Scandals and Loneliness*] show the political life in Argentina since the coming of power of Peronismo in 1945, centering on the "disintegration of two families belonging to the oligarchy under the influence of characters and political facts taken from real life."

Corina S. Mathieu studies the novels of Silvina Bullrich from the vantage point of a woman author exploring the intricacies and most pointedly, the innermost feelings of women in love. The critic stresses that this is always done within a specific frame of reference, which is Argentinian society: "Above all, however, Silvina Bullrich's narrative has been primarily promoted to projecting the individual aspirations, anxieties and needs of women in contrast to the role society has called upon them to play." Corina Mathieu points out that Bullrich's female protagonists are rebels constantly questioning the established mores and searching for new avenues, but who find happiness is elusive. Included in the works analyzed are the volumes *Entre mis viente y treinta años* [*Between My Twenty and Thirty Years*], *Mañana digo basta* [*I Will Rebel Tomorrow*], *Tres novelas* [*Three Novels*] and *Mal don* [*Misdeed*].

Gloria Waldman's study is well defined in its title: "Three Female Playwrights Explore Contemporary Latin American Reality: Myrna Casas, Griselda Gámbaro, Luisa Josefina Hernández." The Latin American reality is considered by the author in the context of her analysis "as that particular situation which accepts as given a series of cultural imperatives, such as an inherently hierarchical societal framework based on class, race, and sex differentiation." She then specifies that such reality "more precisely includes the concept of the traditionally submissive and dependent female and the corresponding dominant, aggressive male, *machismo* — the cult of virility and power, and the sanctified states of marriage and motherhood."

Eleanore Maxwell Dial's article, *Los papeleros* [*The Garbage Collectors*], analyzes the Brechtian technique used by Isidora Aguirre, the Chilean playwright, first by filling the stage with society's marginal people. The *papeleros* are men and women who live near a garbage dump. They earn their meager living by going out in the morning to collect paper and other refuse before the municipal garbage trucks make their rounds. They also forage in the garbage dump. Anything that can be retrieved is sold through a middle-man to poor people. It is the lowest employment, "but marginal as it is, there are people in the place who are lower down the social scale than the garbage pickers are." The play is a satire directed to an unjust society — the critic tells us — with the garbage heap representing the microcosm of the society which produces it. Among music and songs the characters are treated mostly with Brechtian detachment. Eleanor Maxwell Dial concludes that Isidora Aguirre "gives the spectator what Brecht calls a picture of the world; she invites the spectator to stand outside and think, as different characters or singers address their complaints or words of wisdom directly to him."

Gabriela Mora, in her essay, "A Thematic Exploration of the Works of Elena Garro," contends that despite the allegations that Elena Garro's works are ideologically weak, the author is indeed "driven in her work by an intense desire to protest the Mexican social situation, particularly that affecting women." Gabriela Mora then makes a division of themes in the author's work, focusing her analysis on four main trends: a) denunciation of socio-economic conditions in Mexico; b) critical exposé of women's situation; c) time; and d) the mysterious and the supernatural. The critic is careful to point out that these themes overlap in the author's works.

Besides the broader outline of these themes described above, specific focuses include those that deal with the misery of the Indians and the betrayed Revolution. The study emphasizes the author's treatment of the repressed and unhappy condition of women within the social Mexican structure.

Among Garro's works examined by the critic are her novel *Los recuerdos del porvenir* [*Recollections of Things to Come*], her short story "La culpa es de los tlaxcaltecas" ["The Tlaxcaltecas are to Blame] and other stories from her collection *La Semana de colores* [*The Week of Colors*], her plays *Felipe Angeles, Los perros* [*The Dogs*], *La mundanza* [*The Move*], *Andarse por las ramas* [*Walking in the Tree Tops*], and *La Señora. en su Balcón* [*The Lady on her Balcony*].

Gabriela Mora concludes that Garro "has both kept and enlarged the Hispanic-American tradition of protest" in the manner of Rulfo, Cortárzar, Fuentes, and García Márquez.

Dale Verlinger analyzes the work of another Mexican writer, Nellie Campobello, in his article "Romantic Revolutionary and Mexican Realist." The critic begins his essay with an insight into the author's personality based on a lengthy interview with the sixty-year-old dancer and writer, in her homeland. He explains that Campobello, like the Romantics, "hates the city and the technology that it represents" and that she longs to escape into the country "which revives the soul." The critic points out that, as the Romantics, she returns to the past of the indigenous tribes and relics, as in her book, *Ritmos Indígenas de México* [*Indigenous Rhythms of Mexico*] where she attempts to record the dances of the early Mexicans. In *Las manos de Mamá* [*Mama's Hands*] she glorifies her Tarahumara ancestors. Other Romantic traits mentioned by the critic are Campobello's subjectivism and her defense of Pancho Villa, a Romantic cause for which to fight. However, the critic stresses that the Romantic characteristic which permeates her novels is *cultural patriotism* expressed in her version of the stark Mexican reality as

captured by Orozco's paintings and described by Azuela. Dale
Verringer associates the author's fragmented style with the chaotic
reality of Revolutionary Mexico which she portrays.

Carmelo Virgillo analyzes Gabriela Mistral's feminine
symbolism in his essay, "Feminine Symbolism in Gabriela Mistral's
Fruta." The poem is included in the collection entitled *Cuentamundo*.
Virgillo states that in this collection "Gabriela defines in symbolic
terms her mission as a woman and a poet, announcing her plan to
reinterpret the world by first fragmenting it and then re-ordering and
redefining it on her own terms." He also affirms that "it constitutes a
mythic reconstruction of the cosmos that is uniquely feminine in the
lexical framework in which Roland Barthes places myth." The critic
probes into the symbolism of the chosen poem, where he finds that the
poet transcends "the familiar sexual connotations of fruit, and
asserting her favorite themes and sub-themes, namely solitude,
maternity and mysticism, with their variants, grief, love, nature and
death, explores the internal reality of an entity emblematic of
woman's ambivalence."

Celia de Zapata focuses her study on two poets, Sor Juana
Inés de la Cruz and Sara de Ibáñez, in her essay, "Two Poets of
America." She characterizes the Mexican and the Uruguayan poets as
two visionaries who shatter the symbols of their respective epochs.
When analyzing Sor Juana's poetry she establishes that alongside the
poet's conscious effort of imitating Góngora in her artistic creation,
there is also a thirst for knowing "this earth, this world, these circumstances." Her poetry is an instrument for achieving this
knowledge. On the other hand for Sara de Ibáñez, who returns to the
traditional Spanish form, by reviving the "lira" — for example
"poetry is an exercise in mystery." The critic then compares the two
women poets through an *explication de texte* establishing similarities
and differences between the authors of *Primero sueño* [*First Dream*]
and *Canto* [*Song*]. She determines that Sara de Ibáñez is closer to
Góngora than Sor Juana, "and that by placing herself in a line of the
most unalloyed surrealist 'neo-culterana relationship' Sara de Ibáñez
opens a breach in contemporary poetry." After focusing on Sara de
Ibáñez' *Tránsito a Sor Juana Inés de la Cruz* [*A Journey to Sor
Juana Inés de la Cruz*], Celia de Zapata concludes that a tenuous
thread unites these two poets "who today walk the ways that light
does not invade."

Julia de Burgos, Puerto Rican poet, is the subject of the next
two articles. Elpidio Laguna-Díaz in his essay, "The Phenomenology
of Nothingness in the Poetry of Julia de Burgos," is careful to point
out that his approach is not philosophical, that he is not concerned
with it, but rather with ontological problems, within the determination of a concept, an idea, in her poetry. "Nothingness, then, is
related to the concepts of time, life, death, the transcendence of the

human person or its permanence beyond the limits raised to existence." He then analyzes those concepts in several of her poems, stressing that the "nothingness" to which he refers is the void that the poet finds in the surrounding world. As the critic expresses it, "Nothingness is in the poetry of Julia de Burgos everything the world — people as well as circumstances — lack as related to herself; everything that has no coincidence with her being, her way of being; everything that when she loves, needs, discovers, gives, creates, is not there to meet her. Be it social injustice, be it her lover, be it vulgarity or misunderstanding; be it shallowness of heart and mind."

Nelly Santo's study, "Love and Death: The Thematic Journey of Julia de Burgos," centers on her lyricism — "a Neoromanticism whose principal characteristics are the full expression of love's agonizing desolation and a petition to death for deliverance from loneliness and despair."

The critic analyzes two of her books *Canción de la verdad sencilla* [*Song of Simple Truth*] which she points out "marks the pinnacle of her amorous expression" and *El mar y tú* [*The Sea and You*], the testimony of her courtship with death, with the sea symbolizing a bed or resting place. The study is corroborated by Julia de Burgos' personal correspondence and statements she made about the poetic works analyzed. Nelly Santos emphasizes the symbolism in Burgos' thematic itinerary, which progresses from self-discovery to love, and from love through suffering to death. The critic points out the effective use of symbols in the poet's lyrical world. Symbols used include river, sea, waves, furrows, birds, wings and sails.

She concludes that even though the themes are "well-trodden", the poet's distinction for posterity lies in the "uniquely expressive form and mythical elaboration with which Julia de Burgos wrested her images from language."

Rosa Valdés-Cruz in her essay, "The Short Stories of Lydia Cabrera: Transpositions or Creations." asserts and proves that the Cuban writer is very modest indeed in calling her short stories "transpositions." The critic's main premise is that the author "re-creates and re-elaborates the sources of African and universal folklore" amplifying or deleting the material to suit her objectives. Rosa Valdés-Cruz remarks that in "juxtaposition with cosmogonical myths are descriptions of her markedly surrealistic nature." She adds that the stories have been adapted to the local folklore and customs of Cuba during the 19th and early 20th centuries.

Rosa Valdés-Cruz chooses some of the stories from among the sixty-nine narratives of Lydia de Cabrera and analyzes the original themes and their variants, as re-elaborated by the Cuban writer. The elements that are found to be constant in her stories are a delicate grace and a subtle irony.

Raymond Williams in "An Interview with Women Writers in Colombia" renders an interesting inside view of two Colombian novelists, Albalucía Angel and Fanny Buitrago. In the introduction to this interview the author notes that "The young Colombian novelist Albalucía Angel gained national attention in the land of García Márquez and Mejía Vallejo, by winning the award sponsored by the magazine *Vivencias* for the best Colombian novel in 1975 with *Estaba la pájara pinta sentada en el verde limón.* On the other hand, her young compatriot Fanny Buitrago had just won the national contest for short story sponsored by *El Tiempo.* "After establishing the treatment of daring themes and innovative techniques by the two young writers, Williams engages in a dialogue with them that discusses their fiction, their situation in Colombia, the myth of García Márquez and their own position as intellectual leaders in their country.

We believe that the mosaic of critical writings and selections of poetry presented in this anthology would be both a source for the scholar interested in feminine literature, as well as a useful text to be used in courses on Women Writers.

A Random Survey of the Ratio of Female Poets to Male in Anthologies: Less-than-Tokenism as a Mexican Tradition

by

BETH MILLER

University of Southern California

To judge from Antonio Castro Leal's *Las cien mejores poesías mexicanas modernas* [*The Best 100 Modern Mexican Poems*] (1939; 2nd ed. México: Porrúa, 1945), only one in a hundred of the best "modern" Mexican poems was written by a woman. The single female contribution to this anthology is María Enriqueta Camarillo's "Paisaje" ["Landscape"], which begins with an image of a burden as painful as Alfonsina Storni's "Peso ancestral" ["Ancestral Weight"]:

> Por la polvosa calzada
> va la carreta pesada
> gimiendo con gran dolor.
> [Along a dusty highway,
> heavily, a narrow cart proceeds,
> with great groans of pain and sorrow.]

In order to explain this ratio (1:100) one could hypothesize that (a) there are not many good poems written by women, at least by Mexican women; or (b) the editor had a sexist bias; and/or (c) sexism has been particularly widespread and virulent in Mexican literary circles; and/or (d) there was little public respect for women writers in Mexico thirty-five years ago, when this anthology was compiled; and/or (e) there were no Mexican women considered to be first-rate poets by contemporary Mexican male critics at the time of the anthology's publication; and/or (f) extremely few "modern" women poets writing in the period covered by the anthology, that is from Nájera's time through the generation of Contemporáneos in the twenties and thirties, had managed to establish reputations by 1939. I would say there is some evidence to support each of the last five statements of the foregoing six.

In Castro Leal's larger anthology, *La poesía mexicana moderna* [*Modern Mexican Poetry*](México: Fondo de Cultura Económica, 1953), 13 of 115 poets are women (more than 10%). This proportion compares favorably, for example, with the one in the recent anthology edited by Frank Dauster, *Poesía mejicana* [*Mexican Poetry*] (Zaragoza: Editorial Ebro, 1970), in which only 5 (Sor Juana, Concha Urquiza, Margarita Michelena, Margarita Paz Paredes, and Rosario Castellanos) of the 63 poets are women (less than 10%).

While it is true that the majority of anthology editors, compilers, and publishers have been men, women have sometimes fared even worse in the hands of female editors. For example, of the 78 poets included in *Poetas de América: Antología de la Poesía Contemporánea Mexicana* [*Poets of America:* [*Anthology of Contemporary Mexican Poetry*](México: Editorial América: 1945), edited by Manuel González Ramírez and Rebeca Torres Ortega, only 2 are women (María Enriqueta Camarillo and Carmen Toscano). This 1-in-39 ratio is actually almost identical to that found in the famous *Laurel* anthology of 1941 (subtitled *Antología de la poesía moderna en lengua española* [*Anthology of Modern Poetry in Spanish*], edited by Emilio Prados, Xavier Villaurrutia, Juan Gil-Albert, and Octavio Paz (México: Editorial Séneca, 1941). The Laurel collection includes only one female, Gabriela Mistral, among its 38 poets.

Were women poets in our own language faced with equal discrimination? A random sampling of anthologies in English shows that they were not. For instance, in *The Best Loved Poems of 1925*, ed. Thomas Moult (New York: Harcourt, Brace, 1925), 17 of 77 selections are by female poets, from Sara Teasdale to Vita Sackville-West, about 1 of every 4 or 5. In *New Poems: 1940*, edited by Oscar Williams (New York: The Yardstick Press, 1941), 5 of the 36 poets are women (about 1 in 7), and Selden Rodman includes 10 poetesses (again about 1 in 7) in his *A New Anthology of Modern Poetry* (New York: The Literary Guild, 1938). One might also conclude, incidentally, that published women (e.g. Marianne Moore, Muriel Rukeyser, Elizabeth Bishop, Amy Lowell, Dorothy Parker, Edna St. Vincent Millay, Elinor Wylie in these two volumes) do not perish as quickly as their unread sister poets.

Yet, perhaps this comparison indicates only that there were a greater number of talented women writing in the United States than in Mexico and that the small proportion of women in anthologies of Mexican poetry is due simply to the absence of good female poets in Mexico. We can adduce evidence to support this claim. In the *Antología de la poesía norteamericana* [*Anthology of North American Poetry*],ed. Agustí Bartra (México: Libro-Mex, 1952), for example, 10 of 48 poets are women. It is also possible, however, to interpret such evidence differently. For one thing, foreign women writers have always done better in Mexico than home-grown or naturalized ones (and the same has been said of men writers). As Emily Dickinson captured hearts in the fifties in Mexico, D. F., so later did Woolf, Mansfield, Beauvoir, and briefly, Sonntag. A recent issue of *Plural* features translations of Sylvia Plath, although I do not believe poems by Rosario Castellanos or fiction by Luisa Josefina Hernández has ever appeared in those cosmopolitan pages.

Even fewer Mexican female poets are exported, in part because of the difficulty they experience gaining recognition in their own country. A case in point: *Poesía en movimiento* [*Poetry in Motion*], ed. Octavio Paz, Alí Chumacero, José Emilio Pacheco, and Homero Aridjis (México: Siglo XXI, 1966), includes 4 women (Michelena, Castellanos, Nava, and Fraire) of a total of 42 poets, or 1 in 10; the reduced English version of this work, *New Poetry of Mexico* (New York: E. P. Dutton, 1970), includes no women at all. Curiously, the 1-in-10 ratio in *Poesía en movimiento* is no better than that found a half-century earlier in the Uruguayan anthology *El parnaso oriental* [*Eastern Parnassus*], (Montevideo: Maucci Hermanos, 1905); but it is certainly an improvement over *El parnaso mexicano* [*Mexican Parnassus*] (México: Maucci Hermanos, 1905), which in its enlarged second edition lists the names of 73 poets, only one of which appears to be female (Rosa Espino). Unfortunately, a footnote (p. 112) indicates the name is a pseudonym of a "very distinguished Mexican man of letters who figures elsewhere in the anthology." Of course, this 1905 anthology is still Romantic, and there were not many famous female Romantic poets, or Modernist either, in Latin America.

In general, one might expect to find a greater representation of women writers in the second half of the century than in the first, partially as an effect of the Women's Rights movement itself, and on the model of such popular nineteenth-century feminist writers as George Sand and Mme. de Staël. José Manuel Blecua's anthology of Spanish poetry, *Poesía romántica* [*Romantic Poetry*](Madrid: Editorial Ebro, 1956), testifies to the correctness of this historical interpretation. Of the 10 poets in the First Volume, born between 1764 and 1808, none are women; of the 10 born between 1811 and 1837, in the Second Volume, about one-third are women (Gertrudis Gómez de Avellaneda, Carolina Coronado, and Rosalía Castro). After all, it was in the thirties and forties of the nineteenth century, elsewhere in the world, that actual political organization on the issues of a sexual revolution began.[1] In the 1850's Avellaneda published in Madrid the first of her articles on women and a biographical piece entitled "Luisa Molina" in the prestigious bi-weekly *La América*. In 1860, as founder and editor of a largely feminist journal for women, *El Album Cubano* [*Cuban Album*], she contributed a number of theoretical feminist essays as well as articles on notable women and women writers, from Sappho to Victoria Colonna and Saint Teresa.[2] In the same

year, 1860, Coronado published articles on Avellaneda and others in the
"Galería de poetisas contemporáneas"["Gallery of Contemporary Women
Poets"] in *La América*.

Yet, some anthologies do not reflect any historical increase whatsoever
in the number of women writers during the last centuries. For instance, *The
Penguin Book of Spanish Verse*, ed. J. M. Cohen, was published the same
year as Blecua's and is also divided into two parts; the first (from the Cid to
the end of the 17th century) contains three selections by Sor Juana (6 of 316
pages, one-fiftieth of the total), and Sor Juana is the only woman among the
65 authors in this section. But it is the book's Part Two ("Modern Times")
which seems most dismaying since its one late-Romantic poetess (Rosalía de
Castro) and one early modern (Silvina Ocampo) add up to less than a woman
per century.

Given the feminism of the 1930's and the burgeoning international
Women's Movement, we might expect to see more women published and
more activity by educated women on Mexico's literary front. In this connection, we should take into account such influences as the nineteenth-
century Anglo-Saxon women who toured the country, the later travelers
attracted to Mexico by the writings of D.H. Lawrence and other primitivists,
the importation of foreign books and newspapers, the international as well as
nationalistic flavor of the period in letters. [3] More importantly, the participation of Mexican women in the Revolution may be presumed to have
prepared them, to some extent, for entrance into the literary arena as well as
the wider public sphere.

Mexican women had begun to participate actively in "Liberal Clubs"
(such as the "Benito Juárez" and the "Society of Mexican Socialists")
around the turn of the century; many of them served as revolutionary
journalists and editors. Concha Michel, to cite one forgotten case, went to
Russia in 1930 to investigate the socio-political position of women and the
famous women who had fought in the Russian Revolution. She later
published a thirty-five page revolutionary and feminist tract in Mexico in
1934 (*Marxistas y "marxistas"*); organized and wrote programs for the
"Casa-Escuela de la Mujer Trabajadora" ["Schoolhouse for the Working
Woman"] for working-class women in 1936 and the more broadly based
"Centro Femenino de Estudios y Acción Social" ["Feminine Study and
Social Action Center"] in 1939. However, her popular revolutionary ballads
and ideological poetry have never appeared in major anthologies, nor have the
works of such poets of the Revolution as María del Mar, Lázara Meldiú, and
Aurora Reyes; nor, for that matter, have prose pieces by Nellie Campobello,
author of the important and popular, "Apuntes sobre la vida militar de
Francisco Villa" ["Notes on the Military Life of Francisco Villa"].

How, then, can we explain this nearly total absence of women writers from the Mexican literary foreground in the twenties and thirties? First of all, the scene was dominated by the Contemporáneos, an all-male, mainly homosexual, literary clique. Thus, there were no women among the poet-critics who edited and contributed regularly to their journal, *Contemporáneos* (1928-31), the most important in its day and the most significant of several literary magazines the members of the group published during their association. Nor did any women figure prominently among the members of the contemporary and rival, but less important, vanguardist group, the Estridentistas. [4] Nor were there any women among the 22 poets in the controversial and famous *Antología de la poesía mexicana moderna* [*Anthology of Modern Mexican Poetry*](México: Contemporáneos, 1928). Nor were there any in the smaller anthology, *Nueva antología de poetas mexicanos* [*New Anthology of Mexican Poets*], edited the same year by G. G. Maroto (Madrid: La Gaceta Literaria, 1928). And, about ten years later, when the Contemporáneos group had officially dissolved, the significant 1939 anthology, *Poesía mexicana contemporánea: Antología de El Nacional* [*Contemporary Mexican Poetry: Anthology by El Nacional*], in its "Tomo II" ["Volume II"]acknowledges the continuation of the bias by admitting no women among the 16 poets chosen to represent the contemporary period in Mexican literary history.

In contrast, in Gerardo Diego's anthologies of 1932 and 1934, *Poesía española contemporánea* [*Contemporary Spanish Poetry*], published in Madrid, there are at least two token women (Josefina de la Torre and Ernestina de Champourcín). Interestingly, the poets in the Contemporáneos group, who were evidently reluctant to recognize or encourage talent in their Mexican female colleagues, were able to admire foreign women writers: Jaime Torres Bodet praises Alfonsina Storni in an essay on contemporary Argentine writers (in *Contemporáneos: Notas de crítica* [*Contemporaries: Critical Notes*], 1928); Xavier Villaurrutia writes enthusiastically of the exotic H. D. (Hilda Doolittle); Salvador Novo translates Marianne Moore.

The obvious discrimination against women writers in Mexican anthologies and in Mexico generally may be considered to have been, at least in part, elitist. In contrast, if the title of the North American anthology, *The Best Loved Poems of the American People*(Garden City: Doubleday, 1936), is a true indication of the criteria of selection, North Americans admired and read a great many women. Over one-third of the poets in this 670-page volume are female. Of course so was the editor (Hazel Felleman), although, as we have seen, not all women editors are fair judges of writers of their own sex, and there is no guarantee that women poets will be well-represented in an anthology edited by a woman.

We take for granted that a compiler's selections will reflect his own tastes and prejudices as well as those of his time and place, social milieu and literary friends. A critic's inclusions and exclusions imply choices, whether or not he makes us aware of his reasons for choosing. However, even when he does explain his sympathies or criteria, we may or may not approve. For instance, Raúl Leiva in his *Imagen de la poesía contemporánea [Image of Contemporary Poetry]* (México: Imprenta Universitaria, 1959), studies seven groups of poets, beginning with the Post-Modernists; of 29 poets, 1 in 10 are women (Concha Urquiza, Margarita Paz Paredes, and Rosario Castellanos). And Emmanuel Carballo, in his *Diecinueve protagonistas de la literatura mexicana del siglo XX [19 Protagonists of 20th Century Mexican Literature]* (México: Empresa Editoriales, 1965), considers two women to be Mexican literary "protagonists" (again 1 in 10): Rosario Castellanos—the first woman writer to be buried in the "Rotonda de los Hombres Ilustres" ["Rotonda of Illustrious Men"]—and Nellie Campobello. Less leftist politically than Leiva and Carballo, Mauricio de la Selva, in a study entitled *Algunos poetas mexicanos [Some Mexican Poets]* (Guadalajara: Finisterre, 1971), chooses not to include or mention any women writers at all.

Tokenism is not, needless to say, an exclusively Mexican tradition. There is only one woman (Ana María Simo) in J. M. Cohen's *Writers in the New Cuba* and just two (Castellanos and Mistral) in his *Latin American Writing Today* (both Penguin, 1967). Of course, tokenism is better than nothing. One would expect to find at least a token representation of women writers in the sixties and seventies. One of many exceptions is Saúl Yurkiévich's *Poesía hispanoamericana 1960-1970 [Latin American Poetry 1960-1970]* (México: Siglo, XXI, 1972), which has none. However, the overall trend does seem to be toward an increasing recognition of women writers, in a ratio of about one women to nine or ten men. This ratio seems to hold generally, even for anthologies not devoted exclusively to the post-World War II period, a time when a greater proportion of writers than ever before are women. [5] For example, in *Mil y un sonetos mexicanos: Del siglo XVI al XX [1001 Mexican Sonnets: From the 16th to the 20th Century]*, edited by a former Contemporáneo, Salvador Novo (1963; 3rd ed. México: Porrúa, 1971), about 12% of the sonnet-writers are female.

However, although a 1:10 ratio for anthologies of contemporary (post-World War II) writings is perhaps more understandable than 1:100, is it one which is significant as an indication of the actual proportion of good women writers? Not according to most of the evidence. For example, Elena Poniatowska, in an article entitled "¿Vamos hacia un matriarcado literario?" ["Are we heading for a literary matriarchate?"] (*El día*, 21 Feb. 1966) comments on the extraordinary number of important works by women writers in Mexico published in 1966, and there is little question that many fine women writers, not only poets, have been passed over by compilers of Mexican literary anthologies, as they once were by exclusive Mexican literary journals and circles.

I believe that the appearance of so many women on the Mexican literary scene in the sixties is due in considerable part to the literary journals of those years which, although not feminist, were run partly or entirely by women. These important literary magazines (*El Rehilete, Pájaro Cascabel, el corno emplumado*) offered many women writers a start and a chance to publish their works regularly as well as a channel for communication with other writers.

If there were no sexist discrimination in literature on the part of critics, editors, historians, and anthologists, there would be little need for such useful collections as *Diez mujeres en la poesía mexicana del siglo XX* [*Ten Women in 20th Century Mexican Poetry*], ed. Grisalda Alvarez (México: Metropolitana, 1974); or earlier ones such as Helena Percas' acclaimed *La poesía femenina argentina, 1810-1950* [*Feminine Argentine Poetry, 1810-1950*], (Madrid: Ediciones Cultura Hispánica, 1958) and many others published in small editions, sometimes paid for by the compiler, and now almost forgotten.

NOTES

[1] See Kate Millett, *Sexual Politics* (Garden City: Doubleday, 1970), Part II.

[2] See Emilio Cotarelo y Mori, *La Avellaneda y sus obras* La Avellaneda and Her Works (Madrid: Tipografía de Archivos, 1930), pp. 349-51.

[3] See Alicia Diadiuk, *Viajeras anglosajonas en México* anglo-Saxon Women Travelers in Mexico (México: Secretaría de Educación Pública, SepSetentas 62, 1973).

[4] On the Contemporáneos group, see Frank Dauster, *Ensayos sobre poesía mexicana* Essays on Mexican Poetry (México: Andrea, Col Studium 41, 1963); Merlin H. Forster, *"Los Contemporáneos" 1920-1932* (México: Andrea, Col. Studium 46, 1964); Beth Kurti Miller, *La poesía constructiva de Jaime Torres Bodet* The Constructive Poetry of Jaime Torres Bodet (México: Porrúa, 1974), Ch. 1.

[5] In some cases the ratio would seem almost to amount to a ''quota.'' For instance, in the highly respected textbook, *La poesía hispanoamericana desde el modernismo* Latin American Poetry Since Modernism , ed. Eugenio Florit and José Olivio Jiménez (New York: Appleton-Century-Crofts, 1968) there is a ratio of about 1 woman to 10 men poets. However, the breakdown by historical periods is as follows: 13 men, no women in Modernism; 18 men, 5 women in Postmodernism; 19 men, 3 women in Vanguardism; 23 men, no women in Postvanguardism. I do not advocate any sort of quota or ''optimum ratio''; nevertheless, the absence of women writers in the contemporary period—the one in which there are most women writing—is, to say the least, a regrettable flaw in a textbook which claims to be representative.

Women Intellectuals
in
Chilean Society

by

MARTIN C. TAYLOR

University of Nebraska, Lincoln

It seems fitting, in view of the specialized papers in this conference on style, theme, and structure, to present a background study on Chile that serves as a historical and cultural counterpoint. While Chile may not be the perfect model against which to gauge all of Latin America, it can serve as a point of departure. By offering pertinent details on the political, social, and educational development of women intellectuals of Chile—how they languished and thrived—it will become apparent that the struggle of Chilean intellectuals—female and male—reflects a parallel struggle of other Latin Americans for the right to make free choices—untrammeled by tradition and taboos—about their creativity, politics, and sexuality.

I should, at first, like to scan some salient points of Chile's population, economics, and geography, and then go on to a review of the attitudes that shaped colonial thought vis-a-vis women. Following that, I will focus on three sectors—education, politics, and literature—in which women fought to gain equality and dignity.

In the late nineteenth and early twentieth century, émigrés from Argentina, Italy, Germany, the British Isles, and the Slavic countries grafted technical and agricultural advances on the retrograde Indian and Spanish substratum. These adhesions did not really promote women's rights, owing, in part, to male politicians who were insistent on keeping women, together with other social groups, ignorant and disenfranchised. It is generally recognized that high literacy in Latin America is in direct proportion to a populace of European origin. In Chile, however, the European stock was not of sufficient numbers, nor was the education system of such quality up until 1917, to keep illiteracy below sixty percent. From 1917 to 1963, education improved and expanded so that illiteracy dropped to twenty percent.[1]

The majority of Chilean women, in the 19th century, worked on farms or in domestic service. With the emergence of a middle class, in the 20th century, women also became employed in factories, department stores, and small shops as well as in education.[2] All the laboring classes benefited from the discovery of nitrates and copper. International trade also accelerated the need for efficient, universal education to equip all the classes for greater productivity. Unfortunately, the invention of artificial nitrates and the discovery of copper elsewhere resulted in a depressed and fluctuating market for the two basic exports. Also, the opening of the Panama Canal (1914), turned Valparaíso into a distant port of call and slowed down economic growth and contact with foreign cultures. Chile has had its share of political tyranny, but during its longer periods of democratic government, like that of Pedro Aguirre Cerda, women, especially, found a hospitable social and intellectual climate.

The Spaniards recognized early on certain hard facts of Chilean geopolitics: Chile could not be developed without overextending supply lines; the territory was indefensible from the fierce Araucanians; and few negotiable resources were available. The Conquerors developed Peru, instead, because of its gold and silver mines, its more compliant Indians, and its great cultural base. For the two centuries following the founding of Santiago by Pedro de Valdivia, in 1541, Chile remained an outpost governed by a captain-general.

In the slowly emerging transculturation of Chile, Spain implanted, along with the barracks, the church, and the town-hall, a philosophy of social and family order that derived from Aristotle's *Politics*. Aristotle held that the Greek male's qualities of intellect, grace, and virility placed him naturally at the center of the universe. Women, like slaves and children, occupied an

---

[1] See "Illiteracy" in A. Curtis Wilgus's *A Historical Atlas of Latin America*. (N.Y.: Cooper Square Publishers, 1943; 2nd ed., 1967), pp. 342-343. The chart on p. 342, taken from *El analfabetismo en América* [*Illiteracy in America*] (Washington: Pan American Union, 1958), contains either a typographical or statistical error on female and male illiteracy for Chile. The given figures are 56% female and 44% male illiteracy, which are definitely out of proportion with the complementary graph showing between 13% and 36% illiteracy for different age groups, and a separate chart on p. 343, from the *New York Times*, with a figure of 20% general illiteracy in 1963. Luisa Zanelli López, in *Mujeres chilenas de letras Chilean Women of Letters*] (Santiago: Imprenta Universitaria, 1917), p. 29, cites, with profound sorrow for Chile's educational system, a 60% illiteracy rate. Howell, Davies, ed. *The South American Handbook* (Bath, England: Trade and Travel Pub., Ltd., 1972), p. 237, cites 33.6% and 9.1% illiteracy for rural and city people, respectively. An average of the two numbers gives 21%, which is close to the previously mentioned *New York Times* figure.

[2] According to Amanda Puz, in *La mujer chilena* [*The Chilean Woman*], colección "Nosotros los chilenos," 22 (Santiago: Edit. Nacional Quimantes, Ltda., 1972), p. 73, only 22% of the total work force is made up of women; about 50% of the women are workers in factories and farms, 7.9% are in the professional/technical category.

inferior position. Saint Paul and the Fathers of the Church, well versed in Aristotle and the Scriptures, considered the woman a subordinate and sinful creature. She might find redemption either in faith or in carrying out God's will to be obedient and fruitful.

The Spanish Crown believed that the needs of God and the King could be best served when Spaniards in the New World raised families and remained to stabilize and legitimize the Conquest. The *Recopilación de Leyes de los · los Reinos de las Indias* [Code of Law of the Indies](1680) indicates that Spaniards who brought over wives, or sent to Spain for their family, or married the eligible spinsters and widows shipped over for their matrimonial potential (that excluded, of course, ladies of the night), received preferential treatment in obtaining a job, Indians, and land. In contrast, the laws penalized, with fines and imprisonment, unmarried Spaniards. Even as early as 1550, eligible females in Peru outnumbered males, and the exhausted Viceroy Hurtado de Mendoza asked for a halt to their immigration.[3]

In the colonial period, four types of women left their mark on Chilean history.[4] First there was the adventuress, Inés de Suárez, Valdivia's companion in the founding of Santiago, who had a morbid idea of how to stop the marauding Indians from freeing some captured chiefs. She personally lopped off their heads, hoisted them on poles, and thus dissuaded the Indians from further attack. There was another woman named Suárez, Ursula Suárez (1668-1749), who, at the urging of her father confessor, wrote the first account in Chile of her experience with the Devil. She glimpsed, darkly, through a mirror, a leering, fire breathing creature dressed in black, invisible upon looking about the room. Surely a case of Freudian fright. The prize for sadism must go to Catalina de los Ríos Lisperguer (1601-1660), called la Quintrala, the 17th century prototype of Doña Bárbara. Seemingly immune from the law because of her wealth and station, Catalina did not hesitate to poison her father or torture her servants. In addition to sadism, religious masochism ran through the veins of the Lisperguer family. A niece, Catalina Iturgoyen (1685-1732), coated her candy with bitters, wore a hairshirt, and cut off her eyelashes, all this self-mortification in the hopes of a union with Christ's suffering. Chilean writers can trace their heroines, mystics, sadists, and self-torturers to these four creatures of the colonial period.

In the ensuing period of Revolution and Independence, Doña Luisa Recabarren de Marín, and her daughter, Mercedes Marín del Solar, illumine

[3] This area is discussed by Sidonia Carmen Rosenbaum in *Modern Women Writers of Spanish America* (N.Y.: Hispanic Institute, 1945), p. 15.

[4] The following paragraph is synthesized from Marta Elba Miranda's *Mujeres chilenas* [*Chilean Women*] (Santiago: Edit. Nascimento, 1940), pp. 11-36, and passim. See also, Zanelli López, *op. cit.*, pp. 15-16.

the pages of history. The mother, a most gracious Chilean version of Mme Geoffrin or Mme Recamier, espoused the cause of liberty and free-thinking in her literary salon. Mercedes followed in her mother's liberal path; she opened a school for girls, in 1840. The program emphasized religious training and proper morality, that is, avoidance of boys. She also stressed subjects that men usually learned: geography, history, astronomy, and reading. She modernized language learning, by abandoning Latin and Greek in favor of French. This program differed radically from the training in the convents founded by the Jesuits, after 1730. There, the nuns taught the basic alphabet, singing, music, knitting and notions of poetry and drama.[6] The bishop, however, in a fit of pique eliminated the religious drama when he learned that the girls actually enjoyed it.

The framers of the Chilean Constitution of 1833 guaranteed to both sexes free education and suffrage. This was a dilemma for the conservative politicians who believed in an elitist male society. In time, it became clear, women capable of reading and writing would eventually demand a ballot. Since education was the key to change and freedom, politicians refused to fund, staff, and plan the educational system. Finally, in 1854, at the urging of Domingo Faustino Sarmiento, President Manuel Montt set up the Escuela Normal de Preceptoras to train teachers for educating the masses at the elementary level.[7] The instructors, however, Sisters of the Sacred Heart, believed that their duties were to inculcate civic and marital fidelity, religious worship, and the proper care of the house, that is, loyalty, obedience, and virtue, qualities for an aspiring novitiate, but hardly the characteristics for leadership and originality.

At the end of the century, three events occurred that transformed the status of Chilean women. First, control of the Escuelas Normales passed to a group of specially hired German teachers skilled in pedagogy, physical education, and the arts. By 1903, Brígida Walker, Chile's most prominent educator, assumed command of these Escuelas. Señorita Walker had studied the educational theories of Jean Aubert, from his book in French, which she translated as *Curso de pedagogía y metodología* [*Course on Pedagogy and Methodology*](1915). This *maestra de maestras* [teacher of teachers] introduced new programs, such as night classes, lectures, and cycles of courses. The second important event took place in 1877, when the University of Chile

---

[5] On these two women see Miranda, pp. 87-90; Zanelli López, pp. 26-34; José Toribio Medina, *La literatura femenina en Chile* [*Feminine Literature in Chile*](Santiago: Imprenta Universitaria, 1923), pp. 15ff.

[6] Zanelli López, p. 13.

[7] Zanelli López, p. 41. See the excellent chapter on education by Felicitas Klimpel, *La mujer chilena: (El aporte femenino al Progreso de Chile)* [*The Chilean Woman: The Female Contribution to the Progress of Chile*] 1910-1960 (Santiago: Edit. Andrés Bello, 1962), pp. 221-234.

permitted women to pursue degrees in Education and Science.[8]   And finally, the most celebrated private school for women opened in Santiago. From the halls of the school Lebrun de Pinochet have come Chile's foremost intellectuals, including Amanda Labarca de Hubertson.

The lofty principles of universal suffrage guaranteed in the Constitution of 1833 became trampled as soon as the educated women of the eighties tried to vote. The Election Law of 1884 promptly disenfranchised them. To add insult to injury, the politicians passed, in 1934, the Ley sobre Organización y Atribuciones [Law on Organization and Functions] , a law that recognized women's participation in municipal elections.[9] The senators reasoned, with their usual irony, that any woman who could run a household had the capability of running or voting for alderman, a post of form, but not of substance.

By the end of World War II, Chile was one of the last countries of Latin America that denied the vote to women in National elections. For seventy five years women had waged a campaign for suffrage. In 1944, their efforts led to the organization of the Primer Congreso Nacional de Mujeres [First National Congress of Women], and two years later, to the Federación Chilena de Instituciones Femeninas [Chilean Federation of Feminine Institutions], headed by Amanda Labarca. This latter group channeled the energy of two hundred organizations and five hundred active members into the formation of the Partido Femenino Chileno [Chilean Feminine Party].[10] María de la Cruz, the fiery orator who headed the Partido, became, in 1953, the first woman senator. However, her senatorial colleagues ousted her from office seven months later for outspoken support of Perón and the trumped up charge of accepting the equivalent of $25 as a political favor.

After a zealous propaganda campaign, the Partido Femenino registered 700,000 women, and finally convinced the Senate to vote favorably, in 1949, on granting them the vote. The irony was not lost on the women themselves that only 400,000 women cast a ballot, and over 50% of these went to the independent male candidate. Most women, it was theorized, harbored a suspicion of the established parties. The lack of participation (43% did not vote) stemmed from the fact that Chilean women had been ridiculed by their husbands for their liberal positions, or feared reprisals from their spouses if they voted. This demonstrates amply that one can be legally free to vote, but one is not free when the taboos of the past, for the men as well as the women, paralyze emotions and good judgment.

---

[8] Klimpel, p. 153, lists 8,377 degrees of various types for women in the Univ. de Chile between 1910 and 1960.

[9] See Klimpel, pp. 115ff., for a lucid discussion of women in politics.

[10] Klimpel, pp. 127-149, outlines the accomplishments of the Partido Femenino Chileno.

It might be worthwhile to look into the formation of the Círculo de Lectura de Señoras [Ladies Reading Circle], established in 1915 by Amanda Labarca de Hubertson.[1] This ladies club seems an anachronism now, but in its time and for Santiago, it represented a daring innovation: a club by and for women. The richest and most influential Santiaguinas [ladies from Santiago] bought a building to house their literary and intellectual events. The husbands, suspicious of what transpired behind its closed doors, need not have worried, for this group symbolized the female counterpart of masculine status quo. They heard, among others, lectures on Santa Teresa, on women in Benavente's plays, on the Spanish poetess Jinés de Alcántara. The Círculo made worthy efforts to elevate the consciousness of its members in Santiago and in neighboring cities by offering grammar lessons, lectures, and prizes for the best poems by women. Yet, the association was politically naive. When the liberal Senator, Luis Claro Solar, spoke to the Círculo of his bill for amplifying women's civil rights, the diffident response was: "El tema...no pudo ser más de actualidad ni más de acuerdo con los ideales lejanos de la sociedad."[12] In short, while suffragettes marched and petitioned in New York, these select Santiaguinas, with time and money, harbored few thoughts of organizing for political power.

The Círculo, at its inception, also titillated itself with safe, Catholic ideas and antiseptic poems. The year after Gabriela Mistral won the Juegos Florales for her vigorous "Sonetos de la Muerte" ["Sonnets About Death"] (1914), the group awarded first prize for the following precious verses: "Alta la frente que, antes ruborosa / a la voz del Señor, Eva culpable / abatió humilde hasta tocar la tierra, / sin oír del perdón acento suave...." ["Her forehead, once ablush before God's voice, now held high, Eve, blameworthy, fell touching the ground, not hearing the soft tone of the pardon...."] Both poems treat Christian redemption and love, but Gabriela's has so much more impact and directness: "Y yo dije al Señor: 'Por las sendas mortales / le llevan. ¡Sombra amada que no saben guiar! / ¡Arráncalo, Señor, a esas manos fatales/ o le hundes en el largo sueño que sabes dar!'" ["And I told the Lord: 'Along mortal paths they are taking him. Beloved shadow, although misguided! Tear him away, Lord, from those fateful hands or you will bury him in the long sleep that you alone know how to give!'"] Gabriela repudiated the Ladies Reading Circle just as she had rejected so many other

[11] Zanelli López, pp. 189-195, dedicates a chapter to the Club de Señoras, and its president, Doña Amanda. Marta Elba Miranda, in *Mujeres chilenas* [*Chilean Women*], outlines the life of this great educator. Further bibliography on her can be found in *Diccionario de la literatura latinoamericana: Chile* [*Dictionary of Latin American Literature: Chile*] (Washington: Pan American Union, 1958).

[12] Zanelli López, p. 168: ["The topic could not be closer to today's events, nor more in accord with the distant ideals of the society."]

institutions that offered the shell of creativity and uniqueness. [13] She labored,
as an individual and as a poet, beyond the sterile confines of ladies clubs. Her
lack of conformity, which led her to smoke, to publish articles on mysticism,
to read proscribed books on love and philosophy, also drove her from the
boundaries of prudish Chile. She left her country, physically, in 1922, but
returned to it in her themes and language, and ultimately to her resting place
in Monte Grande.

I should like to conclude this talk with a brief comparison between
Mistral and Marta Brunet, who, some have said, was to the novel what
Gabriela was to poetry: virile, direct, realistic, and endowed with
psychological discernment. Marta, like Gabriela, read widely, had sympathy
for the poor, and became attuned to the secret sounds and sights that nature
imparts to only a few. Unlike Gabriela, Marta forged a career within the
confines of a Victorian Chilean morality. Brunet could only hint, in her novel
on homosexuality, *Amasijo* [*Intrigue*] (1962), of an element that remained
underground in both women. [14] Both had discarded the usual trappings and
entrapments of the man-centered female: husband, children, and church.
Where that left them in terms of emotional and psychological sustenance can
only be ascertained in the most veiled argument.

The struggle in Chile, then, as in the rest of Latin America, concerns
itself less with the narrower issues of the ballot and schools for boys or girls,
than with the more pertinent struggle for free choices in an intellectual,
sexual, and political medium that, at once, forced Mistral into exile, stifled
Brunet's sexuality, and extinguished Pablo Neruda's hope for a more just
society.

[13] On her dilemma, see Martin C. Taylor, *Gabriela Mistral's Religious Sensibility*. Series in
Modern Philology, Vol. 87 (Berkeley: Univ. of Calif., 1968), pp. 3-15. Margaret Rudd's forth-
coming biography of Gabriela, on which I collaborate, describes Mistral's antagonism towards
Amanda Labarca.

[14] See María Monvel's prologue to her *Poetisas de América* [*Poetesses of America*] (Santiago:
Edit. Nascimento, 1929), p. 10. "Amasijo," is in *Obras completas de Marta Brunet* [*Complete
Works of Marta Brunet*]. prologue by Alone (Santiago: Zig-Zag, 1963), pp. 789-859. Alone
(pseud. of Hernán Díaz Arrieta) captures, in the prologue, the mysterious Brunet: "Solitaria y
sonriente, con su angustia, resiste el asedio cordial refugiada en esa otra soledad que es el
silencio" ["Solitary and smiling, living with her anguish, she resists the cordial siege sheltered in
that other solitude. silence."] (p. 16).

Clorinda Matto de Turner and Mercedes Cabello de Carbonera: Societal Criticism and Morality

by

JOHN C. MILLER

Gettysburg College

The last fifteen years of the Nineteenth Century in Peru are very turbulent. The devastating effects of the War of the Pacific and the divided state of Peru geographically stimulate a spirited debate as to the future. Two women novelists, Clorinda Matto de Turner and Mercedes Cabello de Carbonera, mirror the national social problems in their works. Their impetus is primarily moral, but, at the same time, their novels provide a positivistic sociological commentary on Peruvian institutions. Clorinda Matto de Turner devotes her attention to the position of the Indian and of the woman while Mercedes Cabello de Carbonera directs her attack against an urban middle class structure based on hypocrisy and political corruption. The two women concur in a critical exposition of the existing political system, and through dramatic statements, they confirm the vices of a vain society without a moral or ethical base.

Clorinda Matto de Turner, from an early age, expresses her concern for the Andean Indian, but her personal experience in the village of Tinta, shortly after her marriage, stresses the necessity of a reform of the three institutions which exercise a powerful influence in the nation: the clergy and the judicial and executive branches of government. Her second preoccupation, one which assumes greater significance in the latter part of her life, is a reevaluation of the woman in Peruvian society.

Her first literary attempts manifest a traditional orientation. In 1876, she founds *El Recreo*, a weekly newspaper of moralizing tendency directed to Peruvian women. In 1881, under the pseudonym of Carlote Dimont, she continues her crusade as editor of *La Bolsa* of Arequipa. Her publication in the same year of the manual, *Elementos de literatura para el bello sexo* [*Elements of Literature for the Fair Sex*], proposes three goals or ideals: the development of a sound society, the healthy upbringing of children and peace in the home. Her post-romantic humanism states that the heart is the source of all eloquence; love can cure many social problems. Nevertheless, there is an initial attempt to relate the role of the woman at home to that of the world beyond, an initial step in Nineteenth Century Peruvian literature.

The initial "leyendas" ["legends"] of Clorinda Matto de Turner, short stories similar to the "tradiciones" ["traditions"]of Ricardo Palma, portray the tragic situation of either the woman or the Andean Indian, both victims of Man. "De cima de horca" ["From the Gallows"] depicts the young Indian who in physical appearance resembles the Virgin Mary who saves from certain death a noble Spanish soldier who has not abused the native women. "El santo y la limosna" ["The Saint and the Handout"] reflects the corrupt practices of church and civil authorities who always succeed in enriching themselves. "Lo que costaba una cauda" ["The Cost of a Train"] describes the circumstances which are later revealed in her novel, *Herencia* [*Heritage*], as well as in the works of Cabello de Carbonera, the tragic situation of the mother who destroys the economic well being of the family in order to marry "properly" the daughter.

The speeches of Matto de Turner, written after these initial writings, continue the same vital interests: the progress of the nation and the status of women. In 1886, on the day of her acceptance into the *Círculo literario* [*Literary Circle*]of Lima, her speech, "Costumbres peruanas" ["Peruvian Customs"]criticizes the Peruvian clergy and the excessive fees which they demand for the performance of religious duties. When she is nominated for membership in the *Ateneo*, her acceptance speech, "Luz entre sombras" ["Light Among the Shadows"], projects a study of the contribution of women, particularly in the role of mother, to the past, present and future of Peru.

The position of Matto de Turner in Peruvian journalism becomes even more noteworthy in May of 1887 when she founds *El Peru Ilustrado*, weekly publication within which she continues her defense of the Andean Indian. Her experiences in the village of Tinta, fictional Killac, Andean settlement where she spent ten years, produces a censure of the Church, particularly of the parish priest who takes advantage of the isolated site and who shows himself immoral and corrupt. The novel, *Aves sin nido* [*Birds Without a Nest*],often compared to Harriet Beecher Stow's *Uncle Tom's Cabin*, reveals the problem of priestly sexuality, the illegitimate children and the women compromised by said circumstances. Matto de Turner declares herself in favor of priestly marriage, considering celibacy a dangerous state for men. In the novel she designates three agents of social corruption: the governor, the landowner and the priest. Noted in the description of the daily lives of the Indians are the varieties of forced labor: la mita, el pongo, la faena y el reparto antelado—the history of Andean Indian exploitation. The protagonist, Don Pascual, village priest, is designated as an individual who needs the institution of marriage. The abuses of his power, particularly through the confessional, exist, according to Matto de Turner because the forced chastity of priests can not exist in the isolating solitude and in the corrupted environment of Andean village life. She does not reject either the Church or the clergy because she depicts the replacement of Don Pascual as an exemplary individual. The declaration of Manuel, bastard offspring of the priest, serves to emphasize the moral purpose of the work. He intends to write his law thesis on the necessity of marriage of the clergy. Every young woman, particularly the Indian woman, lives under constant threat of sexual assault by powerful men. Criticism of the system of government of Peru directs itself to both the courts and civil authorities. Matto de Turner not only complains of the corrupt state of officials, but further emphasizes the ineffectiveness of the "zorros de la camisa blanca" ["the white-shirted foxes"]. The military politician is well known in the nation "...por gozar de influjos conquistados en torneos del estómago o banquetes, como por sacar con frecuencia las manos del plato de la Justicia" ["...for having certain influences won in eating contests or banquets, as well as for frequently abusing Justice."] [1]

Indole, published in 1891, continues the author's preoccupation with the manipulation of power by the clergy and civil authority. Eulalia López, protagonist, represents the desired object of the priest, Don Peñas. Basing the plot on the theory that spiritual intimacy produces a rapid and strong physical attraction, Matto de Turner once again presses for the revision of the celibate state of the clergy. In a secondary plot, she presents the need for land reform; the landowners and foreign businessmen rob the Indians of their lands.

A dramatic work of 1892, *Hima Sumac*, reveals the historic circumstances of the Indian woman in love with a codicious Spaniard, an exemplary woman whose resistance, faced with betrayed love and torture, represents an ideal for women. In contrast, the novel, *Herencia*, published in 1895, depicts and analyzes the falsity, the pretentiousness and the ostentatious display of the aristocratic social climbers of Lima. Doña Lucía Marín, protagonist of *Aves sin nido*, exemplifies model family life. Maternal affection is more present than societal demands. Matto de Turner does not limit herself to a portrayal of the upper classes, but also criticizes the socioeconomic conditions of the urban proletariat woman.   Her most bitter criticism is directed at the mothers who try to create an ostentatiously unnecessary world for the debut of their daughters. Selling furniture and even mortgaging properties, the social climbers attempt to capture a husband of certain social status for their daughters. The marriages fail because they have no emotional base, but rather exist as a deceptive financial arrangement. The opportunist husband is a playboy, a gambler or an emigrant with an easily bought title. On the other hand, the daughter of Doña Lucía, Margarita marries a poor man, made rich through the lottery. He is a good worker, a strong figure representative of the Christian ethic, the triumph of good in a Manichean world. Politics is not omitted in this novel because Don Sebastián Pancorvo, weak and corrupt official of *Aves sin nido*, has become a senator, a clear indication of the little honesty which exists in politics.

The lectures of Matto de Turner in Buenos Aires about women: ''The workers of thought,'' ''The working woman,'' as well as the essay, ''The woman, her youth and her old age,'' direct their attention to the position of the woman in society, active participant in a total development, particularly of her intellectual capacity, but never denying the revered role of mother. [2]

A dichotomy of thought exists in the life and works of Clorinda Matto de Turner—a representative of traditional conservative moral values and a revolutionary in a new sociopolitical awakening.

Mercedes Cabello de Carbonera is a contemporary and a friend of Matto de Turner. Her moralizing novels are directed to an urban population vitiated by pleasure: social pretentions and vanity, political wheeling and dealing, gambling, and the lamentable forced position of women in society, wife-mother or prostitute. Each of her novels: *Blanca Sol, El conspirador* [*The Conspirator*] and *Las consecuencias* [*The Consequences*] begins with a positivist declaration, the study and presentation of the imperfections, the defects or the admitted vices, sanctioned or admired by the society. The novels strive, as in the works of Matto de Turner, to illustrate the excesses of money, the abuses of power and the consequences manifest in the society of Lima.

In *Blanca Sol*, published in 1889, the most outstanding defect of the society is hypocrisy. It appears in two aspects of behavior of the upper classes: the ostentatious parties and religious practices, both characterized by the manifestation of artificial display. Blanca Sol, elected directress of the Daughters of Maria, only wishes the position in order to outdo, during the religious ceremony, the pretentious display of her friend, directress the previous year. *Las consecuencias* is the expansion of a plot first explored by Cabello de Carbonera in ''Los Amores de Hortensia'' [''The Loves of Hortense''], published in *El Perú Ilustrado*, later emerging with the influence of Ricardo Palma's ''Amor de madre'' [''Maternal Love''] to reach a second stage of development as *Eleodora*. The final format is *Las consecuencias*. The work, a novel of forbidden love of a young woman of a respected family, depicts as protector of the protagonist, a mysterious figure who vacilates between a celestina-like spinster, who projects her erotic fantasies, for a price, onto the young woman and a second role as a woman respected in the Lima society for her social and benevolent activities.

The evil individual is, once again, the pretentious woman, in exterior appearance, a good Catholic, however lacking in charity and unwilling to attend mass in the summer because of the presence of the lower classes. She intermingles commentaries on the style of the clothing of the women in church with her ''avemarias'' of the rosary. Cabello de Carbonera criticizes the hierarchy of the Church only in its lack of commentary and admonition among its religious leaders.

Politics is the second area in which the interests of Cabello de Carbonera and Matto de Turner coincide. Matto de Turner examines the microcosmos of the Andean village while Cabello de Carbonera explores higher levels of government in the capital city. The successful attempt of Blanca Sol to obtain a cabinet post for her husband provides a penetrating study of those who live dependent on political vacilation. The newspaper industry only renders hommage to money: flattering syncophants people the houses of the powerful; officials get rich through fraudulent means. They obtain great titles in order to become the distinguished Mr. Nobody. All life is reduced to an extended game in which the noted gentleman, through bribes, attains success, fame and prestige. The political phenomenon of the conspirator is detailed in the novel of the same title, *El conspirador*, published in 1892 with the subtitle, *Autobiography of a Public Man*. The circulation and popularity of the book was such that a second edition was published in Mexico in 1898. Frauds and speculations, all the egotistical goals of a political being, are revealed. Politicians feed on conspiracies, revolutions and changes in government. Jorge Bello, protagonist and conspirator, defines politics as one's conscience in one's stomach, one's opinions hidden in a pocket. According to Bello, politicians ''...saben dar saltos mortales y caer parados en las cabezas de los que los protejen'' [''...know how to summersault and land on their feet on the heads of those who protect them.''] [3] The whole society is corrupted by these politicians. Widows sell the rights to their pensions because they know that government red tape lasts years. Military men and civilian employees live off the ''buscas''—advantages which represent the corruption within the government agencies. The civil code is so elastic that it is difficult to prosecute a friend, but easy to condemn an enemy.

The vices of society: the pleasure of the ostentatious and the meaningless roles of prestige, title and wealth characterize Peruvian and Limeñan society. In the works of the two writers, the homeopathy of certain postromantic tendencies as well as nascent naturalism project a condemnation of a cultural milieu. The two moralizers hope that the medicine, i.e., the societal portraits depicted in their works, smells and tastes so bad that it will cure or, at least, ameliorate certain societal illnesses. ''Mercedes Cabello de Carbonera y Clorinda Matto de Turner son, en la segunda mitad del siglo pasado, las representantes de una novela que ya surgía. La primera, con analizado estudio de la descomposición de las capas altas: panfleto hecho vivisección, tal vez con carencia de emocionado marco, o con mal uso de él. Clorinda Matto de Turner trae al terreno nuestra realidad social con más romanticismo, con la fuerza de la chacarera que ha mirado el sol y que ha visto reventar el trigo en los mismos Andes: con espíritu y tradición. Ambas sostienen agitado momento de emancipación femenina. Tal vez si el no vivir metidas en la acción, les da autoridad de novelistas, capacidad para ello.'' [4] [''Mercedes Cabello de Carbonera and Clorinda Matto de Turner are, in the second half of the last century, the representatives of a novel which was already emerging. The former, with an analytical study of the decomposition of the upper crust: a pamphlet which turned out to be a vivisection, perhaps lacking an emotional framework, or with poor use of it. Clorinda Matto de Turner brings our social reality to the foreground with more romanticism, with the strength of the farm worker who has looked at the sun and has seen wheat burst in the Andes themselves: with spirit and a sense of tradition. Both of them affirm an exciting moment of feminine emancipation. Perhaps not having experienced the action gives them the authority as novelists and the capacity for such.'']   The two women are outstanding in the veracity of their statements. Their own lives are changed by the reactions of the society to their works. Clorinda Matto de Turner is excommunicated and publicly censured; she seeks refuge in Argentina and Europe. In 1900 Mercedes Cabello de Carbonera is institutionalized for depression and melancholy in the asylum of Cercado, her exile during the last nine years of her life. The abuses of women and Indians reveal the excesses of a pretentious, social climbing, opportunistic society. Clorinda Matto de Turner and Mercedes Cabello de Carbonera, together with the Baronesa de Wilson, Carolina Freire de Jaimes and Juana Manuela Gorriti publish numerous articles on the role of women in modern society. They hope to correct the problems of their society; their literary works expose the needs of Peru, victim of a disastrous war and a corrupt past.

NOTES

[1] Clorinda Matto de Turner, *Aves sin nido* (Cuzco: H. G. Rozas, 1948), page 140.

[2] Clorinda Matto de Turner, *Cuatro conferencias sobre América del Sur (Four Conferences on South America)* (Buenos Aires, Juan Alsina, 1909).

[3] Mercedes Cabello de Carbonera, *El conspirador* (Lima: E. Segui & Co., 1892), page 215.

[4] Augusto Tamayo Vargas, *Perú en trance de novela (Peru in a Novelistic Trance)* (Lima: Ed. Baluarte, 1940), page 20.

Bibliography

Mercedes Cabello de Carbonera (1845-1909).

Cabello de Carbonera, Mercedes. *Blanca Sol* (novela social). Lima: Lib. del Universo de C. Prince, 1889, 2nd ed.

Cabello de Carbonera, Mercedes. *Las consecuencias.* Lima: Imprenta de Torres Aguirre, 1892.

Cabello de Carbonera, Mercedes. *El conspirador* (autobiografía de un hombre público) novela político social. Lima: E. Segui & Co., 1892.

Cabello de Carbonera, Mercedes. *El conspirador.* Mexico: La Patria, 1898.

Cabello de Carbonera, Mercedes. *La novela moderna* (estudio filosófico premiado con la rosa de oro, primer premio, en el certamen hispanoamericano de la Academia literaria de Buenos Aires). Lima: Tipografía Bacigalupi & Co., 1892.

Cabello de Carbonera, Mercedes. *La novela moderna* (estudio filosófico). Lima: Ediciones Hora del hombre, 1948 (Primera edición) *sic.* prólogo de Augusto Tamayo Vargas.

Tamayo Vargas, Augusto. *Perú en trance de novela* (ensayo crítico-biográfico sobre Mercedes Cabello de Carbonera). Lima: Ed. Baluarte, 1940.

Clorinda Matto de Turner (1854-1909).

Matto de Turner, Clorinda. *Analogía.* Buenos Aires: Juan Alsina, 1897.

Matto de Turner, Clorinda. *Apostulcunac ruraskancona panan chis Clorinda Matto de Turner castellanonanta runa sim iman tticrasccan.* Buenos Aires: Sociedad Bíblica, 1901.

Matto de Turner, Clorinda. *Aves sin nido.* Lima: Imp. del Universo de Carlos Prince, 1889.

Matto de Turner, Clorinda. *Aves sin nido.* Cuzco: H. G. Rozas, 1948.

Matto de Turner, Clorinda. *Aves sin nido.* Cuzco: H. G. Rozas, 1958, tomo I.

Matto de Turner, Clorinda. *Aves sin nido.* New York: Las Americas, 1968 Estudio preliminar de Luis Schneider.

Matto de Turner, Clorinda. *Aves sin nido.* Buenos Aires: Edit. Solar, 1968 Estudio preliminar de Fryda Schulz de Mantovani.

Matto de Turner, Clorinda. *Birds without a nest.* London: Charles J. Thynne, 1904. Trans. J. G. Hudson.

Matto de Turner, Clorinda. *Bocetos al lápiz de americanos célebres.* Lima: Editores Matto Hermanos, 1890.

Matto de Turner, Clorinda. *Boreales, miniaturas y porcelanas.* Buenos Aires: Juan Alsina, 1902.

Matto de Turner, Clorinda. *Cuatro conferencias sobre América del Sur.* Buenos Aires: Juan Alsina, 1909.

Matto de Turner, Clorinda. *Don Juan Espinosa Medrano o el doctor Lunarejo.* Lima: Editores Matto Hermanos, 1887.

Matto de Turner, Clorinda. *Elementos de literatura. Para el uso del bello sexo.* Arequipa: La Bolsa, 1884.

Matto de Turner, Clorinda. *Herencia.* Lima: Imprenta Masías, 1895.

Matto de Turner, Clorinda. *Herencia.* Lima: Instituto Nacional de Cultura, 1974, Segunda edición.

Matto de Turner, Clorinda. *Hima Sumac.* Lima: La Equitativa, 1882.

Matto de Turner, Clorinda. *Indole.* Lima: Bacigalupi & Co., 1891.

Matto de Turner, Clorinda. *Indole.* Lima: Instituto Nacional de Cultura, 1974, Segunda edición.

Matto de Turner, Clorinda. *Leyendas y recortes.* Lima: Editores Matto Hermanos, 1893.

Matto de Turner, Clorinda. *Perú. Tradiciones cuzqueñas. Leyendas, biografías y hojas sueltas.* Arequipa: La Bolsa, 1884.

Matto de Turner, Clorinda. *Tradiciones, crónicas y leyendas.* Lima: Bacigalupi & Co., 1886.

Matto de Turner, Clorinda. *Tradiciones cuzqueñas.* Cuzco: H. G. Rozas, 1958.

Matto de Turner, Clorinda. *Tradiciones cuzqueñas y leyendas.* Cuzco: H. G. Rozas, 1917.

Matto de Turner, Clorinda. *Viaje del recreo.* Valencia: F. Sempere & Co., 1910.

Carrillo, Francisco. *Clorinda Matto de Turner y su indigenismo literario.* Lima: Biblioteca Universitaria, 1967.

Cuadros Escobedo, Manuel. *Paisaje i obra; Mujer e historia: Clorinda Matto de Turner.* Cuzco: H. G. Rozas, 1949.

Tapia Olarte, Eulogio. *Cinco grandes escritores cuzqueños en la literatura peruana.* Cuzco: Universidad Nacional, 1946.

Life and Early Literary Career of the Nineteenth-Century Colombian Writer Soledad Acosta De Samper

by

HAROLD E. HINDS, JR.

University of Minnesota, Morris

The Colombian literary historian and critic Gustavo Otero Muñoz has written: "Era llegada la época del romanticismo.... La mujer más interesante de esta nueva época, la precursora del tipo moderno de la Colombiana intelectual, fue, sin duda alguna, (Soledad Acosta de Samper)''. ["The epoch of romanticism had arrived.... The most interesting woman of this new epoch, the precursor of the modern Colombian intellectual woman, was, without any doubt, (Soledad Acosta de Samper)''] [1] Despite this undisputed judgment, neither her life nor her literary works have yet been the subject of serious scholarly study. This paper will briefly sketch the life and works of Doña Soledad; will then suggest a number of factors in her life which may have contributed to her development as Colombia's only prominent woman writer in the nineteenth century; and will conclude with an examination of her early journalistic efforts.

1

Soledad Acosta was born in Bogotá, the capital of Colombia, on May 5, 1833, the daughter of Joaquín Acosta and the Englishwoman Caroline Kemble. As a young lady she pursued her education abroad, first in Halifax, Nova Scotia during 1845 and then in Paris for the following three years. Following her marriage to José María Samper in 1855, she began her literary career by translating works of Alexander Dumas and George Sand for Bogotá's *El Neo-Granadino* [*The New Granadan*], a liberal newspaper edited by her husband. She would continue translating French and English works all her life. Meanwhile, she began what to her was the other important role of her life, that of mother, with the birth of two daughters in 1856 and 1857.

Between 1858 and 1863 the Sampers traveled in Europe and Peru, due to an inhospitable political climate in Colombia. On this second trip abroad, Doña Soledad began to publish her own works. She wrote a column for the literary magazines *Biblioteca de Señoritas* [*Young Ladies' Library*] and *El Mosaico* [*The Mosaic*], both of Bogotá. The column described the latest French fashions and reviewed recent plays, operas, and literature. These columns clearly reveal the remarkable breadth of her intellectual formation. French, English, Spanish, Italian, Swedish, German, Danish, and Russian works all commanded her attention. She also penned a short travel sketch of their trip to Switzerland and published a few short *costumbrista* [sketch portraying everyday life and prevailing customs] pieces. (Later in life she would return to both of these literary forms. For example, when she again traveled to Europe in the 1890's, she recorded her impressions in a two-volume work entitled *Viajes de España* [*Travels through Spain*]. And local color and typical characters are encountered in many of her later romantic novels.) During their residence in Peru, Soledad assumed the joint editorship with José María of the *Revista Americana* [*American Review*], a fortnightly literary supplement to the prestigious Peruvian daily *El Comercio* [*The Commercial Journal*]. Meanwhile, she had given birth to two more daughters.[2]

The Sampers returned to Colombia in 1863. Following a brief hiatus, a torrent of works began to flow from Doña Soledad's pen. At first, she devoted most of her considerable energy to writing romantic historical novels and short stories. According to the nineteenth-century Colombian literary critic Isidoro Laverde Amaya, she used almost every subject susceptible to treatment in a novel. However, she was particularly attracted to the dramatic episodes of the conquest and colonial periods and to *costumbrista* themes. Doña Soledad was a popularizer, who did not do original research, but reworked old chronicles or drew on her personal knowledge of local landscapes, customs, and character types. However, her work is void of autobiographical content, since she was an exceedingly private person. She paid careful attention to the known historical facts, and developed probable episodes based on those facts. She also worked within contemporary literary conventions, and was evidently much influenced by the romantic novels of Walter Scott, Honoré de Balzac, and Victor Hugo, as well as by the Colombian *costumbristas* José Manuel Marroquín (1827-1908) and Eugenio Díaz (1804-1865). Doña Soledad was a devout Catholic, who never missed an opportunity to defend the faith. In her works Christian moral themes always predominated, and often became long, cumbersome asides, disrupting an episode's development. [3]

Although she continued to write historical novels the rest of her life, beginning in the 1880's Doña Soledad increasingly wrote biographies and histories. She now added Independence themes to the dramatic episodes of the conquest and colonial periods, and emphasized studies of their heroic actors. Her portraits were historically accurate, but one-dimensional. She ignored the private lives, character blemishes, and imprudent actions of her heroes, focusing only on the positive in their lives. Despite her attention to accurate historical detail, these biographies bear a strong resemblance to saints' lives. Yet most other Colombian historians of the day portrayed national heroes in a similar manner. Several of Doña Soledad's biographies and historical studies were critically acclaimed. Her portrait of her father won a prize in Bogotá on the occasion of the one hundredth anniversary of the Liberator Bolívar's birth, and her biography of the Independence hero José Antonio Sucre won a prize in Caracas. During her stay in Europe following her husband's death in 1888, she was selected to represent Colombia at the Congress of Americanists held in Spain to commemorate the four hundredth anniversary of the discovery of America. Several of the studies she presented at this Congress were published. She was also honored by election to numerous European and Latin American academies, and was a founding member of the Colombian Academy of History. [4]

Doña Soledad was always interested in women's topics and issues. Some of her earliest essays pointed to the need for studies in women's history and for acceptance of women as equals of men. She fervently believed that giving women a sound education and involving them in intellectual life would moralize mankind and ensure the pursuit of Christian ideals. Among her many feminist publications, two especially stand out. In *La mujer en la sociedad moderna* [*Woman in Modern Society*] she sought to illustrate for Colombian women the achievements and careers of women in the nineteenth century. They too, she exhorted her readers, could undertake such honorable, self-satisfying careers and need not feel compelled to marry if no morally upright man proposed. If virtuous career women were able to refuse offers from immoral men, then the men would be forced to change their ways to win a wife, and the world would be morally uplifted. In 1878 Doña Soledad founded *La Mujer* [*Woman*], the first Colombian periodical edited and sustained entirely by women. It lasted a remarkable three years. Historical studies, novels, short stories, and didactic articles especially directed at *señoritas* [young ladies] filled its columns. During the remainder of her long life, she founded and edited three other such feminist journals. Doña Soledad died on March 17, 1913 at the age of 79. [5]

II

Clearly Soledad Acosta de Samper was an extaordinary figure in an age when most Colombian women were illiterate. Even in the upper classes, few women had more than a rudimentary education. A few of her female contemporaries did publish an occasional volume of poetry or a novel,[6] but none were significant or prominent literary figures and certainly none could even begin to compare with her more than one hundred and fifty literary and historical works. [7] In fact, probably no other figure, male or female, in nineteenth- or twentieth-century Colombian letters was more prolific, save her husband. This paper will suggest a number of factors in Doña Soledad's life which tentatively explain why she became nineteenth-century Colombia's only prominent woman writer.

Growing up an only child in the Acosta home partially accounts for her intellectual development. Virtually nothing is known about her mother, Caroline Kemble, and she and Soledad were not close. However, her mother did teach her English, which opened the world of English literature to Soledad and which allowed her later to become a successful translator. Her father, Joaquín Acosta, must have had a major influence on her. He had fought in Colombia's Independence wars and later rose to the rank of general. He had a very active political career. He was frequently elected to Congress, and also served as ambassador to Ecuador (1837-1839) and the United States (1842-1843), and as Minister of Foreign Relations (1844-1845). Joaquín Acosta was also exceptionally well-educated, having spent several years in Europe studying the sciences; and was the author of important scientific and historical studies. Due to his busy public and scholarly life he was often absent from their home in Guaduas. However, their house was a constant center of intellectual activity and discussion, due to Acosta's prominence in political, scientific, and cultural circles and to the fact that Guaduas was a favorite travelers' resting place on the main road between Bogotá and the Magdalena River. Feeling closest to her father and being the only child, Soledad was quite likely to have been an observer of, perhaps an active participant in, the home's intellectual gatherings. Her father also served as a scholarly model for Soledad. His history of the conquest of Colombia is a carefully researched, historically accurate work. Doña Soledad's interest in history, and especially in the conquest period, as well as her insistence on historical accuracy, undoubtedly reflects her father's influence. Most certainly his involvement in the independence wars was responisble for her interest in writing biographies of Independence heroes. Doña Soledad's fervent Catholicism, moral emphasis, and insistence on striving for ideals also reflect similar attitudes held by her father. Her father's travels provided Soledad with the opportunity for an education far superior to that available to women in Colombia. Although the content of the education she received in Halifax and Paris between 1845 and 1849 is not known, if we can judge from the breadth and erudition of her earliest writings, it at least included a mastery of the English and French languages, a broad acquaintance with classical and contemporary European letters, and some knowledge of world history and affairs. [8]

Of equal, if not even greater, importance in explaining Doña Soledad's literary career is her marriage to José María Samper. Her husband was a prominent politician, poet, dramatist, essayist, and journalist of incredible productivity, who bragged, quite accùrately, that he had written more in one life-time than most diligent men could have in two life-times. José María had an ambivalent attitude towards women, which led him to encourage Soledad's career. When speaking of women in general, even after his marriage to Soledad, he viewed the "second sex" as intellectually inferior, politically incompetent, and best suited to homemaking. Yet he recognized exceptions. He pointed with pride to the fact that his mother had learned to read and write. He subsidized the publication of some of the poetry written by his sister, Agripina Samper de Ancízar. And he obviously had considerable intellectual respect for Soledad, since he had her translate English and French works for the newspapers he edited, edited the *Revista Americana* with her, and strongly encouraged her to publish her first novel in 1869. Nevertheless, it seems evident that Doña Soledad chose to restrict her creative work to areas which did not duplicate, that is, challenge, her husband's talents and considerable ego. This, obviously, did somewhat restrict her, but it also left considerable room for her main interests. While he concentrated primarily on political journalism and poetry, she focused largely on historical works, literary criticism, and feminine topics for a feminine audience. This division of intellectual labor was evident as early as their 1858-1862 European sojourn, when José María principally wrote political and social commentary, while Soledad wrote on fashions and the arts, subjects on which José María viewed himself as incompetent. [9]

Doña Soledad's literary career also was helped by her personality. While she was extremely reluctant to reveal her personal feelings and private life, she did have a strong, assertive personality. For example, in her youth she refused to follow her maternal grandmother's wishes to convert to the Protestant faith; and she adamantly denied José María's wish to be married in a non-Catholic ceremony. In fact, it was largely through her influence that he returned to the Church in 1865. Upon her marriage to José María, she was concerned -- as she revealed in her diary -- with being superior to his first wife, whom he had not married in a religious ceremony, and also with encouraging his writing by striving to keep abreast of him intellectually. She further revealed, in the same diary, that she believed women were capable of and suited to literary careers. Her determination to be intellectually worthy of José María, together with her strong personality, her excellent education, and feminist attitudes, must have contributed considerably to producing her remarkable literary career. [10]

III

Soledad Acosta de Samper, as is evident from the first section of this paper, had a long and most prolific writing career. While many of her works are worthy of extended comment, this paper will explore only the beginnings of her literary career. Between 1856 and 1863, while traveling abroad, Doña Soledad published a number of columns and other pieces in Colombian and Peruvian periodicals. She commented upon a wide range of topics. For example, the escapades of the rich and powerful, furniture styles, holiday celebrations, politics, photography, crime, company towns, psychology, reform movements, religion, and oratory all drew her attention.[11] However, most of her writing dealt with travel, fashion, literature and the arts, and women.

Doña Soledad was an experienced traveler, and she found a ready audience for her travel columns. She reviewed travel books, dubbing one English attempt as not bad for fiction; cautioned against expecting too much from tourist services, e.g., the Swiss were experts at exploiting a traveler's credulity; and described in considerable detail the physical and cultural landscape, especially of Switzerland. Other travelers particularly caught her attention. She found the English either insufferably rich or ill-mannered, uncultured, and souvenir thieves. Americans fared little better. They were only interested in eating and drinking. Of all the European countries that the Sampers visited, France particularly fascinated Doña Soledad. French ideas were very popular in Colombia and from a distance France seemed cultured and progressive. She warned her Latin American audience that France up close was decadent and even barbarous. She especially was critical of an upper class which was conspicuously wasteful, irreligious, and sexually promiscuous; which married for convenience, and which valued sumptuous décor above real substance. For example, she was scandalized by the great ladies' need for twenty-eight fancy dresses to pass a week with the Empress; and believed that a mother who sued for support money after her son was killed in a duel was positively barbarous. Certainly, she assured her readers, no South American mother would ever do such a mercenary thing.[12]

Doña Soledad's columns also introduced Latin American readers to the latest European, especially French, fashions. For the most part she found them so extravagant and ornate as to be of little practical use in less affluent societies. And the bright colors offended her conservative tastes. Women, she admonished, ought not to dress like parrots! Interestingly, she perceived a connection between fashion and political systems. If a people dressed simply and conservatively, the government was democratic, and if their costumes were ornate and revealing, they surely lived under a tyranny.[13]

French literature was widely read among mid-nineteenth-century Colombian youth, who believed it provided a model for progress. In numerous essays of literary criticism, Doña Soledad scoffed at this fashionable literature. Offering a mother's counsel, she warned that scarcely anything written in France was fit for *señoritas* to read. Too many novels degraded marriage and popularized divorce. Doña Soledad was certain that these anti-social works would ruin the family. She especially singled out the works of George Sand and Gustave Flaubert as idealizing sexual license. Equally deplorable, contemporary literature was not respectful of religion, e.g., Eugène Sue's *The Wandering Jew*. She further commented that while the works of romanticism were generally acceptable reading, those of the more recent school of realism were not. Realism, Doña Soledad believed, was common, vulgar, and trivial.

Furthermore, it failed to portray honorable characters and the ideals all should strive for. Although she thought that good literature should not distort historical reality, yet it should not concentrate on sordid events, but should show ideals. Above all, a book must have a clear moral message. [14]

Perhaps Doña Soledad's most interesting early writing was her feminist columns. She perceived her audience as being primarily women and her role as educating them. Women, she believed, were equal to men in intelligence. Give women a decent education, she admonished the other sex, and their intellectual equality will be self-evident. And furthermore women were superior to men in imagination, memory, and intuition. They were inferior, however, in physical strength -- thus women ought to avoid the battlefields of war and politics. Doña Sodedad thought that women should be virtuous models -- especially for their spouses and children, or if not married, for society -- and believed that in this way they would have far greater influence than if they involved themselves in politics. But she also stressed that women should not see themselves as wives only. For careers should certainly be open to them as well, as long as a career did not destroy their femininity, that is, the qualities of delicacy, modesty, and timidity. At every opportunity she described successful career women as possible role models and she called for a history of women which would catalogue their achievements -- a history which she herself later wrote. Doña Soledad also based her feminism on the belief that men and women were equal before God. She thought that religion was indipensable for women. It consoled them in their suffering, and convents offered a refuge from the disappointments of secular life. Together with education, religion also saved women from immorality. Despite her support for improvements in women's condition, her concern did not always extend to the lower classes. She did understand that lower-class women needed jobs if they were not to be forced into prositution. But she also disapproved of maids organizing to protect themselves against unscrupulous employers, as was the case in London. This, she feared, would mean that some upper-class women would be without maid service; and she expressed satisfaction with ignorant Colombian maids who knew their place. Yet, on the whole, Doña Soledad's writing on women's place was progressive. In the middle of the nineteenth century, equality for women was still a novel idea. And among Colombians, few could be found who would forcefully argue that women were not frivolous homebodies, but rather intelligent people with an interest in serious subjects. [15] In Doña Soledad's words, "La mujer no es un niño que se puede manejar con paliativos" ["Women are not children that can be managed with palliatives"]. [16]

NOTES

[1] Gustavo Otero Muñoz, "Soledad Acosta de Samper," *Boletín Cultural y Bibliográfico* [*Cultural and Bibliographical Bulletin*] (Bogotá), vol. 7, no. 6 (1964), p. 1063.

[2] Gustavo Otero Muñoz, "Doña Soledad Acosta de Samper," *Boletín de Historia y Antigüedades* [*Bulletin of History and Antiquities*] (Bogotá), vol. 20, no. 229 (April 1933), pp. 171-175; Soledad Acosta de Samper, *Biografía del General Joaquín Acosta: Prócer de Independencia, historiador, geógrafo, hombre científico y filántropo* [*Biography of General Joaquín Acosta: Founding Father, Historian, Geographer, Scientist, and Philanthropist*](Bogotá: Librería Colombiana, Camacho Roldán y Tamayo, 1901), pp. 395, 427, 457; Bernardo J. Caycedo, "Semblanza de Doña Soledad Acosta de Samper" [Bibliographical Sketch of Doña Soledad Acosta de Samper"], *Bolívar*(Bogotá), no. 15 (November-December 1952), pp. 970, 976, 978; Gustavo Otero Muñoz, "Soledad Acosta de Samper," *Boletín de Historia y Antigüedades*, vol. 24, no. 271(May 1937), pp. 259, 263; Soledad Acosta de Samper (Andina), "Revista parisiense" ["Parisian Review"], *Biblioteca de Señoritas* (Bogotá) (March 26, 1859), pp. 89-91; Otero Muñoz, "Soledad Acosta de Samper" (1964), pp. 1063-1064; José María Samper, *Historia de una alma, 1834 a 1881* [*History of a Soul, 1834-1881*] (2nd ed.) 2 vols. (Bogotá: Publicaciones del Ministerio de Educación de Colombia, vol. 1, Editorial Kelly, 1946; vol. 2, Prensas del Ministerio de Educación de Colombia, 1948), vol. 2, pp. 142, 280, 332, 356.

[3] Otero Muñoz, "Doña Soledad Acosta de Samper" (April 1933), p. 173; Caycedo, "Semblanza," pp. 965, 976, 978-980; Isidoro Laverde Amaya, "De las novelas colombianas ["On Colombian Novels"], *La Revista Literaria* (Bogotá) (June 1893), pp. 83-84; Otero Muñoz, "Soledad Acosta de Samper" (May 1937), pp. 263-264, 266-269; Soledad Acosta de Samper, *Episodios novelescos de la historia patria. La insurrección de los Comuneros* [*Novelistic Episodes of the Fatherland's History: The Commoner's Insurrection*](Bogotá: Imp. de La Luz, 1887), p. vii.

[4] Otero Muñoz, "Doña Soledad Acosta de Samper" (April 1933), pp. 174-175; Caycedo, "Semblanza," pp. 981-982, 984; Otero Muñoz, "Soledad Acosta de Samper" (May 1937), pp. 259, 261.

[5] Otero Muñoz, "Doña Soledad Acosta de Samper" (April 1933), pp. 173-175; Caycedo, "Semblanza," p. 983; Otero Muñoz, "Soledad Acosta de Samper" (May 1937), p. 262; Soledad Acosta de Samper (Bertilda), "Historia de la mujer" ["History of Women"], *El Tiempo* [*The Times*](Bogotá)(May 8, 1860), p.(3); Soledad Acosta de Samper, *La mujer en la sociedad moderna* (Paris: Garnier Hermanos, 1895), pp. vii-xi.

[6] Gustavo Otero Muñoz, in *Resumen de historia de la literatura colombiana* [*Historical Résumé of Colombian Literature*], 4th ed., rev. & augm. (Bogotá: Librería Voluntad, 1943), pp. 296-306; and Laverde Amaya, in "De las novelas colombianas," p. 86, n. 1., list some twenty post-Independence women writers, who together did not publish a fraction of the literature written by Acosta de Samper.

[7] For a bibliography of Acosta de Samper's works, see Otero Muñoz, "Soledad Acosta de Samper" (May 1937), pp. 270-283.

[8] Caycedo, "Semblanza," pp. 965-974; Robert Henry Davis, "Acosta, Caro, and Lleras: Three Essayists and Their Views of New Granada's National Problems, 1832-1853" (Ph.D. dissertation,Vanderbilt University, 1969), pp. 92-166; Acosta de Samper, *Biografía del General Joaquín Acosta*, pp. 394ff.

[9] Samper, *Historia de una alma*, vol. 1, pp. 68-69, 210; José María Samper, *Ensayo sobre las revoluciones políticas y la condición social de las repúblicas colombianas (hispano-americanas): Con un apéndice sobre la orografía y la población de la Confederación Granadina* [*Essay on the Political Revolutions and the Social Condition of the Colombian (Hispano-American) Republics: With an Appendix on the Granadan Confederation's Orography and Population*], (2nd ed.) (Bogotá: Publicaciones del Ministerio de Educación de Colombia, Editorial Centro, n.d.), p.158; José María Samper, *Pensamientos sobre moral, política, literatura, religión y costumbres* [*Thoughts on Morality, Politics, Literature, Religion, and Customs*](2nd ed.) (Caracas: Imprenta de G. Corser, 1858), pp. 23, 40; José María Samper, *Ecos de los Andes: Poesías líricas.*

Segunda colección, de 1849 a 1860[*Ecos of the Andes: Lyrical Poems. Second Collection, 1849-1860* (Paris: E. Thunot y Ca., 1860), pp. 343-396; Otero Muñoz, "Soledad Acosta de Samper" (May 1937), p. 259; José María Samper, *Viajes de un Colombiano en Europa* [*Travels of a Colombian in Europe*], 2 vols. (Paris: Imprenta de E. Thunot y Ca., 1862), vol. 1. p. 353.

[10] Caycedo, "Semblanza", pp. 965, 971-973, 975-976; Samper, *Historia de una alma*, vol. 1, pp. 209-210.

[11] Acosta de Samper's writings on these topics may be found in the issues of January 29, 1859; February 5, 1859; February 19, 1859; March 5, 1859; March 26, 1859; April 23, 1859; May 14, 1859; June 4, 1859; June 18, 1859 of the *Biblioteca de Señoritas*; in the issues of September 17, 1859; October 1, 1859; March 17, 1860; and March 26, 1864 of *El Mosaico* (Bogotá); and in the issues of January 20, 1863; February 20, 1863; March 5, 1863; April 5, 1863; April 20, 1863; May 5, 1863; May 20, 1863 of the *Revista Americana* (Lima).

[12] Soledad Acosta de Samper (Andina), "Recuerdos de Suiza," ["Memories of Switzerland"], *El Mosaico* (October 1, 1859), pp. 310-311; Soledad Acosta de Samper (Andina), "Recuerdos de Suiza," *El Mosaico* (March 17, 1860), p. 82; Soledad Acosta de Samper (Andina), "Revista parisiense," *Biblioteca de Señoritas* (January 29, 1859), pp. 26-27; Soledad Acosta de Samper (Andina), "Revista parisiense," *Biblioteca de Señoritas* (February 19, 1859), p. 51; Soledad Acosta de Samper (Andina), "Revista parisiense," *Biblioteca de Señoritas* (May 14, 1859), p. 145; Soledad Acsota de Samper (Bertilda), "Revista femenina" ["Feminine Review"], *Revista Americana* (January 20,1863), p. 46; Soledad Acosta de Samper (Bertilda), "Revista femenina. (Conversación familiar.)" ["Feminine Review. (Domestic Conversation.)"], *Revista Americana* (March 5, 1863), pp. 118-119; Soledad Acosta de Samper (Bertilda), "Revista femenina. (Conversación familiar.), "*Revista Americana* (April 5, 1863), p. 164.

[13] Soledad Acosta de Samper (Andina), "Revista parisiense," *Biblioteca de Señoritas* (February 5, 1859), pp. 33-34; Soledad Acosta de Samper (Andina), "Revista parisiense," *Biblioteca de Señoritas* (March 5, 1859), p. 66.

[14] Acosta de Samper, "Revista parisiense" (January 29, 1859), pp. 27-28; Acosta de Samper, "Revista parisiense" (March 26, 1859), p. 90; Soledad Acosta de Samper (Andina), "Revista parisiense," *Biblioteca de Señoritas* (June 4, 1859), p. 14; Acosta de Samper, "Revista parisiense" (February 19, 1859), p. 51; Acosta de Samper, "Revista parisiense" (May 14, 1859), p. 145; Soledad Acosta de Samper (Andina), "Revista parisiense," *Biblioteca de Señoritas* (April 23, 1859), p. 122; Soledad Acosta de Samper (Bertilda), "Revista femenina," *Revista Americana* (February 20, 1863), p. 94; Acosta de Samper, "Revista femenina. [Conversación familiar.]" (March 5, 1863), p. 119.

[15] Acosta de Samper, "Historia de la mujer," p. (3); Soledad Acosta de Samper (Andina), "Ecos de Europa" ["Ecos of Europe"], *El Mosaico.* (March 26, 1864), p. 83; Acosta de Samper, "Revista femenina" (January 20, 1863), pp. 45-46; Acosta de Samper, "Revista parisiense" (June 4, 1859), p. 14; Acosta de Samper, "Revista femenina. (Conversación familiar.)" (April 5, 1863), p. 164; Soledad Acosta de Samper (Bertilda), "La mujer orador" ["The Woman Orator"], *Revista Americana* (April 20, 1863), pp. 190-191; Soledad Acosta de Samper (Andina), "La monja" ["The Nun"], *El Mosaico* (June 25, 1864), pp. 188-191.

[16] Acosta de Samper, "Historia de la mujer," p. (3).

Teresa de la Parra
Venezuelan Novelist and Feminist

by

RONNI GORDON STILLMAN

Fairleigh Dickinson University

While Teresa de la Parra is best known for her novel *Las memorias de Mamá Blanca* [*The Memoirs of Mama Blanca*], an artistic and nostalgic reminiscence of a happy childhood spent on a Venezuelan sugar plantation, it is another literary endeavor, long neglected by critics, that I direct myself to in this paper. While *Memorias,* written in 1929, is a minor literary masterpiece worthy of an exhaustive intrinsic analysis, the other novel of De la Parra, *Ifigenia,* written in 1924, stands out not so much for its literary qualities as for its ideas. The language is not so effective, the characterizations not so synthetic and universal, and yet there is a brilliant portraiture here. *Ifigenia,* subtitled *Diario de una señorita que escribió porque se fastidiaba* [*Diary of a Young Lady Who Wrote Because She Was Bored*], is the work of Teresa de la Parra feminist and it is a valuable contribution to the cultural anthropology of Spanish America. The partially autobiographical tableau allows us to abstract truths about the upper-class Spanish-American woman especially in the first 25 years of this century. The novelist is innovative in her attempt to appraise and criticize the role of women and she is one of the first apologists in Venezuela and Spanish America to argue the cause of feminism.

Born in Paris in 1890, Ana Parra Sanojo was brought to the family sugar plantation near Caracas where she spent her early childhood. She left Venezuela to study in a convent school in Spain until her eighteenth birthday when she again returned to Caracas. María Eugenia Alonso, the protagonist of *Ifigenia,* is also a young woman from a comfortable family who, when we first meet her, is on her way home to Caracas after a long stay in Europe.

It is the return to Caracas, a city in transition at the time, that prompted the novelist to write *Ifigenia.* She saw a dynamic change taking place in the economic and social structure of the country during her lifetime. Under the dictatorship of Juan Vicente Gómez (1908-35). the exploitation of petroleum resources by foreign oil companies led to unprecedented economic prosperity in certain sectors of society. Before her death in 1936, De la Parra saw Venezuela thrust into the 20th century with its overriding spirit of materialism. She attacked materialism as the force that created some inimical social problems and was most troubled by the social position of women in Caracas, a problem she realized was generalized throughout all the major cities of Spanish America. The young woman of means was awakened to the promises of modernity but she was not allowed to participate in that new freedom; she continued to be repressed by a society full of prejudices and restrictions. The novelist painted such a woman in *Ifigenia* and criticized her captors: men, the embodiment of materialism, selfish perpetuators of the social order. The young woman was primed for marriage to which she gave herself, in body if not in spirit, and spent the rest of her life in hopeless submission to her husband, children and the rules of society. In a letter to an unnamed friend, dated Leysin (Switzerland), December 29,1932, Teresa writes: "My character María Eugenia Alonso was really a synthesis, a living copy of several types of women I had seen suffering in silence all around me and whose true nature I wanted to reveal, 'make talk,' as a protest against the pressure of the social milieu." [1]

Teresa de la Parra offers an apology of *Ifigenia* and reveals her feminist views in a series of lectures she gave in Colombia in 1929, entitled "La influencia de las mujeres en la formación del alma americana" ["The Influence of Women in the Formation of the American Spirit"]. In the first of these lectures the writer defends her novel from those critics who call it "Volterian, treacherous and extremely dangerous in the hands of contemporary young ladies." (p. 684) She explains that she is reflecting an important social phenomenon in these young women of the upper classes who contain within themselves a María Eugenia Alonso in rebellion. They strike out against the submission and self-denial that women have known throughout history, demanding that women be free, responisble to themselves alone, useful to society in ways of their own choosing, and financially independent, that is, supporting themselves through their work. Teresa clarifies that by work she does not mean the humiliating and badly paying jobs in which women are exploited, but rather positions that require study and preparation, suitable for a woman's talents and abilities, for which she will be fairly compensated. Contrary to popular belief, the real enemies of feminine virtue are not books, work and exposure to life, Teresa argues, but rather boredom and aimlessness. Too many women -married and of marriageable age- are bored and unhappy with their lives but society denies them the right to seek out the roots of their dissatisfaction and explore new paths of self-realization. Instead, they acquiesce to the dogma that an uryielding society has transmitted to them: marriage is woman's *raison d'etre* and the source of her fulfillment. The novelist did not accept this end for herself choosing instead to write, travel and, lecture.

In the second lecture, the novelist defends the intellectual woman who devotes her life to study. She expresses her admiration for Madre Teresa, a nun she knew in Caracas, and for Sor Juana Inés de la Cruz, two women who entered the convent for intellectual as well as religious pursuits. The convent was the only place where a woman could devote herself to her books without being criticized and made to feel unnatural. Women were commonly admonished: ''Women who know Latin end up badly''(p. 719), that is, spinsterhood was the terrible and inevitable end that awaited the intellectual woman.

In the third lecture, Teresa de la Parra treats the issue of divorce justifying the conduct of Doña Manuelita Sáenz, a Venezuelan noblewoman who brazenly left the husband she never loved to be with Simón Bolívar. She challenged the idea of the indissolubility of marriage and was consequently rejected by her friends, protectors of the social order.

Teresa is progressive in her ideas about feminism, sympathetic to the needs and propensities of women, and yet her method by which women will achieve independence is more conservative. She rejects a destructive revolution in favor of a process of evolution that will conquer by educating and by making use of the forces of the past. Furthermore, politics, which she ranks with coal mining as the hardest and dirtiest occupations, has no place in her plan and she gratefully leaves the duties of politicians to men.

Turning to *Ifigenia*, we can examine the portrait of the young woman in Caracas in 1924. In this traditional narration the omniscient authoress tells us about the characters and expresses her views through them. Focusing on María Eugenia's aunt we learn what was prescribed for the young married woman. Her husband watched her constantly, censored her entertainment, did not allow her to go out alone, dance, draw attention to herself, establish close relationships with anyone, use make-up or wear provocative clothing. As a young unmarried woman María Eugenia is also expected to live by a strict code. Her grandmother and maiden Aunt Clara, representing tradition, make sure that she measures up and criticize her incessantly for the unladylike way she sits, stands, speaks, for the friends she has and for painting her lips. She is reprimanded harshly for writing to a male friend because self-respecting young women do not send letters to men other than their fathers, brothers, husbands or fiancés. What *is* expected of her is that she will, as an honorable and domestic woman, master the art of making lace and perform other homely duties. María Eugenia's grandmother blames the protagonist's spirit of independence and ignorance of household chores on her reading too much and too indiscriminately.

Some of the characteristics prized in a woman are forgiveness, indulgence, sacrifice, and virtue. María Eugenia is scandalized by her grandmother's many admonitions about the role of the woman as for her it means being a non-entity, a personality-less thing that can only be respected by society if her husband esteems her. Total obedience to a superior or elder male -husband, father, brother, uncle- is expected of the woman just as much as her unquestioning faith and belief in God. The deification of the male figure is in fact the woman's second religion.

Customs related to death and mourning also illustrate the woman's role in society. Only two years after the death of her father is María Eugenia permitted to remove her mourning attire and sit at the window. This is the proper way she will see and be seen by society. She feels as though she is on exhibition: "I am on sale!...Who will buy me?" (p. 312) The question of marriage arises at this time but the heroine's Uncle Pancho opposes his niece marrying without seeing the world and enjoying herself first; once she has had more exposure to life she can marry if she chooses. This unconventional idea meets with the disapproval of María Eugenia's grandmother and Uncle Eduardo who plan to marry off their ward at once. They fear that all the good catches in Caracas will be snatched up if María Eugenia waits too long. Besides, they agree that what their charge needs, and the sooner the better, is a husband to guide and teach her and keep her in her place; she must be broken of her willfulness, her excessive independence, and her disdain for everything that represents authority. César Leal is the candidate proposed by Eduardo for he has all the attributes necessary in a good husband including money, good family, education, and professional position. Marrying for money and social position is the norm in this society of pre-arranged marriages.

Male-female relationships are well developed in the novel. The protagonist's Uncle Pancho is the only male to escape the novelist's criticism; he is the voice of reason and speaks largely for the novelist. He is also the conscience of the heroine, the voice within her that fights back when society threatens her independence. Pancho explains that women are in an inferior social position for economic reasons, that if they do not have their own fortune they must depend upon the male to support them. María Eugenia has been cheated out of the remainder of her inheritance by Eduardo and she anticipates total dependence on her spouse. Pancho admires his niece for her self-esteem and cautions her that society will attempt to belittle her by making her worth dependent upon male esteem for her. He criticizes the system of honor whereby the slightest deviation from society's rules of conduct on the part of the woman leaves a stain on the man's honor. Speaking about the women of Caracas in particular, Pancho accuses women of being too submissive, of steeping themselves in sacrifice and flagellation like martyrs, and not trying to secure the rights to which they are entitled. The death of the curiously (given the time and place) enlightened Uncle Pancho precipitates the protagonist's tragedy.

The plight of the unhappily married woman is treated in the figure of Mercedes Galindo who lives the lie of the happy, loving marriage never daring to betray her true feelings. María Eugenia defends Mercedes from the calumny of César Leal and the others but finally gives up in defeat realizing that their argument, sanctioned by society itself, cannot be discredited. They maintain that a woman coming from a good background, even though disappointed in her marital union, must not make her feelings known, protest or create a scandal with divorce. It is prescribed that she will continue to discharge her wifely duties all the time suffering in absolute silence. De la Parra demonstrates time and again that honesty is not the guiding principle in this society. The case of Gabriel Olmedo suggests what it is like to be trapped in a loveless marriage from the masculine viewpoint. While he considers himself to be the victim, since he has no grounds for divorce, it is clear that Olmedo's wife is the sacrificial lamb in this union. Olmedo can run from the situation, be out of the house day and night if he chooses and still be beyond reproach in society's eyes. His wife, on the other hand, remains at home caring for that domain to which she naturally belongs. Olmedo laments his predicament but is consoled by the fact that he is not the woman: "Fortunately in this hideous misunderstanding I am the man, and for that reason, instead of staying at home to face that ever-present person, I go out and I stay out all day. But if unfortunately it were the opposite, that is, if being the victim as I am, I were besides the woman instead of the man...alas!...I would have already died of despair and boredom." (p. 388)

Like the other male personages in the novel (except Pancho), Gabriel Olmedo is portrayed unfavorably. He is ambitious and materialistic; he marries a woman he does not love to increase his wealth and power thereby sacrificing his feelings for María Eugenia on the altar of Mammon. Once his ambition is sated he returns to the protagonist and begs her to run away with him. She chooses to remain with her fiancé, César Leal, a foolish, arrogant, selfish, tyrannical man. His negative attitude toward women and their place in society is generalized as the male position. When María Eugenia recites one of Silva's "Nocturnos" to Leal, he responds with disgust: he hates Romanticism and recitations and most of all he hates women who display erudition. According to him, "a woman's head was a more or less decorative object, completely empty inside, made to gladden men's eyes, and equipped with two ears whose only function was to receive and collect the orders that men dictated to them." (p. 357) Furthermore, a woman must be religious and guided by faith because she has no power of reason. Leal succeeds in extinguishing what is left of María Eugenia's once independent spirit. As the instrument of an implacable society he is triumphant in reducing the thoughtful, self-assertive young woman to an obsequious coward who takes great pains to prove her ignorance. Once she took delight in reciting *The Divine Comedy* in Old Italian, in speaking French and English, in reading voraciously, in writing. Now she even denies knowing who Dante is and claims that all the writing she ever did involved copying recipes.

In parts I and II of the four-part novel, María Eugenia manifests a spirit of rebelliousness admired by the novelist. She rails at timidity and the object-like existence of the well-off young woman. She laments that she was not born a male so she could be free to do as she pleases: "But I am a woman... and being a woman is the same as being a canary or a linnet. You are locked up in a cage, taken care of, fed and not allowed out while men are merry and flying free. How hateful it is to be a woman!" (p. 129) She sees women as victims, pariahs, slaves, destitute of all rights in the social order. She takes refuge in books and is able to feed her intellectual interests thanks to an accomplice who secures books for her from the library. María Eugenia's grandmother and Aunt Clara would never permit this indulgence and the protagonist takes delight in imagining the scandal if Clara found out she were reading Voltaire's *Philosophical Dictionary*. Both ignorance and innocence are expected in the woman but María Eugenia curses them as having the power to keep women in chains. "Innocence is the humiliating symbol of obedience and bondage which almost all honorable women are used to living in after they get married."(p. 179)

By the time we reach part III two years have elapsed during which the heroine has undergone a transformation. She has learned to live with innumerable social restrictions and has adopted the traditional role of the unmarried upper-class woman. She prides herself on her embroidery, lacemaking and culinary skill. Her prowess in domestic affairs has paid off as she now has a fiancé and freely admits that marriage is her all-consuming interest. In her relationship with her fiancé María Eugenia is submissive and servile. She recognizes his tyrannical hold over her but refrains from defending herself rather than displease him. She indulges him in every way blindly obeying all the restrictions and orders he dictates to her as to whom she will see, what she will wear, etc. Though the protagonist dares not express her thoughts to Leal, she confesses to Gabriel Olmedo that she is terribly unhappy but resigned. She bemoans the fate of all women as she laments her own: "we, poor women, who always go through life under the burden of submission... you see, resigned to be bored, resigned to forget the ideals that cannot be, resigned to be silent so that everything within us is silenced forever." (p. 386) But the alternative if she does not marry Leal is far worse to her: the imminent death of her grandmother ushering in years of prohibitive mourning, perhaps the loss of her beauty -"my only guarantee and my only reason for being." (p. 482)-, finally a humiliating, lonely existence like her unmarried Aunt Clara's. She realizes that marriage to Leal means the total suppression of her will and a hateful servitude to a man she cannot love, and although she hates herself for being a coward, she feels too impotent to repel the forces that have conspired to bring her to this end: the inexorable laws of society as seen in the rigid male-female roles. In agreeing to marry Leal, the protagonist surrenders to the social pressure that will govern the rest of her life. She sees her tragedy personified in the sacrifice of Iphigenia, but the god to whom she will be sacrificed is a "ferocious and ancestral god: venerable monster with seven heads that invokes: society, family, honor, religion, morality, duty, conventions, principles. Omnipotent deity that embodies the cruel selfishness of men." (p. 493)

In *Ifigenia* Teresa de la Parra succeeded in revealing the nature of the upper-class Spanish-American woman of her time and in registering a strong protest against the male-dominated society. The half-century since the appearance of the novel has seen a certain reconsideration of the role of women and some signs of change in the area of options open to women. Marriage and family have not ceased to be society's consecrated goals for women but new alternatives are arising as women are educated into the 20th century. John P. Gillin, an anthropologist, observes:

> In conservative circles and in some provincial centers women are still expected to follow the older pattern, confining their activities mainly to the home and the church. In the middle groups, however, their emergence into business and public affairs has been spectacular. Middle-status women work in clerical positions, as teachers, as trained nurses and hygiene experts, as physicians and lawyers, and in a variety of other callings. . . . From the traditional point of view, one of the most startling phenomena is the rise of prominent women politicians. [2]

Teresa de la Parra foresaw the participation of women in these areas although she did not advocate the sharing of the political burden.

This novelist and feminist, an extraordinary phenomenon in the Venezuela of the 1920's and 1930's, integrated her art and spirit of reform in the hope that women would no longer be sacrificed to that ferocious deity of male supremacy-society-family-honor, as was the protagonist of *Ifigenia*.

NOTES

[1] Teresa de la Parra, *Obras completas* (Caracas: Editorial Arte, 1965), pp. 929-30. All quotations are from this edition of *The Complete Works of Teresa de la Parra*. The translations are my own.

[2] John P. Gillin, "Some Signposts for Policy," *Social Change in Latin America Today* (New York: Vintage Books, 1960), pp. 49-50.

Elena Poniatowska's
Hasta No Verte, Jesús Mío
[*Until I See You, Dear Jesus*]

by

CHARLES M. TATUM

New Mexico State University

Elena Poniatowska is one of many contemporary Mexican writers whose works are firmly rooted in post-revolutionay Mexican social reality. Even the casual reader will have little trouble finding an abundance of novels and short stories which graphically portrays the plight of the rural and urban poor exploited by rich and powerful landowners, industrialists, and government officials masking as leaders of the Revolution. These works provide a description of the downtrodden, of the suffering and the misery of Mexico's masses, but few succeed like Poniatowska's *Hasta no verte, Jesús mío* in presenting this reality from the inside-out, from the point of view of the feminine participant-narrator who reflects the attitudes, values, and behavior of her society.

But Poniatowska's novel is not merely a social documentary. Its value does not reside only in its proletarian conception of a period of Mexican history. The focal point is not the external aspects of social institutions but the evolution and fate of Jesusa Palancares, the first person narrator who is endowed with picaresque traits. The chronicle of her life experiences is not a pretext to scan society critically, condemning its weaknesses and hypocrisy, revealing its seamy underside. It is to present a particular view of the world, that of a lower class working woman whose upbringing and early encounters with brutality and egotism determine, in large part, her independence and strength of character as an older woman. She resists the taming influence of the Mexican male and social institutions — the church, school, the army, and marriage — which attempt to thrust her into a submissive role. While not suggesting that the novel offers a feminist interpretation of reality, it does present a different view than other contemporary Mexican novels of the rural woman, the *soldadera* [camp-follower], her participation in the bloody civil strife of the Mexican Revolution, and her adaptation to the social turmoil which followed.

In the tradition of Lizardi's *El periquillo sarniento* [*The Itching Parrot*] and José Rubén Romero's *La vida inútil de Pito Pérez* [*The Useless Life of Pito Pérez*], Poniatowska's work falls squarely within the picaresque mode. [1] Very early in the novel Jesusa refers to herself as a Lazarina, a young girl of typical picaresque origins, abandoned in death by her mother and destined to follow her father in his meanderings from job to job, from city to city, and from one army detachment to another during the early part of her life. She has very little family life and consequently does not receive the domestic training common to the other female children of her social class.

Like the many *pícaros* before her, Jesusita is dumped into a chaotic world in the midst of savage civil war, a world far worse than our own where, in order to survive, she rapidly matures to adopt an essentially defensive stance in the face of the uncertainties which constantly confront her. From Tehuantepec to Salina Cruz, from Acapulco to Mexico City, she finds herself having to adjust to the vicissitudes of her father's life and the whims of his many mistresses who seem bent on shaping Jesusita in their own image. She soon realizes that she must strike out on her own, even knowing that leaving her father will be fraught with pain and difficulty.

Characteristic of the picaresque novel, *Hasta no verte, Jesús mío* has a panoramic structure as opposed to being a novel of incident or character. Within that structure, the Mexican work is further characterized by the "eternal falling afresh to the task of survival in the landscape of the discontinuous, paralleled narratively by a continuously discontinuous (episodic) fictional form." [2] In the novel's 29 sections, Jesusa is forced to confront some form of adversity and thus finds herself in a situation which threatens her survival. She extricates herself from the situation utilizing her ever-growing repertory of tricks. Taken collectively, the 29 episodes illustrate the continuous dis-integration of an already chaotic world in which Jesusa exists.

Like other *pícaros*, Jesusa always struggles to make the best of seemingly intolerable circumstances as she resists efforts on the part of her employers and others to exploit her. Jesusa works for a time as a housekeeper in her godmother's pharmacy but leaves suddenly when she realized she is rapidly becoming subservient to her. She enters into the employment of an American and his Mexican wife, but this relationship is also cut short by Jesusa's refusal to be exploited.

Rather than ennumerate the many different instances in which she finds herself entangled, suffice it to say that the precipitous changes which occur in her life and in her relationships make her more cautious of the ways of the world. Very soon Jesusa develops an armor, a defensive cynicism which allows her to tolerate life in a chaotic revolutionary society.

One of the most important aspects of the picaresque novel is its implicit criticism of the social institutions and trends of a given historical period. You will recall the *Lazarillo's* mordant satire of the Church and the Spanish nobility of the sixteenth century. Lizardi's *El periquillo sarniento* paints a detailed picture of Mexican society during the final days of the viceroyalty. Lizardi guides his *pícaro* through several social strata and at each point we are given a penetrating view of the corruption, decay, and hypocrisy he encounters.

Poniatowska offers us a similar view of Mexico from the time of Madero through the sixties. Jesusa comments freely on the Catholic Church, the prison system, education, the medical profession, the failure of the Revolution, and the Mexican national character.

As a child, she attends a religious school taught by nuns, an experience which turns her away from the rigid dogmatism of established religion and leads her to develop a deep anti-clericalism which persists until the moment, years later, of her own conversion to a fanatical religious sect. Jesusa recalls bitterly her years in the religious school: "A las condenadas monjas yo les echo rayos y centellas porque me hincaban en unos balcones por el lado de la calle, sobre unos montoncitos de frijoles, o maíces o garbanzos y si no sobre granitos de hormiguero, y en la mera choya me ponían las orejas de burro. Y claro que yo me hice más rebelde y me vengaba colocándoles bolas de chicle en las bancas y les pegosteaba las naguas. Luego les jalaba el capirucho. No sabía yo otra cosa pero si me las presentaran ahora, capaz que barría yo las calles con ellas, al fin que andan muy hilachudas y parecen escobas." [3] ["Those nuns really make me angry because they would make me kneel in the balcony on the street side on a little pile of beans, or corn or chickpeas or if not that, then on grains of sand, and right on my head they would place donkey ears. And of course I became more rebellious and I got even putting gum balls on the benches which would stick to their rear ends. Then I would yank the hoods of their habits. That's the only thing I knew and if you showed them to me now, I would be capable of sweeping up the streets with 'em; since they are always so tattered and they look like brooms."]

She also condemns the nuns and the priests for what was thought to be a common practice in pre-Revolutionary days: their illicit sexual activities. The Church, in Jesusa's opinion, serves only to deceive and therefore should be destroyed.

Turning her criticism to education, Poniatowska satirizes the literacy campaign undertaken by the revolutionary government. Jesusa and her fellow hospital workers are visited by a contingent of young teachers from the Ministry of Education. Although well-intentioned, the young instructors prove to be woefully naive in their

efforts to teach the seasoned and cynical working-class women. While
wanting to learn to read and write, the women resent the clumsiness
and patronizing attitude of their teachers:

> Estos maestros y maestras querían divertirse con
> nosotros porque estábamos grandes. ¡Quíen sabe si sería un
> nuevo sistema de educacíon pero yo no les hice caso! Que
> ¿cómo se llaman los pájaros de siete colores? ¿Cómo se llaman
> los pescados que están debajo del agua? Pues pescados ¿no?
> ¿Y esas flores que según ellos eran hembras y machos? Dije:
> "No, conmigo no, a mí no me gusta buscarles chiches a las
> culebras. Así es de que hasta aquí le cortamos a la
> alfabetizda." Y me salí del Hospital de las podridas porque en
> primer lugar me pagaban muy poco y luego llegaron estos
> maestros a querer tomarnos el pelo con sus exámenes dizque
> de biología comparada y los mandé al carajo. (202)

[These teachers wanted to have some fun at our
expense since we were grownups. I don't know if it was a new
system of education but I didn't pay any attention to 'em!
Like, "What's the name of the bird with seven colors?" and
"What's the name of the fish under the water?" Well, some
fish, huh? "And those flowers which according to them were
males and females?" I told 'em: "Not with me you don't; I
don't like looking for bedbugs or snakes." So pretty quick this
whole literacy thing came to an end. And I left that fleabitten
hospital because, to begin with, they payed very little, and
these teachers arrived to pull our leg with their so-called
biology exams and I told them where to go."]

The Revolution and its leaders come under harsh criticism.
Jesusa reminisces about the confusing period after Madero's
assassination when alliances and loyalties were in a constant state of
flux: one day a *carrancista,* (a supporter of President Carranza), the
next an *anti-carrancista;* feuding between *caudillos* [military leaders]
jealous of each other's influence and power; soldiers deceived into
sacrificing their lives in the bloodbath in which they have no real
stake. As many other post-Revolutionary writers, Poniatowska
demythifies the Revolution by painting some of its most horrible
aspects as dominant features of a period when savagery and greed,
not idealism, were prime motivating forces. Jesusa comments: "Yo
creo que fue una guerra mal entendida porque eso de que se mataran
unos con otros, padres contra hijos, hermanos contra hermanos;
carrancistas, villistas, zapatistas, pues eran puras tarugadas porque
éramos los mismos pelados y muertos de hambre. Pero ésas son cosas
que, como dicen, por sabidas se callan." (94) ["I think it must have
been a poorly understood war what with some people killing others,
fathers against sons, brothers against brothers, *carrancistas, villistas,*

zapatistas; well the whole bunch of 'em were just plain crazy because we were the very ones dying of hunger. But that's the way the things are, it goes without saying."]

As Jesusa looks back to the turbulent years of the Revolution and its afermath, she concludes sadly that conditions have not changed. In spite of this high-sounding rhetoric and the thousands of dead, the people have been betrayed by their leaders: "La revolución no ha cambiado nada. Nomás estamos más muertos de hambre." (126) ["The Revolution hasn't changed anything. We're just starving more now."]

Lázaro Cárdenas' land-reform program is described as a pretext to expropriate lands for self gain. Instead of redistributing the large holdings among the rural peasantry they are doled out as political favors to those officials who support the president. In one final bitter comment Jesusa characterizes the deception of land reform and the subterfuges employed to fool the people. The former owners are driven from their lands and then pacified with empty promises:

Los del gobierno les dijeron que tomaran el terreno que quisieran; que era regalado. Fueron a medirles tantos metros a cada quien y le hicieron sus escrituras. Como quiera que sea, Cárdenas les dio dado el terreno. Nomás que no tienen derecho de vender. Así se están muriendo de hambre, no pueden vender. La tierra sigue siendo del gobierno. Mientras ellos viven, tienen su casa, pero si se mueren y no hay quien represente a la familia, la pierden. El gobierno es el dueño. (268)

["The government people told them to take the land they wanted, that it was a gift. They measured out so many meters per person and gave everyone the titles. Whatever the case, Cárdenas gave them land alright. Except they don't have the right to sell it. So they're dying of hunger but they still can't sell. It's still the government's lands. While they're alive they have a house but if they should die and there is nobody to represent the family, they lose it. The government is still the owner."]

A theme which appears often in *Hasta no verte, Jesús mío* is the inferior status of Mexican working-class women. While Poniatowska does not present a well-defined feminist position in her novel — I am sure this was not her intention — she does create in her *pícara* a combative, aggressive figure who is unwilling to conform to the constraints and expectations of her society. Jesusa exhibits qualities and attitudes which run contrary to those of the passive female character who fills the pages of contemporary Mexican literature. As a *Lazarina* who has been forced, because of the circumstances of her life, into a defensive stance vis à vis her employers, her husband, her family, etc., it is natural that this stance also manifest itself in her attitude toward men, marriage, the mistreatment of fellow-females, and her role as a *soldadera*.

It is significant that Jesusa, whose mother died when she was a child, was not raised to fulfill a woman's role. Her father treated her more as a son than a daughter. Jesusa recalls: "Decía que a manazos tenía que enseñarme, pero pues no nací para echar tortillas y nunca he sabido toretear." (29) ["He said he had to hit me to teach me, but, well, I wasn't born to make tortillas and I haven't learned since."] When her sister-in-law tries to teach her the domestic arts, she rebels: "Quería que me enseñara a hacer tortillas y yo estaba acostumbrada a andar corriendo. Como desde chiquilla no me hallé sino con la libertad, todo mi gusto era andar sola en el campo o arriba de un cerro." (28) ["She wanted me to learn to make tortillas but I was already used to running free, because since I was a child I had always been free, and I loved to walk in the country or high in the mountains."]

As a child Jesusa witnesses the cruel physical abuse of women by men. Her own brother Efrén deals with his wife Ignacia in the traditional way, beating her into submission when she dares to question his authority. Her sister Petra dies of fright, terrorized by her husband for resisting his beatings.

Based on what she has witnessed as a child and her father's treatment of her as a male, Jesusa stubbornly refuses to assume a traditional female role as an adolescent and adult. Her various employers find her militantly opposed to performing domestic female tasks such as caring for small children, cooking, and cleaning house. In the words of one or her mistresses: "Nació para no dejarse." (60) ["She was born not giving in, but resisting."]

Jesusa's relationships to men are clear examples of the redefinition of the female role in Poniatowska's work. With the outbreak of the Revolution, Jesusa begins associating with the troops but not in the fashion common to the legendary *soldadera*. In general, this female figure accepted her submissive female role as sexual partner, cook, and laundress alongside her soldier-man. [4] She accepted her misery with relative tranquility since she was totally adapted to this condition and incapable of aspiring to improve her circumstances. The *soldadera* practiced as a guiding principal the blind allegiance to her man, for this was the accepted pattern passed on to her by her mother.

In her study of the psychology of the Mexican woman, Juana Armanda Alegría describes the *soldadera* as an unconscious being:

...aun más inconsciente que su soldado, a tal grado que si éste va a la guerra a veces sin tener definidas sus razones, ellas en cambio lo hacen sin base alguna, sin ninguna idea específica que las motive. Estas mujeres son en realidad verdaderos casos enfermizos de inconsciencia. El hecho de llevar a sus hijos a la guerra y exponerlos a la muerte implica una grave falta de responsibilidad y una irracionalidad sin precedente. Por seguir a sus hombres las soldaderas sacrifican sus más íntimos principios de mujeres, su sumisión no tiene límites, ellas son las *lumpens* de la femineidad. [5]

[...even more thoughtless than her soldier-companion, to the extent that if he goes off to war without sometimes clearly defining his reasons, they, on the other hand, go without any basis at all, without any specific idea which motivates them. These women are truly extreme cases of thoughtlessness. The very fact of their taking their children to war and exposing them to death implies a grave lack of responsibility and irrational behavior without precedent. By following their men, the camp-followers sacrifice their most intimate principals as women, their submission is limitless; they are the *lumpens* of womanhood.]

Jesusa displays none of these traits. She recognizes men — especially soldiers — for what they are: "¿A poco los hombres no son putos siempre con el animal de fuera, a ver a quién se lo meten?" (78) ["...men are always on the make seeing who they can lay next."]

Jesusa is pursued by a handsome young officer, Pedro Aguilar, who courts her because he sees her aggressiveness as a challenge to his macho powers. Her relationship to him is that of an adversary rather than that of a weak female companion. When she marries Pedro her position becomes more vulnerable, but she responds by denying him sexually in order to maintain her integrity and independence developed over the many years of having to fend for herself. He never affords her the respect she feels she deserves as a woman, and Jesusa continues to deny Pedro his sexual gratification.

Instead of assuming the passive role of the loyal *soldadera*, she sets up a store and continues her own active life, drinking and singing with her *compañeros* [companions]. It is important to note that Jesusa is not a loose woman for she continues to guard herself carefully from being exploited.

Pedro is enraged by what he perceives to be Jesusa's disrespect and defiance. He tries to bend her will through the threat of physical violence, but he has not yet learned to reckon with her female strength and will. Instead of receiving his punishment meekly Jesusa brandishes a gun in Pedro's face, promising to use it if he persists.

Jesusa's previous experiences and relationships have allowed her to develop in a non-traditional mold and have given her values which allow her to maintain her non-submissive role as a woman. In the eyes of the other soldiers she is more of a comrade than a camp-follower and they treat her with the deference she demands.

Whether as a humble barmaid or factory worker, Jesusa
successfully continues to resist attempts by males to tame and
domesticate her. After Pedro's death in battle she does not remarry
because she considers the institution severely disadvantageous for the
woman who gains little and loses her independence:

Como padecí tanto con Pedro dije yo: "Mejor me
quedo sola". Dicen que el buey solo bien se lame ¿y por qué la
vaca no? ¿Como podía adivinar si me iba a ir bien, casada con
un extranjero? Para ser malo el hombre, lo mismo es extranjero que mexicano. Todos pegan igual. Todos le dan a
uno. Son como el león y la leona, la relame, la adula, la busca
y todo. Nomás la tiene en sus garras y le pega sus buenas
tarascadas. Así son los hombres. Apenas la tienen a uno, y
adiós Tejería. Ahorita mientras no le digo que sí, no halla
dónde ponerme; el cedacito cuando está nuevo no halla uno
dónde colgarlo. Ya cuando está viejo: "¡Talísimo cedazo!
¿Dónde te aventaré? ¡Ya estás todo agujerado!" Por eso
nunca me ha llamado a mí la atención la casadera. Mejor pasar
necesidades que aguantar marido. (173)

[Because I suffered so much with Pedro I said: "I'm
better off alone. They say that the bull takes care of himself
and why shouldn't the cow? How would I know if it would go
well for me married to a foreigner. Man is bad whether he's a
Mexican or not. They all hit you the same. They all give it to
you. They are like the lion and the lioness: he licks her and
praises her and everything. But once he has her in his clutches
he really gives it to her. That's the way men are. They barely
have you and good-bye, they're off. Now, while I don't give in
he doesn't know where to put me. One doesn't know where to
hang the sieve when it's new. But when it gets old... "This
sieve! Where will I throw you? You're all full of holes!" That's
why this marriage thing has never attracted me. Better to
suffer want than to put up with a husband.]

Her view of herself as a woman, of woman's relationship to
man, and of man's innate exploitative tendencies are reflected clearly
in a number of her observations which appear almost as epigrams
sprinkled generously throughout the novel: "Esa la enfermedad de los
mexicanos: creer que son muy charros porque se nos montan encima"
(178) ["That's the sickness that Mexicans have: believing they're
manly because they climb all over you."]; "Los afeminados son más
buenos que los machos" (186) ["Effeminate men are better than
machos."]; "Para todas las mujeres sería mejor ser hombre porque es
más divertido, es uno más libre y nadie se burla de uno" (186) ["It
would be better for all women to be men because it's more fun, you're
freer and nobody takes advantage of you."]; "Los hombres son muy

ventajosos, no los guía más que la pura conveniencia. Nadie estima a
su mujer ni la cuida." (314) ["Men take advantage of you; only their
selfishness guides them. Not one of them appreciates his woman and
takes care of her."]

Through continued mistreatment and abuse — much of it
brought upon herself by her persistently aggressive resistance and
assertiveness as a woman — Jesusa develops a consuming cynicism of
the world. Unable to continue tolerating the evil which she feels
surrounds her, she finally converts to a fanatical religious sect — *la
Obra Espiritual* [The Spiritual Work] — where she finds comfort
within a context in which order seems to reign.

Through her religious conversion, Jesusa is transformed
from the lively *Lazarina* into a tame and foolish dupe. Her positive
confrontation with the world and its injustices is compromised; her
combative energies as a *pícara* are siphoned off into empty pietistic
slogans and self-deception.

Jesusa's conversion constitutes a betrayal of the positive
values which directed her behavior as a younger woman. The world,
while making her more wise to its ways and thereby more able to deal
with it, has also worn her down, exhausted her capacity to contend, to
continue her struggle to assert her individuality and integrity. The
odds have been too great.

While in her own mind her new found commitment to God
and the religious life constitute a positive step toward her salvation,
she has regressed in our eyes by surrendering the ethical values which
saw her through a lifetime of difficulties. Jesusa shuns her responsibility as a non-passive, non-submissive Mexican female. Post-
revolutionary society in the form of persistent male dominance and
pre-revolutionary social and political patterns have done her in. Her
retreat to *la Obra Espiritual* only serves to highlight the futility of
trying to change centuries of deeply rooted values.

While Poniatowska's female protagonists holds forth against
a pattern of male domination, Jesusa falls short of providing a model
for today's working class woman who struggles to free herself from a
web of oppressive social behavior. Jesusa believes herself to be
reincarnated, sent back to earth for a third time in order to regain her
original state of grace. This aspect of the novel appears to be in-
consistent with the hard life and coarse language which characterize
Jesusa; as a younger woman she is anything but a faithful servant of
God and a loyal member of the fanatical religious sect.

Jesusa is convinced that she has been condemned to the life
of a *Lazarina* as a form of expiation for her past transgressions. This
religious dimension of the novel adds a decidedly pessimistic tone to
Jesusa's life and fate because *la Obra Espiritual* represents for her the
only means of reintegrating herself into society. Believing it is her

very rebellious nature which has led her astray and caused her to be shunned by man and God alike, she must tame this nature, reject her past "anti-social" and "anti-religious" acts in order to end her life in a way acceptable to both human and divine expectations. Having surrendered her freedom and self-assertiveness — this surrender is viewed as desirable by Jesusa herself — she thereby reverts to the passive, submissive role of the traditional Mexican woman. *Hasta no verte, Jesús mío* is, then, the tale of failure, the autobiography of the dismal fate of a woman whose life contained the potential for both spiritual and social liberation. The novel, set against the backdrop of the Revolution and the subsequent chaos, chronicles the defeat of a revolutionary — Jesusa — not an ideological or social defeat but one more absolute: a spiritual one.

NOTES

[1] Ulrich Wicks, "The Nature of Picaresque Narrative: A Modal Approach," *PMLA*, Vol. 89, No. 2 (March 1974), pp. 240-249.

[2] *Ibid.*, p. 242.

[3] Elena Poniatowska, *Hasta no verte, Jesús mío* (Mexico: Era, 1969), p. 52. All subsequent page references to this work will appear in parentheses in the text.

[4] Juana Armanda Alegría, *Psicología de las mexicanas* [*The Psychology of Mexican Women*] (México: Editorial Samo, 1974), p.131.

[5] *Ibid.*, p. 132.

María Angélica Bosco and Beatriz Guido: An Approach to Two Argentinian Novelists between 1960 and 1970

by

ESTHER A. AZZARIO

Wayne State University

On the list of Argentinian narrative writers of the decade of the 1960's, there is a group of women novelists that has attracted the attention of the critics and deserves ready acceptance by the readers. Among them we have chosen two female authors who appeared in the world of Argentinian letters in 1954, coincidentally brought together at a novelists' contest. Editorial Emecé, S.A., which organized the competition (thus taking a step forward in the evaluation of the female writer) granted the first prize to Beatriz Guido for *La Casa del Angel* [*The House of the Angel*],[1] an incursion into a social topic, and the second prize to María Angélica Bosco for *La muerte baja en el ascensor* [*Death is Coming Down in the Elevator*], a detective story.

The promising quality of the two beginners was fulfilled in the following years by an indefatigable activity which, during the decade we have chosen, produced several significant works, four by María Angélica Bosco and three by Beatriz Guido.

In chronological order, this work begins with María Angélica Bosco, who in 1960 published *La trampa* [*The Trap*] under the auspices of ''Fondo Nacional de Las Artes'' [''National Fund for the Arts''], in 1963 *El comedor de diario* [*Everyday Dining-room*], in 1965 *¿Dónde está el cordero?* [*Where is the Lamb?*], and in 1968 *La Negra Vélez y su Angel* [*Blackie Velez and her Angel*]. Meanwhile Beatriz Guido published in 1961, *La mano en la trampa* [*The Hand in the Trap*], a ''nouvelle,'' together with a series of short stories in the same volume. In 1964 appeared *El incendio y las vísperas* [*The Fire and the Days Before*] and in 1970 she produced her last work of this decade, *Escándalos y soledades* [*Scandals and Loneliness*].

In the prize novel María Angélica Bosco had shown her skill as a writer of detective stories, but in *La trampa*[2] she began analyzing the upper middle class of Buenos Aires, the theme which was to become the permanent motivation in her four novels of that decade.

The attitude of this portion of Buenos Aires society towards life, love, loneliness, and incommunicativeness, and the solutions they try to find for their problems constitute her topic. She shows her sharp critical sense and her fine sense of humor, often sprinkled with touches of irony.

In this brief essay we will confine ourselves to the attitudes assumed by the Argentinian woman and to the solutions she finds within this society, because according to our criterion this is one of the aspects that this writer mostly concerns herself with. The proof of this is a "crescendo" in the importance of the evolution of the female characters in the above mentioned novels.

In *La trampa*, Corina, a wife whose husband is having an affair with another woman, sets the trap by means of which she will succeed in estranging the lovers and thus regain her husband. She does this merely to defend the integrity of her home, though the love between her husband and herself is dying because of boredom and a complete lack of imagination. Her apparent triumph is valid in the eyes of the social circle in which they both move and the rules of whose game they accept. According to a second level of interpretation, this very world would be the real trap in which they are living and in which they are forever caught.

The history of the Rossi family, in *El comedor de diario*,[3] is presented in the form of a frieze covering thirty-five years from 1920 to 1955. They are members of the lower middle class who have become wealthy home-owners. The effort of the Rossis   to become a part of the upper middle class con-stitutes the backbone of the narrative sequence and has the structure of a symphony; there are five well-connected movements ranging from the "Allegro ma non troppo", the establishment of the family in the wealthy and fashionable neighborhood, the "Barrio Norte" ["The North Quarter"], down to the "Finale," whose theme turns around the dying moments of the mother.

Among the individuals of this multiple-character novel Adela stands out, the authoritative and introverted mother whose "ambition without ideals"(22) shapes the behavior of the whole family. Life in the "petit-hotel," managed by her rigid rules and her "stuffiness" develops in a stifling atmosphere of demands and quarrels, where there is neither tenderness nor understanding. Adela has put up a barrier between herself and her husband Aquiles, a barrier of resentfulness; and in their bed there can only be respect for each other ,not love. She is isolated in a world of her own which is her home and she ignores whatever does not relate to her petty ambition—that she and her family may become "somebodies." To that end she harasses them all; they must learn how to act like distinguished people! As the years go by the gaps widen, and within the family there is nothing but hate or in-difference.

After the deaths of Aquiles and Carlos A., her favorite son, Adela lies on her death-bed surrounded by the three remaining children, who have by now drifted wide apart; all they have in common is the weak economical link of a diminished inheritance. Each one in turn has lapsed into different forms of dishonesty in order to remain within the social circles which they succeeded in reaching; the lives of these introverts are filled with coldness and a deep sense of loneliness.

The everyday dining-room set, consisting of a few pieces of old furniture brought over from the old home, remains through the years as a symbol of that part of the family that could not evolve because Adela, in spite of her ambition, failed to guide her family along the way to self-improvement or to love.

In *¿Dónde está el cordero?*[4] the narrative sequence develops along two lines which alternatively constitute two plots. One of them, with the characteristics of a detective story, has a provincial town as a background. The other plot is its counterpoint in the city and assumes the form of a long dialogue in the course of which the "alter ego" makes the remarks and the heroine listens passively.

In the detective story the wife takes revenge on the husband who has repeatedly deceived her. When she finds out she has terminal cancer, she prepares and carries out a plan to have him accused of murdering her without leaving any chance of his proving his innocence; in fact, she commits suicide. The plan works out and she has her revenge.

In the other plot Cecilia, married to Gusy, the spoiled child of a wealthy middle-class family, discovers that her husband is homosexual. She brings herself to accept this situation so as to retain her social position. Gusy, trying to conceal his problem from his parents, travels to the U.S. and shortly afterwards asks Cecilia to divorce him. Cecilia tries to compensate for her frustration by seeking to be herself in her old vocation as a writer. And what she writes is the detective story, the story of a physical sacrifice—that of the condemned husband—but which actually functions as a counterpoint since she, Cecilia, has been the "lamb" of a spiritual sacrifice. There are two women, two social spheres, two solutions; there is the woman who resorts to all her ability and intelligence in order to achieve revenge because in the eyes of the whole town she has been a deceived wife, and there is the woman who has been frustrated and disoriented in a large city and seeks the way to recovery and self-identification.

La negra Vélez y su Angel,[5] the last novel which María Angélica Bosco wrote during this decade, presents a female character whose importance stands out from the title onward. The narrative sequence is structured from the point of view of an omniscient witness narrator in the form of an angel who gives a report to God in which he tries to understand and justify the behavior of "La Negra," the human being whose custody has been assigned to him and whose double image confuses and overcomes him.

By means of a series of flashbacks the angel brings together visions of the past and views of the present, focusing upon several situations, both temporal and spatial, of the process which shaped the personality of "la Negra" towards "un clasicismo burgués y porteño" ["Buenos Aires middle class norms"] (p. 191), with this society's own scale of values and a veiled predominance of the female figure. "¿Qué falta hace que uno les tenga respeto a los hombres? ¿Por qué admirarlos? Pero siempre están reclamándolo..." ["Why treat men with respect? Why admire them? Yet they always demand it..."] (p. 19) "la Negra" says to herself in the "now" of the narrative, which is the year 1965.

In 1938, when she was young, candid, and in love, she married Ignacio Vélez and was proud to bear his old family name. That is why she decided to maintain at any cost the formal integrity of the home, since this was demanded by the rules of the social class she had attained and with which she wanted to be integrated.

In the eyes of the world and of the in-laws who sometimes indulgently humiliated her, "la Negra" accepts and plays the part assigned to her, concealing herself behind the idealized image of a virtuous, good-natured, and somewhat silly woman demanded by bourgeois society.

In keeping with this attitude, she appears before Ignacio as the ignorant woman who failed to understand his intellectual nonconformism, who has gone to the world of the "others" and accepts his infidelities and does not even reject him physically when he comes home after having an affair. In the eyes of Alberto she is the sister, his junior by ten years, who knows nothing of his homosexual habits—the mainstay of his political power—who listens to him without expressing any opinion, and whose social life and economical stability depend on him; and in the eyes of her children "the old lady" is rather candid, but very dear.

Behind this conformist image of a virtuous martyr there lives the other "Negra," the one that worries and amazes the angel because she overlooks her sins or just ignores them without the slightest misgiving. She assumes an attitude of deliberate ignorance and neither despairs nor regrets, thus avoiding the ways that lead to God.

The process from which this second personality emerged was slow but it made her feel sure of herself. She took as good care of her figure and of her looks as she did of her children and her home. As a reaction to her husband's unfaithfulness and to her disillusionment she sought the means of acquiring self-confidence. She ceases to care for Ignacio, but she wins the battle because he always comes back to her and they remain together in the eyes of society. She never refuses to fulfill her "matrimonial duties" but discovers the possibility of sexual enjoyment devoid of love in the first love affair she has, and this affair with Javier paves the way for others. "Y de los otros, Señor, sólo recordó estadísticamente los nombres" ["Of the others, my Lord, she only remembered the names as if they were statistical records"] (p. 186), the Angel sadly remarks.

"La Negra" gets used to the exquisite luxury that comes in the wake of Alberto's professional success, she shines at his receptions and dinner parties, and indifferently observes, with a half smile, the world of gossip and favoritism of *Jornada*, the newspaper founded by Alberto and which, untouched by the political avatars, forever turns wherever the political winds blow. Isn't it the tribune which expresses the opinion of the public? "La Negra" not only approves of her brother but she cleverly supports him, and her children have found in him a substitute for a frustrated father. "La Negra" says cynically to herself: "Uno se puede confiar en Alberto, sabe esconder sus errores, y cuando los chicos los descubran...bueno, ya serán bastante grandes para entender lo que les conviene..." ["Alberto can be trusted, he knows how to conceal his faults, and by the time the children find out the truth about him...well, they will be old enough to understand what is convenient for them..."]. (p. 159) Besides, Ignacio and her two boys get paid for doing nothing in the office of the newspaper. They are three useless men, protected by the power of Alberto, whom she wins with her complacency and apparent submission. God only knows what would become of them were it not for her subtle protection!

These two opposite ways of behaving are integrated, and Marta Delfino de Vélez—"la Negra" to her friends—is the character by means of which María Angélica Bosco upholds her thesis that in the society she is concerned with it is the woman, from a secondary position, who actually controls the situation.

We will now consider the novels by Beatriz Guido, who shows us a vision of another Argentinian reality. In the short work, *La mano en la trampa*[6] she insists on the use of her recurring themes and she presents, with the intensity of a confession made by the heroine, the violent reaction of the youths who will not be kept away from what is forbidden or mysterious, even if the price to be paid for such knowledge may prove to be self-destruction. Repression and violence are the two extremes which determine the drama within a traditional provincial middle-class family which lives its memories of past generations and shuts its eyes to reality.

Nevertheless her two next novels are more significant because the writer, without any reticence, faces the reality of political life in Argentina since the coming of power of Peronismo in 1945, showing the disintegration of two families belonging to the oligarchy under the influence of characters and political facts taken from real life.

In *El incendio y las vísperas*[7] the plot sequence moves along a linear development with the exception of one flashback, and chronologically covers the period from October 17, 1952, to April 15, 1953. Both dates appear on the subtitle and correspond to two historical facts: the first one commemorates the action taken by the masses which, in 1945, liberated Juan Domingo Perón from his prison on the island of Martín García; the second one marks the night when the mobs burnt down the Jockey Club, which was exclusively for the gentlemen of the upper middle class of Buenos Aires. The ending of the novel thus acquires a symbolic characteristic.

The third reality is the expropriation, decreed by the Pernonista government, of the homestead and the parkland of the finest and largest "estancia" in the Province of Buenos Aires which belonged to the Pereyra Iraola family. The grounds were renamed "The Park for the Rights of the Aged" and opened up for the recreation of the "justicialista" workers during their vacations, in memory of the dead Eva Perón.

In the novel the expropriation of this land is what triggers the drama of the aristocratic Pradere family. They try to save the "estancia" ["country place"], (named "Bagatelle" in the novel) because they have inherited it from their ancestors, even though in order to do that they have to come to terms with the "judicialista" régime which they hate.

"Bagatelle"—with its name suggesting a French mistress—and the Carrara marbles that adorn the parkland, and the collection of paintings and sculptures in the Jockey Club, all obsess Alejandro Pradere, the father, a book-lover who is passionately fond of beauty and art; all this is what he lives for and all this justifies his surrender before the demands of the régime as he accepts the position of ambassador to Uruguay; that is, as the representative "de un gobierno que desprecia" ["of a government which he despises"]. (p. 179)

His wife Sofía and his two children, José Luis and Inés, agree with his decision, and the family, spiritually ruined but brought close together by the misfortune which had befallen them, leaves Argentina. In a sense, the family runs away towards what is to be a prison without bars, whereas in Buenos Aires "Bagatelle," the land of their dead, remains as a hostage.

In the meantime, José Luis and Inés have been involved with other university students in the resistance movement against the dictatorship which has brought together, in the "underground," the most variegated political and ideological groups. Doing his duty as a "cell" José Luis has had to save the life of Pable Alcobendas, a law student who is a socialist and an enemy of the wealthy classes. When José Luis takes the wounded Pablo to the attic of his own home in the fashionable "Barrio Norte" ["The North Quarter"] Inés and the young man meet and they are caught in a passionate love which overcomes social barriers.

Months go by. The night when the Jockey Club is burnt down, Ambassador Pradere, who has come over to Buenos Aires for a few days in order to enjoy his books and works of art, commits suicide in the face of the crimes which are being perpetrated against art and culture. The decree for the expropriation of ''Bagatelle'' is signed two days later. Sofía and her children come to the mansion in the ''estancia'' for the last time and then calmly walk out, leaving behind them all its treasures with the exception of the father's favorite night-table clock, to the amazement of the government officials who have been sent there to arrange for the moving of the furniture.

The mother goes off to exile in Paris; José Luis and Inés, together with Pablo, go on struggling in the resistance movement. As the Pradere family disintegrates, there rises the love of Pablo and Inés overcoming all barriers: social, ideological and even physical, because as the result of another political activity Pablo has been imprisoned and tortured by the police, and José Luis has had to resort to his money and his influence in order to save his life after Pablo has undergone horrible mutilations.

Beatriz Guido's last work during this decade is *Escándalos y soledades*,[8] a novel in which she breaks away from the traditional form of the narrative which she had never done before. She makes a ''collage'' in which the accumulation of diverse materials is no obstacle to the development of the plot which the reader reconstructs and thus fulfills the function of a collaborator which is assigned to him in the modern novel. The writer insists on the theme of political facts and characters, this time within a family of men.

The point of view is that of the narrator-hero, Doro, who states his wish to become a writer, thus becoming a witness-narrator, ''a taciturn spy'' (82) as he describes himself.

The chronological period extends from 1957 to 1967, but the continuous flashbacks and the interweaving of passages from the works of other writers (to the long list of whom she expresses her thanks at the end of the novel) create a background going as far back as the days of President Alvear in the 1920 decade.

At the time Gaetano Strada, a former anarchist, changed his attitude in time and turned his great ability to the making of a fortune. He established his family in a large old house at 527 Mexico Street, across the road from the Public Library.

Doro, the child of a second marriage (his widowed father having married his sister-in-law) came into the world on June 7, 1942; by that time his father was dead and his mother died in childbirth. This unusual situation of his four older brothers acting as his parents, and the two men-servants, the Valenzuela brothers, will be the world around him.

Ramón, whose hairy arms affectionately hold the baby, works as a secretary at a court of justice and becomes the head of the family, one of his duties being the upbringing of Dorito.

Alberto has a laboratory (or invention room as they call his powerful amateur broadcasting station) and by means of his radio apparatus he travels all over the world without moving from Mexico Street.

The family tragedy will break out between the eldest brother, Rodolfo, a socialist, a professor at the Institute of Higher Studies, and Martín, the lawyer of the politicians whose catechism is doing a good turn whenever he can.

In the opinion of Martín, if the country is on the verge of disaster "hay que salvarlo a cualquier precio"["it must be saved at any cost"](p. 32),and he decides to go abroad in order to obtain the support of Perón, exiled in Caracas and under the protection of the dictator Pérez Giménez. If Perón is willing to come to terms and to give Frondizi the votes of his party, Frondizi will triumph and in that case he has promised to allow Perón to return to Argentina. This is a historical situation—the agreement was actually made although Frondizi afterwards failed to keep his promise. Martín, in search of a bridge that will pave the way for the interview with Perón, will travel to the U.S. taking Doro with him even though the boy is an adolescent who is still in high school. On the day fixed for their departure an anonymous letter reveals to Rodolfo the real reason of Martín's trip, and in an outburst of despair on discovering his brother's treason and the surrender of his ideals, Rodolfo loses his mind. "Rodolfo, el Santo, el Puro, el Romántico, el que enmudeció de angustia, el que se quema en la vida por una traición" ["Rodolfo, the Saint, the Pure, the Romantic, the man who became dumb with anguish, the man who burns himself up on account of a betrayal"]. (p. 194) From that moment on until his death ten years later Rodolfo will live just like a doll that can be rocked in its cradle. Martín's mission fails because he never gets to see Perón, the latter having to flee from Caracas at the downfall of Pérez Giménez. But Martín, the traitor of the family, can never return home since neither his brothers nor the men-servants will ever forgive him. From now on he will travel between London and Paris, accompanied by Doro, hoping that his country will return to normality.

When Doro hears about the death of Rodolfo he comes home alone and decides never to go away again. In the old house the two other brothers and the old servants are under the loving care of Elisa who divides her attention between them as if she were the daughter of all of them. Galileo, the former keeper of the National Library, who adopted her when she was a little girl, has also joined the family and lives with the obsession of killing the assassin of Leon Trotsky. Doro realizes he is in love with Elisa, who is his only hope of recovering the self-respect which his role as a "spy" has deprived him of. Maybe he can now also hope for the recovery of his country, because after all, "lo peor que tenemos los argentinos es la Argentina; pero es lo único que tenemos" ["the worst we Argentinians have is Argentina but it is all that we have"]. (p. 299) This is the author's thesis. She denounces and accepts the frustrations arising from so many years of bad policies, the "scandals" which cause so much anguishing "loneliness"; yet she has hopes for the recovery of a national solidarity which may lead the country along the way to prosperity and success.

As a conclusion, after looking into the works of these two novelists during the decade we have chosen, we have tried to give proof of the indefatigable activity which attracted the attention of the critics and, from the point of view of literary analysis, of the existence of two interesting constant themes, clearly outlined amidst the social problems which became the backbone of the novels. In the works of María Angélica Bosco her concern with all the aspects of the upper middle class of Buenos Aires gradually narrows down to the subtle behavior of the female within the bourgeois society where the male plays an outstanding rôle. Beatriz Guido, on the other hand, delves deeply into the dramatic consequences which the complex political situation that has been troubling the life of Argentina since the early forties have had upon the Argentinian family.

NOTES

[1] All translations from Spanish texts are mine.

[2] María Angélica Bosco, *La trampa* (Buenos Aires: Emece S.A., 1960).

[3] María Angélica Bosco, *El comedor de diario* (Buenos Aires: Emecé S.A. , 1963).

[4] María Angélica Bosco, *¿Dónde está el cordero?* (Buenos Aires: Emecé S.A., 1965).

[5] María Angélica Bosco, *La Negra y su Angel* (Buenos Aires: Cia. General Fabril Editora S.A., 1968). All page references are from this edition.

[6] Beatriz Guido, *La mano en la trampa* (Buenos Aires: Losada S.A., 1961).

[7] Beatriz Guido, *El indendio y las vísperas* (Buenos Aires: Losada S.A., 1964). All page references are from this edition.

[8] Beatriz Guido, *Escándalos y soledades* (Buenos Aires: Losada S.A., 1970). All page references are from this edition.

Argentine Women
in the Novels of Silvina Bullrich

by

CORINA S. MATHIEU

University of Nevada, Las Vegas

Silvina Bullrich, a prolific Argentine novelist, has continuously displayed evidence of an interest in exploring the intricacies of the feminine soul. She has done so from the vantage point of a woman who was not only able to profit from a cultured, upper-middle class background that offered her a wide range of experiences, but who was also unwavering about not conforming to a predetermined destiny dictated by society. Her novels reflect these circumstances through theme development and in some of the recurring qualities with which she has endowed her characters.

By way of illustration, the prologue to *Entre mis veinte y treinta años* [*Between My Twenty and Thirty Years*] [1] declares that the world she discovered in her early twenties interested her on the basis of two standpoints--money and love--that are after all its ruling forces. This statement makes evident the motivation underlying her novels, although of these pivotal elements the latter constitutes the major thrust.

The totality of her literary production reveals an unabated interest in analyzing the innermost feelings of women in love. She has done so over and over, but always within a specific frame of reference, i.e., Argentine society. Depending on how the theme has been focused, the work takes on different dimensions. In *Los pasajeros del jardín* [*The Travellers*], for example, the allusions to locale and secondary characters are kept to a minimum because it is essential that the reader's attention not be diverted from the protagonist's drama, but in *Mañana digo basta* [*I Will Rebel Tomorrow*] the qualities of society are strikingly apparent, since the conflict facing the main character is in many ways a consequence of society's expectations.

Within this format, there is also an awareness of social differences on the part of the characters that underlines the power of money in society. Moreover, in the last several years, Bullrich has proven to be particularly sensitive to the chaotic conditions prevailing in Argentina, which is not surprising for she has stated about her country that:

> Sometimes it is as if its air and earth are running through my veins,
> mixed with my blood. It elicits both my love and hate. I cannot help
> standing as my country's judge while at the same time rebelling
> against it. It is a love relationship. [2]

Above all, however, Silvina Bullrich's narrative has been primarily
devoted to projecting the individual aspirations, anxieties and needs of women
in contrast to the role society has called upon them to play. She makes no
effort to conceal that her viewpoints are always those of a female author. Miss
Bullrich, a member of the generation born during the First World War,
published a great number of her works in the 1940's and 1950's. The
allusions to the social status of her female contemporaries are clearly set forth
in her later novels through comments from middle-aged women who cannot
help comparing the limited horizons that they first encountered to the op-
portunities available to their daughters.

Bullrich's female protagonists are usually restless individualists who,
because they are unable and unwilling to settle for an average destiny, constantly question established mores and search for new paths, but find that
happiness may be elusive. Yet, it is the satisfaction of being true to their
needs that is all important. Their attitudes often defy what is socially expected
in a traditional society, but they willingly accept the consequences.

Interestingly enough, her characters' remarks on this subject echo her
own statements scattered throughout the prologues to some of the seven
novels included in the volume entitled *Between My Twenty and Thirty years,*
which concludes with a short, frank, and appropriate autobiographical note.
In one of those prologues she points out that the only future a woman of her
class and generation could count on was marriage and motherhood. Worse
yet, being born a woman was considered a sort of punishment both for the
newly-born and for the parents who were pitied for such a misfortune.
Nothing could change that feeling and, even though her own father was
eventually content with his three daughters, the mother never resigned
herself. In vain, Miss Bullrich says, she tried to prove her worth through
personal accomplishments, although in her mother's eyes not even the Nobel
Prize could erase the original sin of being a woman.

Likewise, the protagonist of *I Will Rebel Tomorrow* wakes up one
morning realizing that a woman almost fifty, without a husband and with
three grown daughters now on their own, can look forward to very little
because, according to society, her mission in life has been accomplished. The
question is how to cope with the loneliness and find new meaning in life;
middle age has confronted her with all its unpleasant prospects, yet her body is
healthy and she feels full of energy. Courageously she faces reality:

> ... in the midst of the emptiness that represents for a Latin woman to
> reach the age of forty-nine, I felt it was necessary to reflect why life

indefectibly drives us women. . . to a period in which we are useless on this earth. Something similar must have happened at the time of our birth. A girl, uttered with resignation the attending physician, the midwife, the father. . . . Nobody probably said, if only out of deference to my human abilities, maybe this woman will become a Madame Curie, or she will do for humanity as much as Florence Nightingale, or maybe she will become a great artist. . . while instead she could have been born a boy who could have turned out to be a ruffian, a cheater, or a complete idiot. [3]

   I Will Rebel Tomorrow embodies this perceptive woman's reflections while trying to grasp the real significance of a turning point in her life, with a painful awareness that society has cheated her of her right of feeling needed as a human being. She isolates herself in a solitary spot on the Uruguayan coast to prove what she has really always known:

   . . . that a Latin woman who is not pressed to earn a living can disappear from the face of this earth for as long as she pleases without anyone, absolutely anyone, thinking for an instant that this woman, still young, full of energies, with a desire to work, could be accomplishing a useful task in place of so many incompetent men who are merely pretending to be useful. [4]

   She feels discriminated against, a prisoner of circumstances beyond her control, for while men are given the opportunity to develop their personal resources, women are restricted to household duties and child rearing, regardless of their capabilities. Men derive a sense of accomplishment vital to their self-respect upon selecting the vocation best suited to their abilities; women experience interminable frustration because they are barred from most endeavors, particularly those associated with men of her social class. The latter were born to become ambassadors, cultural attaches or board presidents, but no matter how hard she had worked, how much she had struggled, all she had earned by the age of fifty was the right to take her grandson for a ride on the merry-go-round. The protagonist of the novel airs her frustrations through a series of interior monologues that reveal details of a rather unsuccessful marriage and a disappointing relationship with three selfish daughters. Two of them, Dolores and Nickie, have married well, thereby satisfying the expectations of their class, but the mother is skeptical about such unions; a good number of them are doomed beforehand because of the superficial basis on which they are founded. She voices her complaint by saying:

   . . . the women of our social class in our country consider marriage a triumph, although it is obvious to any who sees them at the marriage ceremony that they are on their way to inescapable failure. [5]

   Several characters utter similar remarks; they allude obviously to dangers implicit both for society and for the individual who disregards human idiosyncracies and expects uniform behavior. In *Bodas de cristal [Wedding Anniversary]*, Luis's wife recalls the dangerous naïveté that characterized her early twenties: "We smilingly approached our inevitable destiny: marriage." [6] Gloria in *Calles de Buenos Aires [Streets of Buenos Aires]* tries to warn her friend Florencia that society has laid out a trap for them:

> Here, in this Buenos Aires where you and I live, we women have been brought up to love. Even though it may sound absurd, we are raised just to love and be loved. Education, intelligence, interests are disregarded. From our childhood we hear talk about the day when we'll get married. We are dressed lavishly and a lot of money is spent to keep up appearances so as to make certain we fulfill our destiny: marriage. We are the vestals destined to protect the sacred fire of love and marriage. [7]

The majority of women find out too late about their ill-founded assumptions concerning marriage. After the first months of marital bliss have passed, they inevitably face the stark reality; but it is too late because disappointment and anxiety have already overwhelmed them. Marriage is an indissoluble tie in a country where the Church has prevented the institution of divorce; moreover, public display of marital differences have traditionally met with open disapproval.

These novels accentuate the lack of individual fulfillment in such sterile relationships, and underscore the premise that society's blind refusal to accept alternatives to the established role for women makes such unions intolerable. Wives became bored and unsatisfied human beings because, according to the author, at the time her generation grew up, the wealthy bourgeoisie had lost many of its solid domestic virtues that may have seemed old fashioned in the 1930's and 1940's, but which had been invaluable during the early years of the Republic. Efficiency was especially frowned upon since it was not a sign of femininity. Girls from wealthy homes learned little or nothing that was practical; rather, they were to cultivate their charms to attract the most eligible suitor. Once married their future was sealed and many husbands either ignored or were unaware of the barrenness of their wives' daily routine. . As a result, the wife continued her role as a social butterfly, perennially concerned about projecting the proper image, forced to keep busy with the mind-dulling trivia of a snobbish social circle. There were no other options.   So-called intellectual women were suspected of being loose; therefore, young women were never encouraged to assume responsibilities outside the household. Such was woman's fate, as Elsa observes in *Streets of Buenos Aires*:

> The real misfortune is to be a woman. Men have interests, different pursuits. For us each day is never ending. [8]

The protagonist of *Wedding Anniversary* suffers anxiety at the prospect of her husband leaving for the office in the morning because she fears the long empty hours:

> During the entire day, during that endless day that stretched before me, I had no other mission than to have breakfast and read the newspaper. After that, I would have to work at filling up those hours. At the age of twenty I found myself morally lost and alone as I never was to feel again. [9]

Many of the women portrayed by Silvina Bullrich fall into that category, although generally they tend to appear as secondary characters. Her heroines, usually strong individuals gifted with great sensitivity, are inclined to examine realistically the discrepancies between the role they are expected to assume and their personal needs as in *I Will Rebel Tomorrow*, where the main figure, after long inner debates, chooses to ignore her family's selfish demands and settles for an independent existence dedicated to the Fine Arts.

As previously noted, marriage rarely turns out to be an enduring and rewarding relationship, and whenever one of the strong female characters finds the man ideally suited for her, a matrimonial union usually proves to be a legal impossibility. This means that even if defying society does not intimidate her, she still faces the decision of risking public displeasure for his sake. Such is the case in *Un momento muy largo* [*A Never-Ending Moment*] and *The Travellers* where, coincidentally, the men die and inflict infinite sorrow and despair on the women. In *The Travellers*, largely an autobiographical story, aside from being reminded that happiness is ephemeral and that the human condition entails much suffering, we must witness the redeeming qualities of the love and tenderness shared by this couple during his prolonged and fatal illness.

Even though throughout her novels Bullrich seems determined to denounce the prejudice that for too long has limited the role of Argentine women in society, her later novels indicate that some changes have broken the *status quo*. Aside from having earned a place among the working force, Argentine women today enjoy a great deal more freedom of action. Nevertheless, directly or indirectly, Bullrich seems to imply that the change is more apparent than real, at least in the areas where it really counts. Alejandra in *I Will Rebel Tomorrow* may have gone off to serve as an interpreter at the United Nations, but she has to work eleven hours a day and still returns home to face household chores. In other words, she has assumed the responsibility of working long hours in exchange for a hurried life leaving no time for herself.

The other phase of women's emancipation clearly stands out in *Mal don* [*Misdeal*], her latest novel. Diego, a gardener's son for Mal don, goes to Buenos Aires to attend the Law School and enters into a circle of wealthy young people. This association allows him to reach several conclusions concerning the habits of the rich, such as that upper class girls equate emancipation with sexual freedom and that men are only too eager to comply. If in the old days it was customary for the landowners' sons to travel to Paris and return with a French mistress, in the 1960's the situation has been reversed and men like Diego have taken the place of the kept woman:

> I was the French mistress of the emancipated society girls, of those who could afford the luxury of going to bed with a penniless student because they could allow themselves anything. Woman's liberation was not much more than that in certain circles. It was only equality with regards to the right to sexual liberties; they asked for more rights than duties and for men, of course, this state of affairs was convenient. [10]

But Bullrich remains adamant on one point: women still have not been given a meaningful chance to share in the important tasks, to be decision makers, or to help steer the country politically, socially and economically. When terrorists capture Diego, now an important corporation lawyer, thanks to his banker father-in-law, he is accused of having double-crossed his people, those who like his uncle Ramón had fought hard for the equal rights of his countrymen. One of the kidnappers passionately addresses himself to women's social inequality:

> I truly admire them, because we men are born to fight and if everything turns out well we are appointed presidents or ministers or something important; women, regardless of the outocme, never get anything. . . they are women, that is to say, nothing, dirt. . . . Believe me they don't have much choice; they say that in time, who knows... for the time being I always tell her . . . "I'm not lying, you are following me out of your own choice, but if we win, I'm not promising you anything. . ." I don't know what women accompanied Che or Fidel, but as far as I know none of them have been rewarded with a laurel crown. [11]

Misdeal, probably Silvina Bullrich's best creation, successfully integrates thematic elements of the past with new ones relevant to the present conditions in Argentina. The result is a novel of greater depth, dispassionately probing into some of the main problems plaguing the country, but not devoid of the intense human element characteristic of all her works.

Through two and a half decades, Miss Bullrich has actively contributed to Argentine letters through novels that are a faithful barometer of some of its social conditions. In her fiction she has attempted to crystalize the dilemmas that faced the women of her generation, many of whom, in spite of their capabilities, found that society had no room for enterprising members of their sex. Above all, through her many fictional women, she has strongly projected the warmth and sensitivity of the feminine soul, the essential qualities of womanhood which prompted Ortega y Gasset to state: ". . . a man's value lies in his actions, a woman's in her inherent nature." [12]

NOTES

[1] Translations of titles and quotes are my own.

[2] Silvina Bullrich, *Entre mis veinte y treinta años* (Buenos Aires: Emecé, 1970), 620.

[3] Silvina Bullrich, *Mañana digo basta* (Buenos Aires: Sudamericana, 1968), 13.

[4] *Ibid.*, p. 17.

[5] *Ibid.*, p. 235.

[6] Silvina Bullrich, "Bodas de cristal" in *Tres novelas* [*Three Novels*] (Buenos Aires: Sudamericana, 1966), 19.

[7] Silvina Bullrich, "Calles de Buenos Aires" in *Entre mis veinte y treinta años* (Buenos Aires: Emecé, 1970), 55.

[8] *Ibid.*, p. 108.

[9] *Bodas*, p. 21.

[10] Silvina Bullrich, *Mal don* (Buenos Aires: Emecé, 1973), p. 161.

[11] *Ibid.*, pp. 251-52.

[12] José Ortega y Gasset, *Ensayos sobre el amor* [*Essays on Iove*] (Madrid: Revista de Occidente, 1959), p. 9.

Three Female Playwrights Explore Contemporary Latin American Realit Myrna Casas, Griselda Gambaro, Luisa Josefina Hernández

by

GLORIA FEIMAN WALDMAN

In the context of this study I am defining Latin American "reality" as that particular situation which accepts as given a series of cultural imperatives, such as an inherently hierarchical societal framework based on class, race and sex differentiation. That "reality" more precisely includes the concept of the traditionally submissive and dependent female and the correspondingly dominant, aggressive male, *machismo* - the cult of virility and power,[1] and the sanctified states of marriage and motherhood. [2]

All the institutions of power that define a person's status in Latin American society - the legal system, the political institutions, the Church, the educational system - construct two very different realities for a woman and a man, with a clear picture of which is the favored group. Most significantly, these definitions of reality are ultimately accepted and adhered to by both groups. [3] Thus an exploration of reality, of the way things are, in the works of these three playwrights is necessarily an examination of the interrelationship between external circumstances and inner forces. [4]

All three, Myrna Casas, Griselda Gambaro and Luisa Josefina Hernández scrutinize areas of Latin American reality that need to be re-examined through different eyes: the anguish of mother-daughter relationships (Hernández' *La hija del rey* [*The King's Daughter*], *Los huéspedes reales* [*The Royal Guests*]); people's cruelty to each other (Gambaro's *The Camp, Los siameses* [*The Siamese Twins*], *El desatino,* [*The Absurdity*]); the destructive power of love (Hernández' *Los sordomudos* [*The Deaf and Dumb*], Casas' *Cristal roto en el tiempo* [*Broken Crystal in Time*]); the struggle for personal freedom (Hernández' *The Mulatto's Orgy*); the essential frustration of the female experience (Hernández' *Los frutos caídos* [*The Fallen Fruit*], *Arpas blancas, conejos dorados* [*White Harps, Golden Rabbits*], Casas' *Cristal roto en el tiempo*). All are themes that deal with conflict, power struggles and coming to terms with internal and external pressures on the self. My intention is to examine, in these three female playwrights, each one's distinct point of view in portraying her characters' situation and in making her statement about Latin American reality.

Most of Hernández' (Mexico) characters are emotionally wounded, drained, in need of affection, of human contact. Some learn to express that need and go on to try and fulfill it (as in *Los frutos caídos* and *Arpas blancas, conejos dorados*), often directly challenging the established order. Others never learn how to reach out and end up alone (*Los sordomudos*), or chose the "wrong people" to love (*Los frutos caídos*), or find themselves face to face with societal taboos (like the father in *Los huéspedes reales*) and commit suicide. Most come to terms with the essentially frustrating nature of life and love, and in particular with the deadening effects of life in the rural provinces of Mexico. Her portrayal of people in a small town situation, with their petty likes and dislikes, their routines and their intrigues reminds us of Agustín Yáñez' *Al filo de agua* [*The Edge of the Storm*], as well as the closed, suffocating world of Galdos' *Doña Perfecta* [*Miss Perfect*].

Hernández creates tortured female protagonists, resolute and determined in their personalities, who try to solve their inner conflicts but are eventually thwarted by the circumstances of which they are a part. Hernández portrays love as essentially unattainable, with obstacles to happiness often imposed by the characters themselves. There is also a distinctly cynical attitude about marriage and human relationships in general (particularly in *Arpas blancas, conejos dorados* and *Los huéspedes reales*).

Hernández' plays challenge numerous norms for Latin American society. She is challenging the society around her by presenting dissident voices, by giving life to situations that *do* exist and that are uncomfortable, such as hostility between mothers and daughters, "dark passions" between fathers and daughters, and the double standard of sexual morality for men and women. Her female characters see themselves first as women, and are therefore conscious of the roles that society expects them to fulfill. Let's examine these situations more specifically.

Celia in *Los frutos caídos* is 27, divorced and remarried, yet basically dissatisfied with her life and forced to face herself in a visist to her country house which she has decided to sell. Also, she must confront her feelings for a younger man who loves her and has followed her from Mexico City to convince her to leave her family for him. She is frustrated and angry as she tells him:

> ¿Así que me sugiere Ud. que me divorcie de nuevo? (*Francisco asiente.*) Que tenga con mi marido una serie de entrevistas preliminares, alevosas de mi parte, porque él no lo espera, hasta llevarlo al punto. Y que luego sostenga una lucha encarnizada por la tutela de mi hijo, y que tenga que fingir, llorar y patear, hasta con-

seguirla por medio de la compasión, porque no hay hombre que
serenamente consienta en ser reemplazado por otro ante su hijo. Y
todo ¿para qué? Para caer nada menos que en un matrimonio con los
mismos defectos de los demás...

[So, you suggest that I get divorced again? *(Francisco nods his head.)*
Have a series of preliminary scenes with my husband, sneaky on my
part because he doesn't expect what's coming, until I get to the
point; have a bitter battle for the custody of my child, and have to
play-act, weep and stamp my feet, until I get what I want, by playing
on his sympathy, because there's no man who is going to agree to be
replaced in front of his child. And all that, for what? To get involved
in a marriage with the same defects as every other marriage...] [5]

We have the sense that the four generations of women in this play are waiting
for old age - for death - to end their pain. Magdalena, true to her name, is the
long suffering wife, always worried about her husband, always protecting him
and yet disgusted with his drunkenness and mediocrity.

Tiene que ser, porque tampoco quise estar sola, ni morir abandonada,
ni ser una vieja endurecida, como Tía Paloma. Ya sé que soy la que
no llora, la que no se ofende, la que no pide nada, pero quisiera
imaginarme, si hubiera podido evitarse todo esto, ¿cómo habría sido
mi vida?

[It has to be as it is, because I didn't want to be alone, or die abandoned, or be a hard old woman like Aunt Paloma. I know that I'm
the one who doesn't cry, the one who doesn't get offended, the one
who doesn't ask for anything, but I would love to imagine myself, if I
had been able to avoid all of this. How would my life have been?] (p.
465).

Paloma, the old aunt, a familiar figure in Hernández' writing, has never
married:

No me casé, ni tuve novios, ni conocí hombres. No me han ex-
plotado, ni he sufrido por nadie, ni nadie me ha exigido nada.

[I never got married, or had boyfriends, or knew men. They haven't
exploited me, nor have I suffered because of anyone, nor has anyone
demanded anything from me] (p. 447-448).

Then there is the 18 year old student, Dora, who insists that her life will be
different. However, in a final note of pessimism and resignation, Celia says:

Para volver aquí cuando haya llegado el momento de encerrarme, de
esconderme, de pudrirme en el suelo ... Me esperarán los muebles

apolillados, esos dos retratos viejos, las rejas y...tú, Dora.

[So I'll return here when the moment comes to shut myself in, to hide, to rot on the ground...The moth-eaten furniture will be waiting for me, as well as those two old portraits, the iron grating and...you, Dora.] (p. 447)

Thus the gap between the four generations of women is closed, by emphasizing the deadly sameness of the possibilities for each woman.

In *Los huéspedes reales* Cecilia sees her inexorable destiny as marrying her insensitive macho *novio* [boyfriend] who says to her: "Hay algo que las mujeres no comprenden...la vida de un hombre tiene dos aspectos..." [There's something that women don't understand...a man's life has two sides...] [6] The marriage is encouraged by Celia's mother, who wants her married - and out of the way of her father and herself. Cecilia has accepted this destiny and in effect rejects Bernardo, the young student who loves her and whom she loves. But her rebellion and her revenge will be exacted, through hating her new husband, being sexually indifferent to him, and forcing him to bring her back to her parents' home.   This play also includes two other favorite Hernández themes: the hostile and competitive nature of mother-daughter relationships,[7] as well as the painful dilemma of a father and daughter caught in an Electra situation: "Eres una mujer y quieres ser una niña, eres mi hija y quieres hacer papeles de esposa..." [You are a woman and you want to be a little girl, you are my daughter and you want to act like a wife...] (p. 105). Later on Cecilia repeats, as if it were a litany: "Viviremos y moriremos juntos, seremos de esos que se insultan y se adoran, de esos que se muerden y se lamen los golpes y moriremos juntos, moriremos juntos y..." (p. 107) ["We will live and we will die together, we will be like those who insult each other and adore each other, those who bite each other and lick each other's wounds and we will die together, we will die together and..."]

Similar themes are developed in the soliloquoy, *La hija del rey*. With regard to the mother-daughter situation, the daughter confronts her deepest self in response to her mother's note asking to see her. She is anticipating her mother's plan to send her away, since the daughter reminds the Queen of past guilt, weakness, hate, and unfulfillment. She says: "Poco placer me has dado como hija. No me reconozco en ti." [You've given me little pleasure as a daughter. I don't recognize myself in you.][8] The Queen personifies those archtypal female dieties who supremely wielded their power, decreeing life or death with aplomb. The daughter, intimidated by her mother, essentially plays the passive role of waiting for the news, of never initiating anything, and of finding her identity in other people's image of her. Her ultimate impotence manifests itself in her Electra-like situation: "De niña, hubieras querido ser su esposa y te morías de envidia (...) De mujer, hubieras querido ser su asesina.'' [As a little girl, you would have wanted to be his wife and you died of envy (...)As a woman, you would have wanted to be his assassin.''] (p. 14) However, through the process of role-playing the imagined interaction between her mother and herself, she anticipated the situation, and confronted her deepest fears about her real motivations in her relationships with her mother, her father, and her step-father. She made her own decision to leave, and thus didn't allow herself to be acted upon, but rather took the initiative.

In *Los duendes* [*The Spirits*], with the help of absurdist techniques [9], and her acute sense of humor, Hernández pits the increasingly mechanized, systematic, rational world of the male characters against the more spontaneous, unexpected and richer reality of her female characters. In the tradition of Ionesco and Albee, Hernández shows us how life is much more absurd, strange and illogical than we know, in protest against people's acting as if life were predictable and mundane. Is it gratuitous that in this play the men represent the ''watch keepers'', the ''schedule keepers'', the self-conscious principle, and the women, the curious, experimental, out-reaching principle? Hardly. As we can see from this brief examination of her works, her point of view is consistent. Her women figures are in conflict with the aspirations that the society at large has for them and they assert themselves in different ways. They generally do not succeed in fulfilling themselves though. This doesn't imply negative aspirations for women on Hernández' part, as much as it does imply her negative assessment of the way reality unfolds for women in Latin America.

Myrna Casas (Puerto Rico) shares with Luisa Josefina Hernández a versatility within the theatre genre in successfully combining Aristotelic and structurally traditional elements, as in *Eugenia Victoria Herrera*, with absurdist elements, poetic language and distinct Brechtian overtones, as in *Absurdos en soledad* [*Absurdities in Solitude*]. Her vision of reality is defined by the inclusion in her writing of such varied themes as: the nature of love; the tentativeness of human contact; the constant interplay between past, present and future; commonality of experience; the arbitrary violence and cruelty inherent in society.

Specifically, in *Cristal roto en el tiempo*, we enter into an atmosphere of doom, disappointment and anguish. We experience ''three dimensions of futility in the juxtaposing of past, present and future.''[10] Doña Laura, member of an aristocratic San Juan family, finds herself the madam of a high class bordello when her playboy brother is killed in a car accident. Laura is tense, worried, bitter and linked to the past, just as Manuela, the servant who has always been with the family, is loyal, anguished at the desperate plight of the rapidly declining business, and also linked to the past. Amelia, the young prostitute who has been convinced to move to New York where she can be more successful, is linked to the future. María, sensitive and self-denigrating, is forever lost in her alcohol-filled memories of the lover who abandoned her. The play belongs to these four women, all from very differnet social classes and backgrounds, who dominate the text with their will to survive - because of their pride, in Laura's case, or their loyalty, in Manuela's case, or their refusal to be poor again, as in Amelia's case.

It is María who falls most into the world of Latin stereotypes. She willingly sacrificed herself for her lover, for his music career, and he took advantage of this and left her. She says, remembering him:

Son manos de ángel...de cristal...de cristal...pero...el cristal se rompe...No...estamos todos hechos de cristalitos pequeños que nos van desangrando...y la vida es una herida larga...una herida larga...honda y lenta...

[They are hands of an angel...of crystal...of crystal...but...crystal breaks...No...we are all made of little pieces of crystal that drain our blood...and life is a long wound...a long wound...deep and slow...][11]

Through the use of voices from the past, we sense the nature of the pull the men exert on the women: Manuela's free-loading husband, who constantly questions why she wants to return to that house; María's lover, who laments his having to leave her to better his career, but adds that he will never forget her; Pepito, the brother who squanders the family's money, all the while insisting that he will always be there to protect his sister Laura.

As in Hernández' work, Casas is also interested in illuminating father-daughter relationships, which she develops both in *Cristal roto en el tiempo* and *Eugenia Victoria Herrera*. In *Cristal roto en el tiempo,* the patriarch's disappointment in his daughter, Doña Laura, in her apparent betrayal of his values by maintaining the ancestral home as a brothel, is revealed through passages where he talks to her from the past. She is guilt-ridden and pained, and at the same time frustrated that she has never been able to disagree with her father, or her brother, and impose her will. The relationship in *Eugenia Victoria Herrera* is similar to Hernández' *Los sordomudos*, where once again, a patriarchal figure controls his children's lives by threats or promises, and generally manipulates them. In *Eugenia Victoria Herrera,* the dying father fails to see that it is not his son or son-in-law, but rather Eugenia, who loves the land as he does and wants to uphold her people's traditional allegiance to the soil, as opposed to the migration to the city. [12]

Casas calls *Absurdos en soledad* "a series of expressionistic, symbolic monologues." Just as Agustín Cuzzani calls his pieces *farsátiras* [satirical farces],[13] Casas refers to hers as *absurdos* [absurdities] and *soledades* [solitudes]. The play is a tour de force of six *soledades* alternating with six *absurdos.* The six *soledades*, composed of two characters, *la niña* [the little girl] and la actriz [the actress], form a unity. As with Coleridge's "willing suspension of disbelief", we long to accept the world of fantasy, imagination, self-confidence and assertiveness of *la niña*, in contrast to the solid world of *la actriz*, with her mundane questions, all referring to her particularly literal search for the entrance to the stage (a metaphor for the search for her personal identity and fulfillment). Underlying the tenuous but affectionate relationship the two share, is the little girl's disappointment that the actress wants to enter the stage, in effect to leave her. This is seen in the following translation of the fifth *soledad* in its entirety:

> The Actress ascends the stage with great determination. The Little Girl follows her and shouts "No!" The Actress enters through the curtains. The Little Girl murmurs a painful "Ay!" and then disappears. [14]

By the final *soledad* the actress has been won over by the little girl and her world, and has passed from her own reality into the little girl's. It is the little girl who leads the actress to the entrance to the stage, that she has been longing to find. But as the actress disappears, we experience an acute sense of loss and separation. The actress is getting what she wanted, but at what price? Both are alone and left with bittersweet feelings of melancholy and nostalgia - essential clues to Casas' view of reality. In the following dialogue from the sixth *absurdo*, the actress clarifies the circular nature of the play. The actress - overdressed, like a star - has finally found the entrance to the stage:

ACTRESS- When do we begin?
MALE ACTOR- We've finished.
WOMAN NO.2- Everything is over.
WOMAN NO. 3- Yes.
ACTRESS- Fine. I'm ready.

(They all leave and she begins to speak as the curtain falls.)

-This is the story of a little girl.   Of course that little girl was this one...I mean...was me. Well anyway, one day I was looking out seated on my Grandmother's fence while the neighbors passed by. We had some of the strangest neighbors. There was a man who... (p. 113)

Reality then, in the *soledades*, is a merging of the two worlds - the stage and the little girl's world - both synonymous with imagination, magic and dreams.

Casas' view of reality, as portrayed in the six *absurdos* is devastating. She makes her statements about war, destruction, gratuitous cruelty and people's inability to share affection, displaying a strong Brechtian influence (as manifested, for example, by the characters' directly addressing the audience and discussing and changing the sequence of events of the play). *Absurdo* No. 1 is an example of a strong statement of despair about the possibility of human relationships. In it a man and a woman reminisce and try to recapture their love, while six people, dressed as *persianas* [window shutters] act as a chorus. The chorus is quite angry and annoyed when the woman says she is happy - and is quite satisfied and laughs cynically when in the end, love and hope between the couple is crushed: "(En una carcajada que se extiende hasta que cierra la cortina.) Sin amor." ["(In a burst of laughter that goes on until the curtain closes.) Without love."] (p. 31)

Griselda Gambaro (Argentina) primarily writes theatre of the absurd. She makes use of absurdist techniques to refocus our traditional expectations about life and theatre and to communicate her vision of the world. She examines the existence of cruelty, hostility, humilliation and people's indifference to each other. Unlike Hernández or Casas, who imply sex-related differences in male-female behaviour, most of Gambaro's characters are despicable and unsympathetic, regardless of their sex. Victims, when given the opportunity, become victimizers. What is interesting though, as seen in *El desatino*, is that the men's particular strangeness, or craziness, if you will, is quite individual and original, while the portrayal of the two women figures, the Mother and the elusive Lily, wife of the protagonist, Alfonso, follow stereotypic patterns. The Mother is a ridiculous, exaggerated figure who wants to be young, have sex with her son's best friend, Luis, and hates her daughter-in-law. Lily, the wife whom we are never sure exists, is mysteriously alluded to but infrequently appears, is apparently a prostitute, and has also had sex with Luis. She is totally indifferent to Alfonso, who idolizes her, and doesn't even know his name.

Most relationships in Gambaro's plays are overtly cruel and hostile, except for the purely sexual relationship between the Mother and Luis. *El desatino* revolves around the bizarre and unexplained circumstance of some kind of a "weight" attached to Alfonso's ankle - an unidentified object which is rotting, and makes him into an invalid. Numerous graphic episodes indicate the gross indifference of his so-called "loved ones" to his plight. They ignore him; leave him out in the rain; don't feed him - with the exception of *el muchacho*, the unknown youth who desperately tries to saw off the object and free Alfonso. In doing so, Alfonso treats him vilely, tells him to leave, and accuses him of being a homosexual. When he finally succeeds in sawing off the "weight", Alfonso dies. Likewise, in *The Camp*, there is an attempt for human closeness between Emma, an inmate, and Martin, an administrator. The attempt is necessarily thwarted though, by the nature of the metaphor of the concentration camp as life; brutality and regimentation are the same inside the camp, as well as outside of it.

Through her use of absurdist techniques, Gambaro induces richer, more varied responses to familiar situations. Everyday reality takes on another dimension as we watch these familiar situations extended to their limits. We are forced to react as we see extreme brutality depicted as a mundane occurrence, rather than singled out as something extraordinary and infrequent. We must come to terms with the unexpected and unfathomed horror that Gambaro presents as everyday life - which , although frightening, is all too recognizable.

What then is the ''reality'' these three dramatists present? All three paint a somber picture of the individual's struggle for coherency in an essentially hostile world. It is interesting to note that all three use the absurd to create their particular versions of reality: Hernández, the most poetic, uses it to emphasize elements of humor; Casas, the most lyrical, to highlight elements of fantasy; Gambaro, the most sparse in her writing style, to create an atmosphere of horror and cruelty.

The following statement, although originally about Gambaro's work, applies equally well to Hernández and Casas. For all three, their perceiving and portraying Latin American reality necessitates ''a relentless investigation of aggression and submission, of love and hatred, of dependence and independence.'' [15] This is especially so in their portrayal of reality for the Latin American woman. For as we have seen, particularly in the plays of Hernández and Casas, within this generally pessimistic view of reality, the possibility for personal fulfillment for the female is significantly lower than for the male. Thus the situation does not differ in kind from the global one, vis à vis women. Certainly, though, it does differ in degree, owing to the distinctive Latin American socio-cultural context previously described.

NOTES

[1] Octavio Paz, *The Labyrinth of Solitude: Life and Thought in Mexico* (New York: Grove Press, Inc., 1961), p. 81. Particularly pertinent is Chapter 4 ''The Sons of La Malinche''.

[2] For further development of these themes, see Ann Pescatello, Editor, *Male and Female in Latin America, Essays* (University of Pittsburgh Press, 1973).

[3] Peter L. Berger and Thomas Luckmann, *The Social Construction of Reality* (New York: Anchor Books, Doubleday and Co., Inc., 1967).

[4] Once again the Orteguian posture, "Yo soy yo y mi circunstancia..." ["I am I and my circumstance..."].

[5] Luisa Josefina Hernández, *Los frutos caídos* (Xalapa, México: Ficción, Universidad Veracruzana, 1958), p. 21.

[6] Luisa Josefina Hernández, *Los huéspedes reales* (Xalapa, México: Ficción, Universidad Veracruzana, 1958), p. 21.

[7] For an exploration of this love-hate relationship, see the section, "Mothers and Daughters: A Mythological Commentary on the Lives" in Phyllis Chesler, *Women and Madness* (New York: Doubleday and Co., Inc., 1972).

[8] Luisa Josefina Hernández, *La hija del rey* in *Cuarta antología de obras en un acto* (México: Colección Teatro Mexicano, 1965), p. 14.

[9] A viable definition of *theatre of the absurd* can be found in Harry Shaw, *Dictionary of Literary Terms* (New York: McGraw-Hill Book Co., 1972), p. 377: "An avant-garde style of playwriting and presentation in which conventions of structure, plot, and characterization are ignored or distorted (...) an irrational quality of nature is stressed, and man's isolation and aloneness are made central elements of conflict (...) characters may appear in different forms and identities and may change sex, age, and personality; the presentation may have no fixed or determinable setting; the sequence of time is fluid and indefinite."

[10] Francisco Arriví, *Teatro Puertorriqueño, Tercer Festival*, (San Juan: Instituto de Cultura Puertorriqueña, 1961), p. 12.

[11] Myrna Casas, *Cristal roto en el tiempo* in *Teatro Puertorriqueño, Tercer Festival* (San Juan: Instituto de Cultura Puertorriqueña, 1961), p. 306.

[12] The following works actually fall outside the purview of this study, whose scope is "contemporary reality": *Eugenia Victoria Herrera* (M. Casas) takes place a few years before the invasion of 1898. *Clemencia* (L. J. Hernández) takes place in 1863. *Arpas blancas, conejos dorados* (LJH) takes place in 1930. *Quetzalcoatl* and *Popul Vuh*, both by Hernández, both pre-Columbian mythology.

[13] Agustín Cuzzani was born in Argentina in 1924. His *farsátiras* include: *Una libra de carne* [*A pound of meat*], 1954; *El centro-forward murió al amanecer*] *The Centerforward died at dawn*] , 1955; *Los indios estaban cabreros* [*The Indians were angry*], 1957; *Sempronio*, 1957.

[14] Myrna Casas, *Teatro: Absurdos en soledad* (San Juan: Editorial Cordillera, 1964), p. 83.

[15] Oliver, William I., *Voices of Change in the Spanish American Theater, An Anthology* (Austin: University of Texas Press, 1971), p. 49.

Brechtian Aesthetics in Chile: Isidora Aguirre's ''Los papeleros'' [*The Garbage Collectors*]

by

ELEANORE MAXWELL DIAL

University of Wisconsin-Milwaukee

In his ''A Short Organum for the Theater (1948),'' Bertolt Brecht writes: ''The theater has to become geared into reality if it is to be in a position to turn out effective representations of reality, and to be allowed to do so.'' Chilean dramatist Isidora Aguirre has, in her 1963 play, *Los papeleros* [*The Garbage Collectors*], endeavored to create theater that is geared into reality, and in so doing is heavily indebted to Brechtian aesthetics. Carlos Solórzano has called attention in *El teatro actual latinoamericano* [*Latin American Theater of the Present*] to Brechtian overtones in *Los papeleros*, and, indeed, the play from beginning to end reflects the dramatist's knowledge of and admiration for the aesthetics and techniques of epic theater. [1]

Nor is Aguirre alone in this regard. She belongs to a generation of playwrights who began writing in the 1950's, a decade in which Brechtian dramaturgy began to make an impact in Chile. As Julio Durán-Cerda has indicated in the Prologue of *El teatro chileno contemporáneo* [*Contemporary Chilean Theater*] a Chilean production of *Mother Courage* (1953) helped bring a new dynamism and vigor to the theater of that country. Indeed, the arrival of Brechtian theater almost coincides with the date Durán-Cerda chooses as the beginning of modern theater in Chile; in that year, 1955, three women playwrights of considerable importance, María Asunción Requena, Isidora Aguirre and Gabriela Roepke, first saw their plays produced. These women, according to Durán-Cerda, represent the three main currents of modern Chilean theater: the evaluation of past history (Requena), satire and social criticism (Aguirre) and transcendalist theater with emphasis on individual perspective (Roepke). [2]

And it is Isidora Aguirre's approach to satire and social criticism with its resonant echoes of Bertolt Brecht that interests us here. She chose, as Brecht often did, to fill the stage with society's marginal people. Here, for instance, the word ''papeleros'' is used in a special way. These are not paper collectors or garbage collectors employed by the city. They are, rather, men and women who live near a garbage dump. They earn their meager living by going out in the morning to collect paper and other refuse before the municipal garbage trucks make their rounds. They also forage in the garbage dump. Anything that can be retrieved is sold through a middle man to poor people. It is the lowest of employments, but marginal as it is, there are people in the play who are lower down the social scale than the garbage pickers are.

Indicating her technique, Aguirre characterizes *Los papeleros* as a ''satire with music and songs, divided in two parts and ten scenes.'' And the music serves, as does the music in *The Three Penny Opera* and *Rise and Fall of the Town of Mahagonny,* as an integral part of the work. Then, too, one encounters titles for scenes. While the stage directions do not indicate that these titles should be flashed on a screen, written on placards or displayed in similar fashion to the audience, it is difficult to imagine their not being dealt with in some such manner. The titles show the shifting emphasis of the play: ''El oficio del papelero'' [''The Trade of Garbage Picking''], ''El negocio de vinos'' [''The Wine Business''], ''La Guatona Romilia'' [''Chubby Romilia''], ''El Tigre aprende un oficio'' [''Tiger Learns a Trade''], ''El mitín de la Romilia'' [''Romilia's Rally''], ''Los pobres presentan reclamo al rico'' [''The Poor Present a Demand to the Rich Man''], ''La Mocha y su guacho'' [''Mocha and her Baby''], ''Fiestas patrias en el basural'' [''National Holidays on the Garbage Heap''], and ''Los pobres quedan más pobres'' [''The Poor Get Poorer''].

The play is a mosaic which centers around the garbage heap, the people who earn their living from it and live near it. Aguirre has created a gallery of characters, nineteen in number plus a general category of garbage pickers and Una Voz, characters who are treated anecdotally and, for the most part, with Brechtian detachment. If there is a spokeswoman, however, it is surely La Guatona Romilia, a character who can take her place alongside such epic heroines as The Mother and Mother Courage. If she resembles The Mother in her ability to espouse a cause, she resembles Mother Courage in her indomitability. When Pinto suggests that women are better off at home tending the stew than out giving speeches, she cuts him off by saying sarcastically, ''That's right. And men off to the cantina to get drunk. No, sir! We women are mothers and we've learned to fight better than anyone when it comes to trying to get decent houses for our children. Who marched in the forefront when the inhabitants of the Zanjón took possession of the lands of the Feria? Women. We aren't back in the old days when man was king. Now we have earned ourselves the right to talk the same as he has.'' (Part II, v, 272) To demonstrate what women have accomplished in the past, Romilia relates that she and another widow once had the good idea of renting a pit that would enable them to have the garbage concession to themselves rather than going through another person. They succeeded in doing this, but, after the death of her friend, Romilia was not able to continue by herself. Her present goal involves rallying the garbage collectors to go with her as a committee to the Futre to demand land which had been promised a year ago, land where they could build new homes.

From the very beginning of *Los papeleros*, the audience knows that this is a play about people who are wretchedly poor, that the playwright has a definite point of view, and that the play's stylized structure is more than mere whim; the audience is being asked to view the poor with something more than charitable concern. In the introductory verses Aguirre says: ''The theater with its licenses/is coming to tell you/in the name of the garbage collector, who cannot tell it,/the story of the scum of man/and man in the scum.'' (p. 247) The story, she knows, is an absurd one, for it is absurd that some men should live poorly so that other men should live well.

Much of Aguirre's satire is directed at a society that allows such divergence in the distribution of wealth. When the youth Tigre steals a watch from a poor girl, his mother, Romilia, is upset, but she decides that the fault lies not with her son but with the garbage dump, a force which reduces the Christian to the level of a beast. A Brechtian chorus of garbage collectors and others points out that sometimes robbing goes by other names, names such as ''speculating.'' One finds in Brecht an elaboration of this theme in *Saint Joan of the Stockyards* in the confrontation between Saint Joan and her poor and Mauler who in his speculating on meat causes workers to lose their jobs.

From the opening song to the closing song, Aguirre reveals her debt to Brecht, as she looks at life among the garbage collectors in Santiago. The garbage heap is a microcosm of the society which produces it in much the same way that Brecht's slaughterhouse is: ''Dehumanized humanity/when there is no end to the unrest in our cities: /Into such a world, a world like a slaughterhosue, as Saint Joan says.'' [3] Here the garbage collectors have their hierarchy, their dreams, their frustrations. In her portrayal of this microcosm, Aguirre adheres to what Brecht calls ''improbability of a constant kind.'' [4] Here the garbage collectors, who are obviously not a group of society's most articulate members, express themselves ably in Chilean tones. For Aguirre the ''pit'' is life, or rather the vicissitudes of living, whereas for Brecht, the garbage pit is Mauler's heart: ''Straight to his heart, Lennox! Straight to his heart! It's a sensitive garbage pit!'' [5]

Also, in *Los papeleros,* Francisco asserts that everyone lives outside or within a pit. For a while he himself was able to live on the edge; then life became too much for him and he, too, fell into the cavity. (Part I, ii, 256) One of the most theatrical, and not the least effective features of the play, is the translation of this metaphor into visual terms in scene iv when the relationship of two characters to the cavity becomes apparent. One old man appears on the edge of the hollow, and the other can be seen with shoulders

still above the cavity, but the rest of his body submerged in it. Carrying out
the image in musical terms in ''Digging,'' the garbage collectors sing in
choral fashion that ''Life is a pit.'' (Part I, i, 251)

Life being what it is, Aguirre's characters take refuge in their dreams and
illusions. Don Núñez's illusion is that a German whom he knows will save
him from his poor condition. Mocha dreams that she will be able to educate
the abandoned baby that she has taken into her care. And while Romilia's
fantasy entails the hope of uniting the people so that theirs may be a better
world, Felipe Mora dreams of receiving the money that is owed him from the
period when he worked in a mine. All these illusions are acknowledged in a
dream sequence song, ''Ballad of the Beggar Girl with the Tramp''; here La
Mocha envisions a beautiful version of the *basural* (world) while someone
sings: ''What can /that white veil like smoke be/here and there/Dreams that
are being dreamed/by sleepers in the garbage dump.'' (Part I, iv, 265)

Aguirre's world of the downtrodden includes those even more wretchedly
unfortunate than the garbage pickers, specifically Don Núñez and Viejo. As
Don Núñez says: ''The garbage collector lives from leftovers, and we from
the leftovers of the leftovers.'' (Part I, iv, 266) Brecht has said that his plays
are for river-dwellers, fruit farmers, builders of vehicles, and upturners of
society. (''Organum,'' p. 185) He would invite these people into the theater
and ''hand the world over to their minds and hearts, for them to change as
they think fit.'' (p. 185) The people who inhabit Aguirre's world in *Los
papeleros* are people who have most to gain from a change in society, yet they
are in the worst possible position to effect change. The Chilean *roto* [a person
who is dirt poor], on seeing this play, would undoubtedly realize that the
predicaments of these characters are akin to his own. The irony and the
imagery would not be lost on him. When, in *Los papeleros*, a garbage
collector whose hands are permanently stained, tries to find some other way of
earning a living, he is rejected by a prospective employer because of his dirty
hands. This anecdote with all of its moral, sociological, and economic implications could perhaps be grasped by the spectator. But would the play, one
asks, lead to greater understanding? Would it lead to action?

Los papeleros is, of course, meant to be instructive; its boldly experimental form is certainly not meant to be an end in itself. Brecht has
spoken approvingly of the experimental theater of Gorky, Chekhov, Haupt-
mann, Shaw, Kaiser, and O'Neill; but if he approves of their ex-
perimentation, it is largely because by it, the problems of our times, problems
such as the emancipation of women, are reshaped into theatrical terms.[6]
And, of course, this reshaping must be effective. Such is Aguirre's
dramaturgical intent. Her didacticism is solemn, but never tediously
academic. The interplay among Chile's social classes is vividly portrayed by a
dramatist who wants to get across to her audience the reality of life for ''the
underdogs,'' and, just perhaps, those viewing the play will reflect that in-

dividuals such as Romilia and Julia Vega are not so powerless after all. And maybe the audience will set about trying to change the world. Brecht says: "The theater now spreads the world in front of him (the person in the audience) to take hold of and use for his own good." [7]

Aguirre's play could have been depressingly *costumbrista* [of a strong regional flavour], but it is not. "Clarity," according to Eric Bentley, "is the first requiste of didacticism." In the *Good Person of Setzuan*, he notes that Brecht makes his instruction into a work of art because he avoids the pitfalls of permitting the work to be too quaint and charming on the one hand and too allegorical and ponderous on the other. [8] Aguirre also manages to avoid these pitfalls. *Los papeleros*, to be sure, has its quaint touches such as the use of Chilean expressions, for example, and the celebration of Chilean national holidays on the dump with the song called "To my Flag." Rigoberta sings her original composition: "They teach us in school/from the moment we learn to read/that no matter how poor we may be/we must be good patriots." (Part II, viii, 280) And yet, whatever quaintness exists here is drowned in the irony of the situation, in the bittersweet quality of the words.

As one ponders Brecht's own listing of epic theater's characteristics as opposed to those dramatic theater, one is struck by Aguirre's adherence to Brechtian tenets, an adherence which if not undiscriminating is certainly ardent. [9] She gives the spectator what Brecht calls "a picture of the world"; she invites the spectator to "stand outside and think," as different characters or singers address their complaints or words of wisdom directly to him. There is, moreover, the continual appeal to reason. In dramatic theater, Brecht says, "thought determines being" whereas in epic theater "social being determines thought." At one point in *Los papeleros*, the chorus sings, "One mustn't apply/sentimental criteria/and judge the poor/as one judges an equal." (Part II, vi, 276)

Social protest, of course, is not new in Latin American theater; *Los papeleros* is thematically allied to scores of plays from Mexico, Ecuador, Argentina, and Puerto Rico in its treatment of the lower depths. But Aguirre's skillful use of Brechtian techniques in a completely Chilean setting is striking. While the structure of the play with its integration of music adheres closely to Brechtian theatrical principles, the language and atmosphere are eminently Chilean. Like Romilia in the play, Aguirre, would organize workers to accomplish just ends. In epic theater, the human being is the "object of the inquiry," Brecht's term. In *Los papeleros,* the garbage pickers are the objects of the inquiry, yet the play could have been written about miners, farmers, laborers. But the satire is not merely a political tract; the play's aesthetic dimensions are deserving of praise. Aguirre perceives, one may conclude, Chilean reality as something that must be changed. As for solutions and options, those are a matter for the spectator, detached and enlightened, to consider.

NOTES

[1] Bertolt Brecht, "A Short Organum for the Theater (1948)," *Brecht on Theater*, ed. and tr. John Willett (New York: Hill and Wang, 1964), p. 186. Isidora Aguirre, *Los papeleros, El teatro actual latinoamericano* (Mexico: Ediciones de Andrea, 1972), ed. Carlos Solórzano. The page numbers will refer to this edition and translations of titles and quotations are mine.

[2] Julio Durán-Cerda, *El teatro chileno contemporáneo* (Mexico: Aguilar, 1970), pp. 29-57.

[3] Brecht, *Saint Joan of the Stockyards, Avant-Garde Drama*, tr. Frank Jones (New York: Bantam Books, Inc., 1969), p. 122.

[4] "Organum," p. 182.

[5] *Saint Joan*, p. 130.

[6] Brecht, "On Experimental Theater," *Theater in the Twentieth Century*, tr. Carl Mueller and ed. Robert Corrigan (New York: Grove Press, Inc., 1963), pp. 96-97.

[7] *Ibid.*, 108.

[8] Eric Bentley, "From Strindberg to Bertolt Brecht," *The Playwright as Thinker* (New York: Meridian Books, 1955), p. 224.

[9] Brecht, "The Modern Theater is the Epic Theater," *Brecht on Theater*, p. 37.

A Thematic Exploration of the Works of Elena Garro [1]

by

GABRIELA MORA

City College (CUNY)

Mexican writers, spurred by a deep cultural schism, have not ceased asking what is Mexico and who is the Mexican. [2] Their works reflect the characteristics cited by scholars as distinguishing Latin American literature: the strong protest against prevailing socioeconomic conditions and the search for self-identity. [3] Judged by what has been said about Elena Garro, her work appears to be an exception to this phenomenon. Her theatre, for example, has been praised for its poetic style, its originality and sense of humor while at the same time criticized for ideological weakness. [4] Of her narrative, Emmanuel Carballo has said:

> In the world of Garro there are no rich or poor, good or bad, there are only happy or unhappy people. There is no class struggle, there are no redeemers or people who want to be redeemed. Perpetual adolescents, her characters fight against death ... and only aspire to be happy. [5]

Despite these opinions, it is our contention that Garro is driven in her work by an intense desire to protest the Mexican social situation, particularly that affecting women. As this brief examination will show, she not only deals with traditional problems like the exploitation of the Indians and the betrayal of the Revolution, but the victimization of woman, as well as alienation and loneliness, the most representative themes of our time.

To simplify our task, we made an arbitrary division of the material into four groups. We stress the term arbitrary because some of the works examined overlap the category in which we placed them, and at least one of our divisions is artificially separated from another to which it could easily belong. The four are: a) denunciation of socioeconomic conditions in Mexico; b) critical exposé of women's situation; c) time; d) the mysterious and the supernatural. It is apparent that the second group belongs in the first. We separated them, however, because in Garro's treatment of women there are specific motifs which deserve special attention.

In the first group we have those works that reveal the misery of the Indians, like the novel *Los recuerdos del porvenir* [*Recollections of Things to Come*][6], the short stories "El zapaterito de Guanajuato" ["The Little Cobbler from Guanajuato"] and "El anillo" ["The Ring"], and the plays "Los perros" ["The Dogs"] and "La Dama Boba" ["The Foolish Lady"].[7] In *Recollections...* and several stories collected in *La semana de colores* [*The Week of Colors*], the Indian is seen nostalgically as a childhood friend who shares secrets and games and infuses life with magic, despite his status as a servant. The warm feeling of camaraderie is especially evident between the white ladies and their maids for they all suffer at the hands of jealous and possessive men as in the short story "La culpa es de los tlaxcaltecas" ["The Tlaxcaltecas are to Blame"][8]. Nevertheless, as Garro demonstrates, the existence of economic injustice and strong racial prejudices make the Indian's lives the most degraded in the society. The author places the newly rich mestizos among the major exploiters of the Indians, as in *Recollections*, where Rodolfo Orizabar and his mother well represent a greedy bourgeoisie that stops at nothing for money and social status.

The theme of the betrayed Revolution is the backbone of Garro's novel and her play "Felipe Angeles".[9] The historical figure of Felipe Angeles gives us, on the one hand, the soldier of noble ideals who must be sacrificed by those afraid of losing the power acquired with the Revolution. On the other hand, the setting of *Recollections*, a forlorn town occupied by the military, emphasizes the emptiness of the soldier's life which he tries to fill with liquor, women and wanton cruelty. Such is the situation of General Rosas, who seems to be incapable of controlling his destiny or stopping himself from inflicting pain on the people under his care and command. A figure more pathetic than odious, this character has a strong resemblance to Colonel Buendía (*One Hundred Years of Solitude*) of whom he could be a forerunner.[10]

Garro uses kidnap and rape as one indication of the low esteem in which women are held by the society she portrays. Kidnap and rape are important motifs in *Recollections* and "The Dogs", especially in the latter where they generate the dramatic action. In both works, the victims are young girls, white in the first, Indian in the second, who suffer sexual abuse and feel only fear and repulsion for the perpetrators. The fact that the offenders are helped in these crimes by their friends and meet no censure when they take up

residence with the victims is used by Garro to indicate how women of
different cultures and social strata endure similar fates. The abusive
treatment of the female sex is further evidenced by other brutal acts
which likewise are confined to no social group: the drunken Indian of
"Los perros", the General in *Recollections*, and the lawyer-husband of
"La culpa es de los tlaxcaltecas" add physical punishment to the
psychological torture of their women.

    The unhappy married woman is another constant in Garro's
work. The female protagonists of "¿Qué hora es?" ["What Time is
It?"], "La culpa es de los tlaxcaltecas", and the plays "La señora en
su balcón" ["The Lady on Her Balcony"], "Andarse por las ramas"
["Walking in the Treetops"], and "La mudanza" ["The Move"] [11]
represent unsatisfied wives who are confined to their homes and
change into lonely, alienated human beings. For example, Elvira
Montúfar, one of the best drawn characters of the novel, considers the
death of her husband the blessing of liberation. Elvira remembers her
married years as a time of solitary tedium when she suffered a total
loss of her personality, a motif also found in the dramas mentioned:

    The widow had no memory of how she had looked in that dark
    period of her life. "How strange, I don't know what I looked
    like when I was a married woman", she confided to her
    friends.
        "Child, don't look at yourself in the mirror any more,"
    the grown-ups ordered when she was small, but she was
    unable to resist: her own image was her way of recognizing the
    world.... When she married, Justino monopolized the words
    and the mirrors and she endured some silent and obliterated
    years in which she moved about like a blind woman, not
    understanding what was happening around her. The only
    memory she had was that she had no memory. She was not
    the one who had gone through that time of fear and silence.
    (23-24)

    When Garro makes the unhappy wives pressure their
daughters into marriage, she is stressing the idea that social and
economic imperatives often leave matrimony the only road open to
women. This situation, developed in *Recollections* and the play "La
mudanza", explains the rivalry and jealousy among women who
cannot afford solidarity because they depend on men for their
sustenance. [12]

    In the social milieu presented by Garro, the woman is at
times ignorant, lazy and vengeful (for instance Carmen in "La
mudanza" and the soldiers' lovers in *Recollections*), but adapts well to
the role of mother, daughter, wife or lover assigned to her. However,
when she is endowed with sensitivity and imagination, the clash
between her spiritual qualities and her monotonous existence creates a
painful alienation. Some, like Titina from "Andarse por las ramas",
leave their men and homes in search of relief and find instead people

and circumstances like those that made them run away. Other women seek self-destruction. Clara in "La señora en su balcón" and Lola in "La mudanza" commit suicide. Isabel in *Recollections* looks for death as punishment for a guilty love, which is in truth the product of the limited possibilities offered to her by society.

Death by suicide or as a result of senseless violence is a frequent theme in Garro's work. Her characters view death as "the solid home", the only state which allows one to achieve all the things attainable, to complete the apprenticeship of humanity begun in life, and to obtain the total freedom desired. [13] The fact that the majority of those who died or seek death are women is a clear expression of the author's views on the condition of the female in society.

As noted earlier, the theme of time is prominent in the work of Elena Garro. Fascinated by the Aztec concept of circular and cyclical time, she uses it in different ways in several pieces. [14] It is an important structural element in *Recollections of Things to Come* (the title itself is meaningful in this respect) in which frequent shifts of time occur and distinct qualities of time are keenly perceived by the characters. The Mondacas, for example, stop the hands of the clock each night in order to submerge themselves into a "new and melancholy time where gestures and voices moved in the past."(14) On other occasions, time is experienced in the context of unmitigated pain shared by the inhabitants of Ixtepec, as the collective voice of the town narrates:

> In those days, I was so miserable that my hours accumulated shapelessly and my memory was transformed into sensations. Unhappiness like physical pain, equalizes the minutes. All days seem like the same day, acts become the same act, and all persons are a single person. The world loses its variety, light is annihilated and miracles are abolished. ... The future was the repetition of the past. (58)

The idea of circular time, reinforced by the similar beginning and ending of the novel, is also used in the drama "Los perros". In this play, the repetition of the same destiny in three generations of women reflects not only the cosmological meaning of time for the inhabitants of an Indian village, but also the injustice of unchanging economic and cultural patterns. [15]

Reminiscing ia a major activity for Garro's characters. The Mondacas, Elvira Montúfar, and others in *Recollections* spend their time reliving memories of childhood and early youth that they very much miss. This nostalgia, an element of several stories in *La semana de colores* also, rests on the memory of a past in which the world was felt to be solid, protected, and marked by an intensity of life since lost. Nicolás, whose incestuous link with Isabel derives from the memory of a shared happy childhood, remembers the passage from infancy to adulthood as follows:

At that time even their mother's thimble shone with a different light as it darted to and fro constructing bees and daisies. Some of those days were singled out and stamped for all time on the memory, suspended from a special air. Then the world turned opaque, lost its penetrating odors, the light softened, each day became the same as the one before it, and people acquired the stature of dwarfs. (27-28)

The cyclical concept of time is also suggested by the ability of the novel's characters to exist in the past as much as in the future, for given their lives of rigid, traditional patterns, they can see or "remember" tomorrow with the precision of what has already been. Isabel, for example, still far from the tragedy that will end her life, "abandons" those around her because in her mind she is "miles away, coursing through a future that was just beginning to be delineated in her memory" (156). Luisa, one of the prostitutes in the novel, knows that her murderer is "stalking her in the farthest reaches of her memory" (218). Likewise, Nicolás in jail "remembered his future, and his future was death in a field in Ixtepec" (259).

The magical and the supernatural are frequently joined with time in Garro's work as in "¿Qué hora es?" and "La culpa es de los tlaxcaltecas", the latter an outstanding example of the skill with which she weaves present, past and future into the narrative structure. In her plays "Un hogar sólido" and "El Encanto, tendajón mixto" she uses temporal dislocations to help create their fantastic-symbolic effects. [16] Since Indians and children take magic as a natural phenomenon, they accept the deeds of a witch, the appearance of elves, or the transformation of humans into dogs without surprise, as happens in several stories of *La semana de colores*. But even other characters show no signs of astonishment when witnessing the wonders, a literary device much in vogue today. [17] In *Recollections*, for instance, the young stranger pulls cigarettes out of thin air, walks in the rain without getting wet, and is able to call forth storms without surprising anyone. In the same work, time stops when the fate of the lovers is about to be decided, and while the sun shines upon the neighboring villages, a long night envelops Ixtepec. One of the remarkable episodes of the novel occurs when the lovers fly away on a horse while a troop of soldiers is helpless to stop them. These events, presented without explanation as the most natural of occurrences predate similar incidents now well known from *One Hundred Years of Solitude*.

As this survey has attempted to indicate, Garro's work is representative of current Latin American literature. Like Rulfo, Cortázar, Fuentes or García Márquez, she has both kept and enlarged the Hispanic-American tradition of protest, and like them she has used her art subtly to reveal the deep layers of complex social reality. In Garro's fiction and theatre, loneliness, alienation and death are to be seen in the context of the socioeconomic exploitation of the people. She links the betrayal of the Revolution with the victimization of women, problems of guilt, and nostalgia for the past. Garro advances the possibilities of political and social satire with her sensitive use of magic and mystery, an approach that has become important in Hispanic-American letters. 18 With demanding artistry, Garro has explored the Latin American self and society in a body of work that deserves a place alongside the better known writings of her peers.

NOTES

1. The definition of theme cannot be examined here. As a point of departure for this paper we used Tomachevski's analysis in which *theme* is considered a unity formed by the meanings of a work's different elements. (B. Tomachevski, "Thématique", *Théorie de la Littérature*, ed. and trans. by Tzvetan Todorov, Paris: Editions du Seuil, 1965, pp. 263, 269). For the meaning of *motif*—a more elemental and schematic unit than theme— we consulted Sophie Irene Kalinowska's *El concepto de motivo en literatura* [*The Concept of Motif in Literature*], trans. by Sonia Romero and José Varela M. (Valparaíso, Chile: Ediciones Universitarias, 1972). In this book there is also a brief exposition on the various definitions of the term "theme".
2. The thoughts of Samuel Ramos, Octavio Paz and Carlos Fuentes, on this subject are well known.
3. Jean Franco, *The Modern Culture of Latin America: Society and the Artist* (London: Pall Mall Press, 1967) maintains that intense social preoccupation has characterized Latin American Art in general. The search for the meaning of the Latin American self has motivated Martínez Estrada, Mallea, Picón Salas, among others.
4. Juan García Ponce, "Poesía en Voz Alta ["Poetry Aloud"], *Revista de la Universidad de México*, XI, 12, August, 1957, pp. 29-30, praises the "ágil, chispeante, humorístico" ["agile, sparkling, humorous"] dialogue of "Andarse por las ramas" ["Walking in the Treetops"]. Alejandro Moreno Ling in "Cuarto Programa de Poesía en Voz Alta" ["Fourth Program of Poetry Aloud"], (*La Nación*, México, July 29, 1957) finds grace and poetry in "Los pilares de doña Blanca" ["The Pillars of Doña Blanca"], but points our the author fails when passing to the thesis level.
5. *Narrativa mexicana de hoy* ["Mexican Narrative of Today"], prologue and notes by Emmanuel Carballo (Madrid: Alianza, 1969, p. 26).
6. *Los recuerdos del porvenir* (México: J. Mortiz, 1963). It was translated into English by Ruth L.C. Simms as *Recollections of Things to Come* and published by University of Texas Press (Austin, USA, 1969). Subsequent quotes will be from this edition in English and indicated by page numbers in parentheses.
7. "El zapaterito de Guanajuato" and "El anillo" are included in *La semana de colores* (Xalapa, México: Universidad Veracruzana, 1964). "Los perros" was first published in *Revista de la Universidad de México*, XIX, 7 (March, 1965) pp. 20-23. Later it was included in *12 obras en un acto* (México: Ed. Ecuador O° O' O", 1967). "La Dama Duende" appeared in *Revista de la Escuela de Arte Teatral*, México: Instituto Nacional de Bellas Artes, 1963, pp. 77-126.
8. "La culpa es de los tlaxcaltecas" is part of *La semana de colores*.
9. "Felipe Angeles", *Coatl* (México, Fall, 1967). This would be the first drama written by Garro: 1954, according to our correspondence with the author.

10. *Los recuerdos del porvenir*, published in 1963, was written in Switzerland in 1950 during Garro's long illness. García Márquez, whose *One Hundred Years of Solitude* appeared in 1967, read and commented upon *Los recuerdos* according to a letter we have from Garro dated December, 1974.

11. "¿Qué hora es?" is in *La semana de colores*. "La señora en su balcón" in *Teatro breve hispanoamericano contemporáneo* (Madrid: Aguilar, 1970). "Andarse por las ramas" forms part of *Un hogar sólido y otras piezas en un acto* [*A Solid Home and Other One-Act Plays*] (Xalapa, México: Universidad Veracruzana, 1958). "La mudanza", *La Palabra y el Hombre* 10, México (April-June 1959) pp. 263-274).

12. We touch upon this aspect in "Los perros y La mudanza de Elena Garro: designio social y virtualidad feminista", *Latin American Theatre Review*, 8/2, Spring, 1975, pp. 5-13.

13. Violent death overtakes several characters in *Los recuerdos*. The mother of Manuela in "Los perros" is beaten to death. Before the Final Judgement, the dead of "Un hogar sólido" will learn to "a ser todas las cosas" ["be all things"] because "en el mundo apenas si aprende uno a ser hombre" ["on earth one hardly learns to be a man"], comments one of the characters (p. 31).

14. Garro has expressed her interest in the problem of time in various interviews; special mention of the Aztec concept of circular time is found in Roberto Páramo "Reconsideración de Elena Garro" ["A Reconsideration of Elena Garro"], *El Heraldo cultural*, México, December 31, 1967.

15. For more on this see article cited in note 12.

16. "El Encanto, tendajón mixto" is found in *Un hogar sólido*.

17. Todorov commenting on "what has become of the narrative of the supernatural in the twentieth century" finds that "the most surprising thing is precisely the absence of surprise" (*The Fantastic: A Structural Approach to a Literary Genre*, Cleveland: Press of Case Western Reserve University, 1973, 169), a feature also found in the so-called "magic-realism" in Latin America.

18. Political satire is illustrated by "Ventura Allende" in *Un hogar sólido*, although satirical allusions of this type are not lacking in "Felipe Angeles", and in *Recollections*.

Nellie Campobello:
Romantic Revolutionary
and Mexican Realist

by

DALE E. VERLINGER

University of Virginia

Revolution is based on liberty and freedom from oppression and is, by that essence, romantic. No author of the Mexican Revolution demonstrates this spirit of freedom and nationalism in both life and works better than Nellie Campobello. Her life is intimately linked to her production as a ballerina and novelist, which must be considered here for Nellie has integrated herself into the artistic world on both levels and they are inseparable.

The now sixty-two-year-old author lives in the Colonia San Rafael in Mexico City where she received me in a disordered, museum-like parlor steeped in the atmosphere of the Golden Age of the Campobello sisters and there she told me of her life: of Pancho Villa, whose name and place in history she championed for more than thirty years, of her Ballet Folklórico begun in 1937 and now directed by Amalia Hernández, of her dance: ''I have been called the Isadora Duncan of Latin America...I dance because I love to, not to make money, but to capture the spirit of my people.'' She spoke of being Mexican, the need to be proud of one's homeland, of her studies of Genghis Khan, T.E.Lawrence, Napoleon, military strategy and its relation to the dance, the history of Europe, the Revolution. We sat for hours in that room as she told me of all these things, as she recited poetry of broken hearts, doomed love affairs, and women dying to be loved; as she told me of Spanish dandies and knights in shining armor.

Despite a definite *joie de vivre*, Miss Nellie is prone to melancholia. A sense of pessimism and despair lingers over her and leaves the first and most fundamental romantic traces upon her work. In the traditional romantic spirit the reaction to this *mal du siècle* is to run into the past when things were brighter. And so it is with Nellie. The 1930's, as she described them in the prologue to her collected works [1], were a time of hatred, revenge and calumny. There was no justice for the true hero and there was no truth. The artistic world was at an all-time low. The picture in general was bleak. In this time of injustice and lies Nellie took refuge in an age when heroes were heroes, when the truth was found in Mama's tales. Sheltered in that heroic past, she wrote Cartucho [Cartridge]. During the days when she was being shoved from one city to another, dancing in stadiums and public squares upon orders of the revolutionary government, days when she saw in the faces of the people of the villages the failure of the Revolution, days of loneliness and despair, she sought out the comfort and inspiration of Mama's skirt, to find the shelter of a time when the Revolution seemed like a ray of hope. Immersed in that past, she created Las manos de Mamá [Mama's Hands]. In an era when theater and dance were nothing more than a sham, when, according to José Clemente Orozco, "the cancer of bohemianism attacked young painters destroying their will power, talent, and lives,"[2] Nellie retreated to the Golden Age of Indigenous Civilization and there, in that era when art was great and art was Mexican and free from European contamination, she created her autochthonous dance.

Nellie, like the romantics who came before her, hates the city and the technology that it represents. She has been unable to come to terms with Mexico City and anxiously awaits retirement so that she can escape to the country which revives the soul; the country where she, like Wordsworth, finds her God.

The romantic reaction to mass civilization and the city, as explained by H.G.Schenk,[3] is illustrated by the interest in indigenous tribes and relics and concern about the extermination of the noble savage. Nellie's reaction is found in her dance and in her literature: her book Ritmos Indígenas de México [Indigenous Rhythms of Mexico] is an attempt to record the dances of the first Mexicans as illustrated in the codices and in sculpture and to purge the dances of the modern commercially-oriented movements. In Mama's Hands, she dedicates several chapters to the glorification of her Tarahumara ancestors, "that beautiful race of the plains of Chihuahua: ...ancient, peaceful, sensitive Indians, artists, exponents of a noble life, resigned by nature, without the white man's civilization." (ML,237)

The title of her first book, Yo [I] , a collection of poems, is indicative of still another affinity between Nellie and her Romantic precursors, the ego cult. Her poems deal with Nellie, with how she views the world. They are very personal creations in which she attempts to explain to the world who she is and tries to explain to herself what she is all about. This dominant sense of self pervades her novels in the autobiographical accounts and the constant narrative intrusion in the first person or in the imperial ''we'': the reader does not doubt for a moment that la Campobello is in control, that hers is the only valid point of view within the world of her novel.

A cause for which to fight is yet another romantic trait which applies to our author. Lord Byron rushed off to war and death in Greece. Nellie rushed head on into battle with her government in defense of a man who had been vilified in the post-revolutionary years, Pancho Villa. He was a defeated man, a forgotten man, an underdog, and therefore, a figure very close to the romantic heart.

Miss Nellie and several influential friends set out to create the "white legend" of Doroteo Arango. The battle was symbolically won in 1966 as Villa was restored to his rightful place in history when the government erected a monument in his honor in the Glorieta de Riviera in Mexico City. The products of her struggle are admirable: Nellie herself launched the first attack in 1940 with the publication of *Apuntes sobre la vida militar de Francisco Villa* [*Notes on the Military Life of Francisco Villa*]. The first taste of triumph came in 1951 with the publication of Martín Luis Guzmán's *Memoirs of Pancho Villa* for which Nellie provided documents and information from her private archives on Villa and the Revolution.

One romantic characteristic which is of the utmost importance in our consideration of Nellie Campobello and which moves us into another aspect of our study is *cultural patriotism*. This, more than any other, is the principle characteristic of Nellie's life and work. Cultural patriotism, as defined by Schenk, is nationalism. It is finding and describing the national reality.

Her works, particularly her two novels, are steeped in Mexican reality. That reality is cruel, morbid, tender, but most of all chaotic and changing. It is the reality painted by Orozco, described by Azuela. With a word, a phrase as brief as the stroke of an artist's brush, the author sketches before our eyes the agony, the horror, and the disasters of war. A character is introduced, we come to know him, and suddenly, brutally, with the stroke of a pen, the shot of a gun, he is gone --like Kirilí from *Cartridge*:

Kirilí wore a red jacket and yellow leather boots. He sang ostentatiously because he used to say to himself, "Kirilí, you've got a good voice." ...He was courting Chagua, a lady with little feet. Kirilí, whenever there was a skirmish, would pass by our street repeatedly, so we could see him shooting. Whenever he got to talking about battles, he would say that he had killed nothing but generals, colonels, and majors. He never killed a soldier. ...They went to Nieves. Kirilí was bathing in a river. Someone told him that the enemy was coming, but he didn't believe it and didn't get out of the water. They arrived and killed him right there in the river. ...He stayed there in the water, his body growing cold, and pressing between the weaving of his porous flesh some burning bullets. (ML, 57)

Or consider the story of Jacinto Hernández from *Mama's Hands*:

Villa's soldiers hit the mark in three shots dealt through the head of poor Jacinto. ...Jacinto Hernández, with his black western-style pants fitted to his straight, strong legs, lay there on the red bridge with open arms that day when they asked "Who goes there?" and he staggered like a child taking his first steps. (ML, 234)

As Ernest Moore has written, her style is brief, bare and brutal; it fits the character of the Revolution which she portrays very well.[4]

Her message is simple: War is hell. War is cruel. War is real...

The reality of Nellie as a child, the reality of Revolutionary Mexico was one of chaos. That turbulence, that instability of the world that surrounded her is reflected in her style of fragmentation. The novel becomes the screeen of a child's mind. Distorted memories fade as quickly as they appear and create an episodic structure similar to that attributed to the picaresque novel by Stuart Miller.[5] The reader is bombarded with one happening after another, one hero after another, in a continuous parade which passes before his eyes. There is no plot. There is no character development: the characters enter the scene, perform their function, and then are cast aside like a child's toy when he has grown tired of playing with it. Amid the chaos and fragmentation stands one stable character --Mama. She presides over both novels. Nellie's works are an elegy to her collection of sweetdeadmenheroes and to Mama: Mama, a flower; Mama, the dawn; the movement of her arms like flowers falling into a mountain stream; a poppy turning in the wind losing its petals; Mama, Nature itself. Mama was provider, protector, creator, and God and in these roles she reflects still another aspect of the chaotic Mexican reality as described by Gary Keller when he states that the Revolution destroyed the tradition of the father-protector-provider and that that burden fell to the woman.[6] Witness *Mama's Hands.*

Mexican reality was death. In her novels, Nellie, the child narrator, views death passively and without compassion, with just a simple curiosity. Her reaction is Mexican if we consider Frank Tannenbaum's explanation of the Mexican indifference to death. He writes that the presence of death is accepted as a matter of course and that it leaves behind much less feeling of horror than in other civilized societies.[7] Octavio Paz explains the Mexican way of death as an impatient face-to-face confrontation. Death, he says, does not frighten us because life has cured us of fear.[8] This attitude is best seen in Nellie's work in the sketch "From a Window" from *Cartridge* in which a man has been executed outside the window of her house. He was there for three days and during that time Nellie grew fond of him:

Since he had lain there for three nights, I had already become accustomed to seeing his crumpled body, fallen on the left side, hands to his face, sleeping there right next to me. He seemed to belong to me, that dead man. There were times when I, afraid that they had carried him off, got up hurriedly and climbed up in the window, he was my nightly obsession, I liked seeing him because it seemed to me that he was very frightened.

One day, after eating, I went running to contemplate him from the window, he was no longer there. The shy dead man had been stolen by someone, the ground was marked by his body and empty. I slept that day dreaming that they would shoot someone else and wishing that it was right next to my house. (ML, 103)

This Mexican concept of death is seen repeatedly in the author's characters -- in the stoicism of Catarino Acosta in *Mama's Hands*, he who was shot without bullets; in the song of Emilio, one of Mama's admirers: "If they are going to kill me tomorrow, let them do it quickly."

Mexican reality was the ominous city so well described in *Mama's Hands* as a place where people have names for every little action; where "store windows are filled with lights, pastries and silk stockings worn by children with withered lips ...where people smoke, drink and lack fresh and healthy air to breathe, where people ignore the fact that in the country a child's bones and eyes are made stong and the body is bronzed by the cold so that it is not dirty white like the stomachs of dead fish or fetuses preserved in alcohol..." (ML, 208)

Mexican reality was brave and strong women, *soldaderas* [camp followers], like Nacha Ceniceros in *Cartridge* who was executed for accidentally shooting her lover: "She cried for her lover, put her arms up over her face, her braids hanging down, and received the bullets. She was a beautiful sight." (ML, 79) This was a reality of strong women like Mama, like the women of the North.

Laughter. Flour tortillas. Coffee without milk. Cuts and bruises. Dead men. Rifle blasts. Wounded men. Men on horseback running through the streets. Screams of soldiers. Filthy banners. Nights without stars, moons, or noonday suns. This is the reality which Nellie confronts with pure innocence by which she exposes very frankly the horror of the adult world, the foolish games that men play. This is the reality --Mexican in its entirety-- unmasked and written in a style that expresses the paradoxical and turbulent Mexican character.

With the publication in 1960 of *Mis Libros* [*My Books*] Nellie Campobello vanished from the literary scene. She has not given up writing and longs to be able to retire from the duties which monopolize her time as the directress of the National School of Dance so that she will be able to reintegrate herself with her social element, with her physical liberty so as to be able to continue paying back her debts, the greatest of which is that of being Mexican.

I reflect now upon this woman who a few years ago I knew so little about and I see her as almost a personification of the romantic quest for national identity. She is a Tarahumara and intensely proud of it: her hospitality, generosity, and kindness are proof of it. She is Mexican: her dance and her literary themes made of the flesh and blood and clay of a people tell us that it is so. She is revolutionary: her break with previous traditions in dance and in literature and her fight with an entire government are illustrations of the fact.

Nellie Campobello is a woman bursting with human warmth and bewildered by the world she sees around her; she is a woman out of her time. Nellie Campobello is the Romantic High Priestess as she bids you enter her parlor, her world, and says: "I may even teach you the secrets of the Nile."

NOTES

[1] Nellie Campobello, *Mis libros* [*My Books*], (Mexico: La Compañía General de Ediciones, S.A., 1960). Further references to this text will be followed by the abbreviation "ML" and the page number. The translations of all quotations from this text are my own.

[2] José Clemente Orozco, *An Autobiography* (Austin: The University of Texas Press, 1962), p. 26.

[3] H.G. Schenk, *The Mind of the European Romantics* (Garden City: Doubleday and Company, Inc., 1969), pp. 30-45.

[4] Ernest Moore, "Novelists of the Mexican Revolution: Nellie Campobello," *Mexican Life*, 17 (February, 1941), p. 22.

[5] Stuart Miller, *The Picaresque Novel* (Cleveland: The Press of Case Western Reserve University, 1967).

[6] Gary D. Keller, "El niño de la revolución mexicana: Nellie Campobello, Andrés Iduarte, y César Garizurrieta" ["The Child of the Revolution: Nellie Campobello, Andrés Iduarte, and César Garizurrieta"], *Cuadernos Americanos*, 170 (May-June, 1970), p. 142. Translation is my own.

[7] Frank Tannenbaum, *Mexico: The Struggle for Peace and Bread* (New York: Alfred A. Knopf, 1964), p. 17.

Feminine Symbolism in Gabriela Mistral's ''Fruta''

by
CARMELO VIRGILLO

Arizona State University

FRUTA
by Gabriela Mistral

En el pasto blanco de sol,
suelto la fruta derramada.
De los Brasiles viene el oro,
en prietos mimbres donde canta
de los Brasiles, niño mío,
mandan la siesta arracimada.
E.tiendo el rollo de la gloria;
rueda el color con la fragancia.
Gateando sigues las frutas,
como niñas que se desbandan,
y son los nísperos fundidos
y las duras piñas tatuadas...
Y todo huele a los Brasiles
pecho del mundo que lo amamanta,
que, a no tener el agua atlántica,
rebosaría de su falda...
Tócalas, bésalas, voltéalas
y les aprendes todas sus caras.
Soñarás, hijo, que tu madre
tiene facciones abrasadas,
que es la noche canasto negro
y que es frutal la Vía Láctea...

FRUIT

by Gabriela Mistral
(Chile, Nobel Prize for Literature, 1945)

Onto the sun-white grass
I free the spilled fruit.

That gold comes out of Brazilian lands
enclosed in dark wicker baskets where it sings
from out of Brazilian lands, my child,
they send the siesta in bunches.
I stretch out the roll of glory;
color rolls out with fragrance.

You go after the fruits on all fours,
like little girls skittering off,
and they are melting-soft loquats
and hard tatooed pineapples...

And everything smells like Brazilian lands,
bosom of the world that nurses it all,
that, if not for Atlantic waters,
would overflow its skirt . . .

Touch them, kiss them, turn them over and over
and you will learn all their faces.
You will dream, child, that your mother
has inflamed features,
that night is a black hamper
and that the Milky Way is a fruit tree.

German Arciniegas has said of Gabriela Mistral: ''The world was to her like a room of lost steps, in which she walked without looking at anything, because she knew everything.''[1] Perhaps one ought to qualify Arciniegas' observation by suggesting that Gabriela's true world was her poetry, and that through the intuitive reality of this medium she spent a lifetime searching for identity, retracing those ''lost steps'' as a woman and a human being.

While much of Gabriela Mistral's spiritual quest can be traced throughout her prolific literary output, the short collection of poems entitled *Cuenta-mundo* [*Who Tells The Story of the World*] must be considered one of her most significant contributions.[2] For it is here that Gabriela defines in symbolic terms her mission as a woman and a poet, announcing her plan to reinterpret the world by first fragmenting it and then reordering and redefining it on her own terms.

Though the collection deserves to be studied as a whole, since it constitutes a mythic reconstruction of the cosmos that is uniquely feminine in the
lexical framework in which Roland Barthes places myth,[3] in this paper we
shall limit our observations to only one poem, "Fruta" ["Fruit."] In it
Gabriela, transcending the familiar sexual connotations of fruit, and asserting
her favorite themes and sub-themes, namely solitude, maternity, and
mysticism, with their variants, grief, love, nature, and death, explores the
internal reality of an entity emblematic of woman's ambivalence. She invests
fruit with new dimensions, making it a symbol of the lonely Messianic role of
the female, implying that grief and self-immolation are necessary for the
creation and survival of mankind.[4] Furthermore, we propose to examine how
Gabriela probes into the primordial enigma surrounding procreativity and
equates it with artistic creativity.

To begin with, let us refer briefly to the four-line enneasyllabic composition "La cuenta-mundo" [She Who Tells the Story of the World] which
serves as her credo while it introduces the conceptual and most of the formal
characteristics of "Fruta" and other poems:

Niño pequeño, aparecido,
que no viniste y que llegaste,
te contaré lo que tenemos
y tomarás de nuestra parte. [5]

One notices immediately that Gabriela speaks with the maternal authority of
one familiar with the world's make-up and ready to pass this knowledge on to
her child. Also evident are two planes: the physical, where Gabriela ex-
cruciatingly confesses her sterility, declaring her death as a person in the
phrase "Niño pequeño, aparecido, que no viniste," and the spiritual, in
which she proclaims her rebirth as an artist, announcing the birth of her
"created child" in the parallel clause "y que llegaste." It is in this antithesis
that one finds Gabriela's paradox and realizes that here mother, child, and
world become abstractions. Interpreted symbolically, they transcend rigid
temporal and spacial limitations and are converted into immanent elements of
eternal truth. She consequently loses the earthly traits of the sterile woman
and reacquires, in this new realm of artistic rebirth, the inalienable rights of
her sex. This introductory quatrain and the poems that follow constitute a
subtle invitation to return via the imagery of her verse to the poetess' own
childhood--a world of innocence, illusion, and dream where objective, adult
logic disappears, and the subjective concept of primal universal order rules. It
posits the world we find in "Fruta."

Almost casually Gabriela announces that she is casting onto a sunny
meadow the fruit presumably brought along:

> En el pasto blanco de sol,
> suelto la fruta derramada. [6]

Following the plan outlined by Gabriela in "La cuenta-mundo," "fruta" becomes a word-symbol for the decomposition of the external world and the creation of a new *poetic* one wherein the more profound connotations of fruit can be examined. In this symbolic framework, *fruit*, understood as *offspring*, discloses woman's maternal mission: *freeing* the life she brought or *spilled* into the world. Underlying this message are further inferences prompted by the rhetorical context in which the verbs "soltar" [to free] and "derramar" [to spill] appear. The first suggestion is that the cleavage implicit in childbirth at some unspecified time in the past (past participle "derramada") is predestined because the act of spilling is involuntary. The second is that a mother gives birth cognizant that the fruits of her love, once liberated from her dark womb into the light, are to be consciously freed like newborn animals scattered in a warm pasture. [7]

The second stanza contains the second and third movements:

> De los Brasiles viene el oro,
> en prietos mimbres donde canta
> de los Brasiles, niño mío,
> mandan la siesta arracimada.[8]

The most discernible variant in this second movement is the introduction of the third-person narrative voice and the addition of yet another poetic person expressed by the directive vocative "niño mío." Both replace the first-person voice of the initial stanza, thus amplifying the poetic dimension. The impression immediately derived from these four lines is that of a cradle song, as the metric rhythm reproduces a swinging and rocking movement which matches the fruit's swaying journey from Brazil, in dark wicker. Ultimately, the singing and rhythm insinuate the image, sound and movement of a mother lulling her child to sleep.

The interior structure of this second movement derives from symbolism and imagery. The noun "Brasiles" or Brazilian lands, is of capital importance, for it gives rise to a long and intricate series of associations further revealing and reinforcing the central theme--woman's ambivalent, mysterious nature which presupposes her ties with earthly and divine power. The figure of Brazil is commonly linked with the legendary, fathomless riches of those dark and secret recesses that have captivated man's imagination for centuries. Aside from this image, Brazil conveys an even deeper symbolism. It recalls the figure of the bare-breasted Amazon, the mythic hermaphrodite whose traits epitomize the strength this vast and complex land draws from the interplay of its many components. Gabriela, by making Brazil--the source of the fruit-- a symbol of pluralistic totality, endows womanhood with the traits of the Amazonic virago. Brazil as source or origin suggests further implications for the Amazonic myth. It becomes an extraordinary place whose integrity rests on the harmonious coexistence of opposites and implies the mythological paradise free of discord, discrimination, unrest, suffering, or conflict. The hermaphrodite, uniting dominant traits of male and female, symbolizes an ideal condition, largely unknown in our world.[9] Thus Gabriela is transcending earthly reality and describing a mythic-mystic journey in a timeless, spaceless context, with Brazil functioning as mother and Paradise and perhaps even God.[10] Such interpretation is supported by the verb-form "mandan" [they send] and by the plurality of the noun "Brasiles." Together, verb and noun suggest the anonymous and magnanymous will that chooses woman's deceptively fragile womb, the "prietos mimbres" [dark wicker baskets], for the purpose of delivering to earth forms of life conceived in His own precious image. The noun "oro" or "gold" is thus used to mean life, reflecting its radiant loving source. In the same framework, the metaphor "siesta arracimada" [siesta in bunches], understood as a reference to the prenatal condition of living beings in which it is still possible to exist in a perfect state of peace and unity, would call to mind the image of the ideal world whence all life originates and flows naturally from one generation to another.

In the third movement, represented by the last two lines of the second stanza ("Extiendo el rollo de la gloria; / rueda el color con la fragancia"),[11] Gabriela reinstates the first-person singular voice and reappears as the dominant figure. It seems that she is retracing her steps to elaborate on what she had stated in the first stanza. She no longer addresses herself to her would-be child but to the reader to remind him how the fruits fall out as a result of her unfolding or opening out their container--traditionally a paper cone.

From a strictly logical standpoint, the conceptual and formal characteristics of the third movement would indicate that this couplet could have followed or been incorporated into the first stanza. In effect, the third movement continues and reinforces the imagery of the first one, for it infers the preestablished natural dictates of childbirth. Moreover, with the introduction of the image produced by the metaphor "rollo de la gloria" of the mother's womb as a cornucopia, the complex levels of symbolism and imagery stratify. At this point, "siesta arracimada" of the second movement previously understood as an allusion to the child being lulled to sleep now suggests that this infant is a "frutita," a "small fruit" himself hanging in a bunch (hence the Spanish "arracimada"--a play on the words "racimo" and "rama") from his mother's breast ("prietos mimbres"), seen as the branches of the dark tree of her body. With this new symbolic dimension, it becomes understood that as the mother is singing her child to sleep she pulls out her breast ("Extiendo el rollo") against which the sleeping child lies while nursing.

The third movement, with the reappearance of the first-person singular voice and the reiteration of the third, also seems to complete a cycle within which one witnesses the image of fruit becoming more and more abstract. What was "fruta" in the first stanza becomes successively "oro" and "siesta arracimada," ultimately achieving complete transparency in the metaphor "rueda el color con la fragancia." This systematic disintegration of fruit as a one-dimensional entity into particles evoking optical, tactile, gustatory, and olfactory sensations can be attributed to the poetess' effort to recreate the synesthetic totality of fruit with her breast and with her child. Subsequently, if we carry one step further the symbolism of the fruit's container within its rhetorical framework--"rollo de la gloria"--a number of other images surface. "Rollo," first seen as the mother's womb-cornucopia and then as her breast, now denotes the female genealogical sphere as well as astrological completeness and even divine perfection. [12]

Structurally, the imagery integrates the superficially fragmentary nature of the first three movements. The strophic order represents Gabriela's reconstruction of the feminine mission in antiempirical, transcendental terms, rejecting any human systematization of the cosmic process. Her view may be summarized as consisting of: 1. *Creation* ("En el pasto blanco de sol, / suelto la fruta derramada."); 2. *Conception* ("De los Brasiles viene el oro,"); 3. *Gestation* and *Sustenance* ("en prietos mimbres . . . mandan la siesta arracimada."). This new poetic logic not only explains the tying of the strophic knot ("suelto la fruta . . . Extiendo el rollo de la gloria") but would also constitute the end of a cycle and the return to the initial process of continous Creation.

The fourth movement reestablishes the multiple symbolic perspectives. On the first level of illusion the child is the object of the mother's scrutiny as he pursues on all fours the elusive fruits which she identifies for him: soft loquats and hard tatooed pineapples. On the second symbolic level, the child is seen groping for his mother's hard breasts with their soft nipples.

> Gateando sigues las frutas,
> como niñas que se desbandan,
> y son los nísperos fundidos
> y las duras piñas tatuadas . . . [13]

The poetess, by making explicit the relationship between "frutas" and "niñas," both feminine nouns, attaches feminine characteristics to fruit. The lack of grammatical elision deliberately makes the poetess' child, as well as the fruits, dependent on the same verb-form "sigues" [you follow or go after] of the main clause. By this means Gabriela links the act of following and that of the fruits' dispersing, fruit and offspring, and, finally, the child of the poetess' imagination and all living beings that abandon their matrix after creation. In the realm of this new logic, the lexical forms of the stanza can only be interpreted in highly polisymbolic terms. "Sigues" corresponds to the effort on the part of the infant to grope for the breasts as they separate from his mouth and from each other as the mother moves her torso. As a dual image, it also corresponds to the fruit following the same predestined path of all little girls whose mission demands that they cut their maternal bond--an idea made explicit by the Spanish "desbandarse" [to disband]. Furthermore, we notice portrayed symbolically in the exotic, soft-molten loquat and hard tatooed pineapple that tolerance for extremes which, by allowing softness and sweetness to coexist harmoniously with duress and indelible strength, emphasizes the feminine, hermaphroditic nature of fruit. The suspension marks ending the stanza suggest that behind the aforementioned polarity of external and internal characteristics of fruit lie the opposite forces of feminine reality, the continuum of life, and, in an even broader sense, the concept of the self-renewing creative process.

The fourth stanza melds the entire relationship between the fruit, breast and child triplicity:

> Y todo huele a los Brasiles
> pecho del mundo que lo amamanta,
> que, a no tener el agua atlántica,
> rebosaría de su falda . . . [14]

We see readily that a fourth level of imagery is now attained with Brazil portrayed as a huge, enormous woman or even as a single breast. Yet, this quatrain could have more logically followed the second movement: "De los Brasiles viene el oro," and "de los Brasiles . . . mandan la siesta arracimada," where "oro" and "siesta" can now be viewed as milk. The strophic dislocation or displacement, therefore, reflects the poetess' own subjective cosmic vision, and one looks, then, for a new poetic logic resting on a symbolic plane: in the interior imagery of the fifth movement. Therein the image of Brazil as a hermaphroditic Amazon, developed earlier, is brought back to complement and highlight that image of feminine completeness of the fourth movement. Furthermore, the reiteration of Brazil as "pecho del mundo" calls to mind the archetypal fertility figure of the tropical Great Mother which all but spells out Gabriela's reestablishment of the vital cycle. This is the transcendental return to the prenatal phase of humanity and the most basic mother-child relationship in which mother and breast are now woman and source of food. It is also Gabriela's way of reaffirming feminine priority in the universal order.

The fourth plane of imagery of woman as *bosom of the world* now establishes the female figure as a complex entity, and this is achieved by the integration of cosmic elements. Here, feminine ambivalence, expressed in the interaction of offspring and mother, mother and earth, earth and water, water and human flesh, dissolves the apparent ambiguity engendered by the relative pronoun "que" [that] at the beginning of the third line. Brazil is now equated at once with fruit and breast, all three overrunning land boundaries to flow throughout the world, for Brazil's milk *is* her fruit.

In the two movements of the last stanza, the mother-fruit motif advances, along with the major and minor themes. Gabriela uses the imperative to assert her motherly and spiritual authority explicitly:

> Tócalas, bésalas, voltéalas
> y les aprendes todas sus caras.
> Soñarás, hijo, que tu madre
> tiene facciones abrasadas,
> que es la noche canasto negro
> y que es frutal la Vía Láctea . . . [15]

The external structure of the stanza indicates that this is the only sextain representing a complete poetic unit. The first two lines are topical and form the sixth movement, uniting with the last four which in turn produce the last movement of the composition. Between these two movements is a continuity that foregrounds the completeness of Gabriela's message before concluding it. Thus, fruit, breast, milk, woman, mother and child, humanity and creation, earth and universe are irrevocably fused. Even the rhythm integrates diverse elements as it echoes the cadence of the earlier cradle song before sounding a slower, reflexive, concluding tempo, indicating the child has fallen asleep.

In the first couplet, the imperative and the reiteration of the same grammatical ending reproduce the rhythm of the fruits or breasts turned over and over. Concomitantly, there emerges the maternal invitation to have her body explored, suggested by the addition of the metaphor "y les aprendes todas sus caras" in the second line. After all, fruit is meant to be touched, kissed, sucked, like a mother's breast. The visual, tactile and gustatory sensations in the phrase "Tócalas, bésalas, voltéalas," coupled with the implications of the following parallel clause "y les aprendes todas sus caras," lead to not only the physical but also the spiritual discovery of woman. At this symbolic level, one visualizes fruit and breasts submitting voluntarily to a predestined task intended to surprise and gratify both the mother's child and the world that partakes of Brazil's abundance. All discover with each touch, each kiss, each turn a new pleasure that will nourish and fortify.

In the last movement, the poetess seems to be whispering to the child of her imagination whom she has finally lulled to sleep in the silence of the night. Here the verb-form "soñarás" on which the parallel clauses "tu madre tiene facciones abrasadas," "es la noche canasto negro" and "es frutal la Vía Láctea" all depend, serves as a key-word. First of all, the allusion to the oneiric experience of the child establishes a bond between the consciousness of the mother and the subconscious mind of the child. Furthermore, the future tense almost confirms that, in this state representing the meeting of two perceptions of human reality, the offspring will discover in dream what the mother as woman already senses. This intuitive capacity so integral a part of the feminine character and so essential to creativity is revealed by the structural function of the verb "soñar" in its symbolic form. It fuses the two movements by disclosing their intrinsic characteristics. Thus the *mother* created by the poetess identifies spiritually with the other half of her artistic creation: the *fruit-child.*

Having linked *Brazil* and *fruit, mother* and *offspring, woman* and *creation*, we now also understand woman's presence, essence and ascendency. This is accomplished by the key-words "facciones abrasadas," "noche," "frutal," and "Vía Láctea" which are employed to integrate externally and internally the structural aspects of the entire poem. The common link between these word-symbols is their relationship to the four basic cosmic elements: air, fire, earth and water. They are also the cardinal points of woman which the poetess uses to accentuate female completeness. [16] Thus woman becomes synonymous with mother nature and associated with complexity, contradiction and mystery. Through the same symbols, the ritual (the innate and natural sacrifice of woman--the freeing of a nurtured child) which had remained implicit up to this point, surfaces in the last three lines where it is ultimately substantiated by the reference to the mythic-mystic ascendency of the female figure. Recalling the ocean voyage of fruit from a remote, bountiful, sunny Brazil; remembering the separation of fruit from its source to make the long trip in tight, dark, wicker hampers--a mission intended to please and nourish the world--it should not be difficult to grasp the symbolic level of the last movement.

As before, the symbology of this last movement is pluralistic. The "facciones abrasadas" could intimate the mother-poetess' point of origin: the sun which symbolizes light, life, Heaven, God. On the other hand, the adjective "abrasadas" could also correspond to *abrased, seared* or *burned* referring to both Brazil's parched soil and the mother's dried breast after she has weaned her child. Moreover, the choice of this particular adjective denotes pain and anguish as well as abuse. "Noche," man's silent reminder of the dark and mysterious infinity that surrounds him above and below, here fulfills a dual function. It is correlative to both "prietos mimbres" and "rollo de la gloria." Both are containers, the former to transport the child to a future he cannot, at this point, visualize--perhaps even his death--and the latter the child's physical and spiritual container, suggestive of the dark, peaceful womb. The last two symbols, "frutal" and Vía Láctea," complete the poem's entire cycle. Both function as coordinates in the dualistic structure of the composition since they imply *source of life* and *nourishment.* They also bring together the two planes on which the composition is constructed: "frutal" the telluric level, "Vía Láctea" the nebulous, distant realm of the imagination--a child's vision of Heaven or paradise. The ensuing imagery portrays the fruit tree and the Milky Way suckling then releasing their offspring--fruit and heavenly bodies--to float all alone in darkness and silence on their eternal mission. The former in their wicker hampers across the great ocean,[17] the latter abandoning their luminous source so that they in turn can brighten up the universe. From their distinctive yet similar acts of cleavage, new fruit trees and new constellations will be formed whose children will carry on the creative, lonely, sacrificial, self-fulfilling and unmistakably maternal assignment.

NOTES

[1] Germán Arciniegas, *América mágica: Las mujeres y las horas* [*Magical America: Women and Hours*](Buenos Aires, Editoral Sudamericana, 1961), II, p. 231.

[2] Gabriela Mistral, *Poesías completas,* [*Complete Poetry*] 3rd ed. (Madrid, Aguilar, 1966). Henceforth, all references to Mistral's poetry will apply to this volume.

[3] Lisa Appignanesi indicates that the term *femininity* is one generally misunderstood because it is vague. "As such it constitutes what Roland Barthes calls a 'myth': a statement which bears no *direct* relationship to the object it describes (woman) and evokes a range of suggestions which is culturally determined." *Femininity and the Creative Imagination* (London, Vision, 1973), p. 2. The implication is that *feminine* is an adjective denoting not sociological characteristics, but rather constituent factors such as *creativity, sensibility, suggestiveness, intuitiveness*, etc.--traits that may be found in *man* as well as women. Consequently, the artist can be said to possess all of these characteristics, regardless of sex. In this respect, *Cuenta-mundo*, more than just a woman's view of the world, is instead a hymn to the spiritutal nature of Creation and to all that is good, beautiful and everlasting on earth.

[4] Gabriela Mistral's view coincides, albeit fortuitously, with Erich Neumann's pronoun-cement that ". . . woman experiences herself first and foremost as the source of life. Fashioned in the likeness of the Great Goddess, she is bound up with the all-generating life principle, which is creative nature and a culture-creating principle in one . . . . Abduction, rape, marriage or death, and separation are the great motifs underlying the Eleusinian (matriarchal) mysteries." *The Great Mother*, 3rd ed. (New York, Pantheon Books, 1963), p. 306.

[5] "Little ghost child, / who never came and yet arrived, / I'll tell you about our world / and you will share it with us." *Poesías completas*, p. 287.

[6] "Onto the sun-white grass / I free the spilled fruit." Ibid., p. 296.

[7] The message conveyed by the imagery of this couplet corresponds admirably to the Spanish *dar a la luz*: to give birth. It is worth noting how a similar imagery representing infants as young animals put out to pasture emerges from *Lecturas para mujeres* [*Rendings for women*]: "Vosotras, madres, decís: ¡Los hombres hacen esto! ¡Los hombres lo han querido! ¡Los hombres se han vuelto fieras! ¿Y quiénes son los hombres? Miradlos, pués: son cosa diminuta que engorda y sonríe a la sombra de vuestro seno, como se agranda y dora el grano de uva a la sombra del parral.

De vosotras salieron; vosotras los cargásteis mientras no pudieron caminar; vosotras los trajísteis de la mano. Ahora os sentís extrañas a ellos; os asustáis de sus crimenes y exclamáis: '-¡Los hombres! ¡Los hombres!' --como gritarían las madres del rebaño devorado en la noche: ¡Los lobos! ¡Los lobos!'"

["You, mothers, say: Men do this! Men have wanted it this way! Men have turned into wild beasts! And who are these men? Well, just look at them: they are diminutive things that fatten and smile in the shade of your bosom, like grapes growing and brightening in the shade of the vine arbor.

They came out of you: you carried them while they were unable to walk; you led them by the hand. Now you feel as strangers before them; their crimes frighten you and you exclaim: 'Men! Men!', like mothers crying: Wolves! Wolves! when their flock is devoured in the night.'']*Lecturas para mujeres*, 3rd ed. (San Salvador, Ministerio de Educación, Departamento Editorial 1961), pp. 111-112.

[8] "That gold comes out of Brazilian lands / enclosed in dark wicker baskets where it sings / from out of Brazilian lands, my child, / they send the siesta in bunches." *Poesías completas*, p. 296.

[9] Juan Cirlot, *A Dictionary of Symbols* (London, Routledge and Kegan Paul, 1971), pp. 40-41.

[10] *Ibid.*

[11] "I stretch out the roll of glory; / color rolls out with fragrance." *Poesías completas*, p. 296.

[12] "Signs and Symbols" in *The Random House Dictionary of the English Language*, College Edition (New York, Random House, 1968), p. 1535. Also, see Neumann, op. cit., p. 141.

[13] "You go after the fruits on all fours, / like little girls skittering off, / and they are melting-soft loquats / and hard tatooed pineapples." *Poesías completas*, p. 296.

[14] "And everything smells like Brazilian lands, / bosom of the world that nurses it all, / that, if not for Atlantic waters, / would overflow from its skirt . . ." *Ibid.*, pp. 296-297.

[15] "Touch them, kiss them, turn them over and over / and you will learn all their faces. / You will dream, child, that your mother/ has imflamed features, / that night is a black hamper / and that the Milky Way is a fruit tree." *Ibid.*, p. 297.

[16] Cirlot appropriately claims that according to most elemental cosmogonies, nature is depicted as a hermaphrodite: "Of the four Elements, air and fire are regarded as active and male: water and earth passive and female. *op. cit.*, p. 4.

[17] By giving the fruits' container a definitive shape, "prietos mimbres," the poetess finalizes her conviction that woman is essentially a mother, whose symbol is the womb. As such she is preordained to *hamper* her children and then *release* them from her bond.

Two Poets of America:
Juana de Asbaje and Sara de Ibáñez

by

CELIA DE ZAPATA

At this historic moment when the woman intellectual of America is coming into her own, it is fitting to recall two persons who, though separated in distance by the length of Latin America and in time by almost three centuries, find common ground in the universal language of poetry. One was Juana de Asbaje—Sor Juana Inés de la Cruz—the Mexican "tenth muse," and the other was the Uruguayan Sara de Ibáñez, one of the most lyrical and moving voices of this century. Juana de Asbaje died on April 17, 1695; and on April 3, 1961, the lyre of Sara de Ibáñez was stilled after the measures of *Canto Póstumo* [*Posthumous Song*][1]—poems written shortly before her death—had sounded.

Spring was just beginning in the Northern hemisphere when Sor Juana went to her last resting place. And in the Montevideo cemetery the leaves were swirling among the tombs and about the feet of Sara de Ibáñez's friends as they came to bid her farewell.

It was in San Miguel Nepantla (a Náhuatl word meaning "amid" that should be understood as among the volcanoes and between the mountain and the valley) that Juana de Asbaje, the most exceptional woman of the 17th Century, was born on November 12, 1651.

Sara de Ibáñez arrived into the world not far from Paso de los Toros in Chamberlain, Uruguay, on January 11, 1909.[2] In his Prologue to *Canto*, Pablo Neruda tells us that "Montevideo, to welcome the Atlantic alongside its immense docks, on the walls of which urchins write the word *poesía* [*poetry*], has raised statues to its great poets—the gravest, saddest, and yet the stormiest of universal poetry."[3]

> Una tierra obediente a mi sonrisa
> un lugar sin raíz que gira y canta,
> donde la muerte nunca tiene prisa
>
> (*Canto*, "Isla en el mar", p. 16)

[A land obedient to my smile,
a rootless place that turns and sings,
where death never rushes.

                    (*Canto*, "Island in the Sea")]

Uruguay, like Chile, is the cradle of richly endowed poets whose in-spiration is born where the continent begins its final turn toward the junction of the two oceans at the southernmost tip of America. Mexico, at the other extreme, rooted in a marvellous and mysterious anthropological past, heard its lutes strummed in colonial times by poets who followed the models of Spanish poetry. But its rich pre-Columbian tradition paved the way, in its concise and flexible Aztec expressions curiously replete with metaphorical inflections, for a future of songs and poems characterized by the distinguished reserve that flows in the docile blood of Indians conquered by haughty Spaniards.

If indeed the Viceroyalty of New Spain was not prepared for the arrival on the scene of Juana de Asbaje, who was destined to penetrate the perplexing question of "appearance and reality" that so much disturbed contemporary philosophers, it must in all justice be concluded that no country or kingdom of the time would have granted any more than Mexico did, nor would have treated her any better as a woman intellectual.

In Sor Juana and Sara de Ibáñez we see two visionaries who shatter the symbols of their respective epochs. Few understood Sor Juana in the 17th Century; many have criticized the cold and introverted nature of Sara de Ibáñez in our times.

As Octavio Paz has pointed out in *Las peras del olmo* [*Elm Pears*], Sor Juana's attitude 'is unusual in the Hispanic tradition. For the Spanish grandees' knowledge is summed up in heroic action or in denial of the world (positive denial, it might be called—action of a higher order because of its sacred nature). For Sor Juana the world is a problem. Everything offers her an opportunity to sharpen her questions; her whole being is sharpened in questions... Within this tradition disinterested knowledge becomes blasphemy or insanity.' [4]

Sara de Ibáñez, in the boundless light which she herself radiates—as when Juana de Asbaje asked that the poet should be changed into a resplendent light—is the trembling flame consumed within her long esthetic agony over her transcendental and religious perplexity.

Traspasé las fronteras de la rosa
pisé caminos que la luz no usa
y entre fríos caminos de medusa

malgasté mi sonrisa más dichosa
Contra el viento solté una mariposa
y ví mis huesos relucir confusa,
Oigo el coro que me acusa
desde mi propia carne temblorosa

(*Canto, De los vivos*, II, p. 57)

[I went beyond the limits of a rose.
I trod upon roads untouched by light
and among cold pathways of Medusa,
I wasted my happiest smile.

Against the wind I left a butterfly loose
and I saw, confused, my bones sparkle.
I hear the cloistered choir accusing me
from my own shivering flesh.

(*Canto, From the Living*, II, p. 37)

Neruda's calling her a "great, exceptional, and cruel poet" perhaps sufficed to consecrate her without understanding her, but when he states that "this woman claims a forgotten inheritance left by Sor Juana Inés de la Cruz: that of rapture strictly controlled, of poetic ecstasy become tangible foam" [5]he had to look backwards and recognize the splendid Baroque tradition that was to be fused in the poetic crucible of Sara de Ibáñez. [6]

Sor Juana, as is well known, was guided by the purest tones of Garcilaso de la Vega, was not indifferent to Lope de Vega, listened to the measured and lucid accents of Fray Luis de León, at times was transported by the crystalline raptures of San Juan de la Cruz, and, above all, was the humble and consummate disciple of Góngora, as she herself has recognized. [7] That "scrap of paper," *El Primer Sueño* [*First Dream*], is the only work that Juana de Asbaje produced (as she herself has confessed) to give herself the pleasure of imitating Góngora. But, in contrast to *Soledades* [*Solitudes*], in which richness of forms and colors leads nowhere (it is "the shining, rainbow-hued serpent that bites its own tail," as Manuel Durán has said) *First Dream* takes off to unattainable heights in a specific search for knowledge. Its point of departure is the dream and as such it anticipates Freud and the forerunners of Surrealism in showing that truth may be found in the revelation of the subconscious. Sor Juana is not interested only in artistic creation. If indeed it is true that she employed dirges, sonnets, lyric poems, Christmas carols, ballads of every kind and form, rondels and other classical forms, for Juana de Asbaje poetry was an instrument for knowing "this earth, this world, these circumstances."

To Sara de Ibáñez, on the other hand, poetry is "an exercise in mystery,'' as she once said over BBC in London. Austere and extravagant, restless and marble-like as ''the dove that was consumed in its own whiteness,'' she recognizes ''no other joy than that of words.'' At the height of the free verse movement in Latin America, the Uruguayan bard rechannels the old Spanish tradition toward the classical forms of poetry. In her is reborn the ''lira'' (combination of seven- and eleven-syllable verses), a form of poetry that no other woman in the American continent had used since Sor Juana. And within her poetic cloister, Sara de Ibáñez, veiled in mystical modesty, allows her emotions to flow under dew-like serenity in a manifestation of genuine perfection. Romances, sonnets, semi-sonnets, *silvas*, ''liras,'' all employing the most daring and dazzling metaphors of the 20th Century, give a magnetic quality to the musical language of Sara from *Canto* (1940) to the apprehensive shuddering of *Apocalipsis* (1971). [8]

The Baroque was a pure bundle of nerves bursting open into strident ideals—pure exaltation of the spirit and the word. The Renaissance had been a broad stream, channeled, navigable at will, and within classical parameters.
Because of the sudden inroads of the extraordinary, those writers and esthetes are correct who have called the Baroque the first excursion into modern romanticism, a kind of ''trial run'' for romanticism. It signifies the triumph of complexity and complication heightened by frequent cultic references to mythological beings. The gods of mythology never have a place in Sara de Ibáñez' writing; rather, her surrealistic images are based on a symbology of Biblical origin.

No te cercan el pecho
disparado,
vivas espadas de ámbar quebradas al tocarte
y labios desprendidos que te endulzan el aire
(*Canto*, ''Vas a tocar tierra'', p. 83)

Se abrasó la paloma en su blancura
Murió la corza en la hierba fría
Murió la flor sin nombre todavía
y el fino lobo de inocencia oscura
(*Canto*, ''Isla de la luz'', p. 17)

[Your fleeing bosom is not fenced,
live swords of amber broken upon your touch,
and loosened lips that sweeten your air.
(*Canto*, ''You Shall Set Foot on Land,'' p. 83)

> The dove burned itself in its whiteness
> The deer died in the cold grass
> The flower died unnamed still
> and the fine wolf died of dark innocence
>   (*Canto*, "Island of Light," p. 17)]

That dove consumed in its own whiteness, that snow recurring as a symbol in all of Sara de Ibáñez' poetry, is none other than the poet herself whose "incomprehensible and frigid" song has to be heard and read "with lingering love," as Roberto Ibáñez advises, in order to be better understood. From the four elements: air, fire, water, and earth, rise the impregnable fortresses of her poetry. These formidable battlements—the austere and narrow range of her poetic images—make even more worthwhile the conquest of her innermost lyrical redoubt.[9]

Juana de Asbaje, in her *Primer sueño*, follows the same metrical form as is found in *Soledades*—the "lira"—and its length, 975 verses, approaches that of *Primera soledad*.

> El viento sosegado, el can dormido
> éste yace, aquel quedo
> los átomos no mueve,
> con el susurro hacer temiendo leve
> aunque poco, sacrílego ruido
> velador del silencio sosegado[10]
>   (Obras completas, *El sueño*, p. 184)

> [The wind is quiet, the hound asleep,
> the latter lies, the former, peacefully,
> does not move the atoms,
> he fears to make noise however light
> and little, sacrilegious noise,
> and watches the calm silence
>   (Complete works, *The Dream*, p. 184)]

> Sólo el menguado aliento
> de una flor bajo el agua, sosegado
> Un bosquejo de viento
> para siempre callado,
> de selvas y de nubes olvidado
>   (*Canto, Liras*, II, p. 23)

> [Only the waning breath
> of a flower under water, quietly,
> a sketch of wind
> forever silent
> oblivious of clouds and woods.
>
> (*Canto, Liras*, II, p. 23)]

There are several happy relationships of both substance and form in these two lyrics. Both deal with ecstatic peace. But what different kinds of peace! The word "wind" [viento] appears in both; "peaceful" [sosegado] appears once in Sara de Ibáñez, twice in Sor Juana. In the Uruguayan's "lira," "peaceful" refers to the breathing of a flower under water, creating a visual image that is reflected in the surface of the water above. The absolute quiet, a marvel of passivity imperfectly discerned as through a clouded glass is evoked by the sketch as if done in Chinese ink of a wind forgotten forever by forests and clouds. That is, the conceptual play of an invisible wind which is neither seen nor felt and which, therefore, does not exist. The image is one of a fascinating detached immobility—of a soul, one might say, losing itself in a stellar landscape through its dreams.

In Sor Juana's "lira" the "wind is peaceful," it does not dare move the atoms even in whispers since such a sacrilegious noise could disturb the silence in which the sleeping dog rests. Here one finds no antithetical transpositions or conceptual variations. Even though her soul is preparing itself for its flight into the undiscovered regions of consciousness and despite the fact that Sor Juana admits that she writes this "lira" under the influence of Góngora, the esthetics of Sara de Ibáñez brings her closer to the author of *Soledades* than Juana de Asbaje was able to do in her own "lira."

By placing herself in a line of the most unalloyed surrealist "neo-culterana" relationship, Sara de Ibáñez opens a breach in contemporary poetry. Behind her rises the chorus of Renaissance and Spanish Baroque voices, but Sara is also the spokeswoman of the 20th Century, as attested in *Hora ciega*, *La batalla*, and *Apocalipsis*, all inspired by the wars of today. With prophetic vision, *Apocalipsis* sings of the final holocaust of mankind, victim of its own hand. She renders her homage of gratitude to three French poets in short poems dedicated respectively to Rimbaud ("Callar"), Mallarmé ("La página vacía"), and Valéry ("Desdén"), all included in *Formas de la agonía* [*Forms of Agony*].[11] Perhaps it was from Rimbaud that she derived the quality of "cruel poet" attributed to her by Neruda; from Mallarmé, her reclusiveness (and music from Verlaine). And from Valéry—oh, from Valéry!—that geometric balance that shines in his poems, that "pure poetry" that the Frenchman offered as a measure of perfection; the poetry a later J. R. Jiménez aspired to write; one that Jorge Guillén sometimes approximated, and the same that, among us, was made quietly hers, forever hers, by Sara de Ibáñez!

It is not enough that Sor Juana Inés de la Cruz should have mourned the vain pomp of the world, sighed for its unhappy and chaste loves, and understood, as few women have, the irreparable wear and tear on matter exposed to the currents of time. Juana de Asbaje believed in God. She was a forerunner in her time of the rationalism of the 18th Century and for the greater happiness of her soul, she believed in God. In spite of her surprising scientific knowledge that was to alter her faith, as happened afterward with the arrival of the Age of Reason and of Positivism, Sor Juana Inés de la Cruz lived and died believing in God. Sara de Ibáñez sought Him in the paths of unpretentious modesty that always characterized her poetry. She sensed the loneliness of man, his existential anguish, the mystery of death fixing its great eyes on her at the end.

> ¿No me ves pordiosera de tus morrales turbios?
> Dime, si puedes ¿dónde mi amor no dará frío?
> Yo que tengo las llaves de la soledad
> mi soledad sin puertas eternamente miro
>
> (*Canto, Diálogos de la muerte y su espejo*, p. 48)

> [Don't you see me, a beggar of your bag of dregs?
> Tell me, if you can, where will my love not give cold?
> I, who have the keys of loneliness,
> my loneliness without doors I watch eternally.
>
> (*Canto, Dialogues of Death and its Mirror*, p. 48)]

Cecilia Meireles expressed her amazement at "that strange woman, so sensitive and so long-suffering, who nourishes her visions and predictions with rare and powerful lyrical images."[12] Cecilia, a Brazilian poet, so expressive in her own inner pain that she asks in her poetry for "one hundred years to cry," can indeed be echoing her sister, Sara de Ibáñez, when she tells us:

> Voy a llorar sin prisa
> Voy a llorar hasta olvidar el llanto
> y lograr la sonrisa
> sin cerrazón de espanto
> que traspase mis huesos y mi canto
>
> (*Canto, Liras*, V, p. 29)

[I am going to cry unhurriedly.
I am going to cry until I forget all tears
and conquer a smile,
without closing on dread,
that goes beyond my bones and my song

(*Canto, Liras*, V, p. 29)]

And that God of Sara Ibáñez whom she questions in "No me ves..."?
How distant are the Christmas carols and sacred letters of Sor Juana, shining
with faith from her 18th Century theological bastion!

Juegos del aire

¿   ?
Dejóme Dios ver su cara
cuando entre paloma y flor
sobre aquel cielo mayor
brotó una blanca almenara;
dejóme Dios ver su cara?

Air Games

[Did God let me see his face
when between dove and flower
a white beacon appeared
on that major heaven,
did God let me see his face?]

The inquiring tone continues in the three stanzas that follow, to
culminate in the fifth:

O yo me estoy descubriendo
los ojos con que algún día
veré lo que no sabía
que en sueños estaba haciendo?[13]

[Or am I discovering in myself
the eyes with which someday
I will see that which I did not know
I was doing in my dreams?]

The Baroque theme of the deceptive play between dream and reality
acquires plastic character in a tone of doubt at the outset that bursts into an
angry cry in "Plegaria" before the nakedness of man face to face with a God

who views his death without concern. ''Plegaria'' is a sonnet that reminds us of the "lovesick powder" of Quevedo shaken now by an internal vibration that asks—or demands—a definitive truce between the Creator and his creature.

Si tú estás allí, en lo oscuro,
Señor sin rostro y sin pausa;
si tú eres toda la causa
y yo tu espejo inseguro.
Si soy tu sueño, y apuro
sombras de tu sueño andando
pronuncia un decreto blando:
líbrame de no pensar,
y echa mi polvo a vagar
eternamente pensando [14]

[If you are there in the dark
Lord without face and without pause,
if you are the cause of everything
and I am your uncertain mirror.
If I am your dream, and I consume
shadows of your dream in being,
pronounce a light decree:
free me from thinking
and set my dust to wander
forever thinking.]

In *Tránsito a Sor Juana Inés de la Cruz*, the poet engages in a direct dialogue with Sor Juana in which she frequently compares her with a dove, one of the numerous symbols that carry the entire pagan, biblical, and Renaissance poetic charge in the works of Sara de Ibáñez. *Tránsito* is a sonnet of sonnets composed of 14 lines,   each inspired by a verse of the first sonnet which serves as the pattern. Here are some selections from *Tránsito*:

Soneto I   Te escucho andar entre la hierba fina
              donde la rosa de tu pensamiento
              en el secreto valle, al duro viento
              cuajaba su escultura de neblina

Soneto VII   Te escucho andar paloma de las nieves,
              que el rubor de los aires apacientas.
              Nácar que el nublo de un suspiro ostentas,
              a la intemperie de tu amor te atreves.

Soneto VXI   Tu sangre en Dios confusa, en Dios ardía
                    y en Dios buscaba sus raíces viejas
                    Eras el instrumento de sus quejas
                    que a la desnuda miel se convertía.

                    Del canto a la plegaria consumiste
                    mujer y arcángel en melado fuego
                    y de gemela muerte renaciste.

                    Orar te oyó cantando el mundo ciego
                    y Dios en la poesía que sufriste,
                    y en éxtasis caudal, bebió tu ruego. [15]

                    [I hear you walk on the light grass
                    where the rose of your thoughts
                    in the secret valley, to the hard winds,
                    curdled its sculpture in the fog

                    I hear you walk, dove of the snow,
                    that the blush of the air that you pacify.
                    Mother-of-pearl that exhibits the cloud of a sigh,
                    to the unsheltered love you dare.

                    You blood, confused in God, in God it burned,
                    and in God it sought its old roots.
                    You were the instrument of his laments,
                    that turned to the naked honey.

                    From the song to the prayer, you consumed
                    the woman and the archangel in honey-colored fire
                    and from their twin death you were reborn.

                    Praying, the blind world heard you,
                    and in the poetry that you suffered, God,
                    in overflowering ecstasy, granted your request.]

God answered the plea of Sor Juana Inés de la Cruz in her overflowing ecstasy in the 17th Century. God, because he is God, must in like manner have anticipated the overflowing ecstasy of Sara de Ibáñez in the 20th Century.

That Sara de Ibáñez should have left in *Tránsito*, such an enduring homage so finely in tune with the poetic spirit and form—the sonnet—that Sor Juana employed with such elegant artistic skill, was perhaps a prodigious magical exercise that transcends simple literary tradition.

A tenuous thread unites them. Two poets who today walk "the ways that light does not invade."

To Juana de Asbaje and Sara de Ibáñez, imperishable muses of America, should go our testimony of poetic faith and most affectionate respect on the joint anniversary of their deaths in this month of April 1975.

NOTES

[1] Poetry with an introduction, "anticipo, umbral y envío" ["anticipation, threshold, and delivery"] by Roberto Ibáñez that consists of *Diario de la Muerte, Baladas y Canciones, y Garilla* [*Diary of Death, Ballads and Songs,* and *Garilla*](Buenos Aires: Losada, 1973).

[2] There are certain discrepancies worth clarifying regarding this point. Domingo L. Bordoli, *Antología de la Poesía Uruguaya Contemporánea* [*Anthology of Contemporary Uruguayan Poetry*], (Montevideo, 1966); Sarah Bollo, *Literatura Uruguaya,* [*Uruguayan Literature*], (Montevideo, 1965); Hugo E. Pedemonte, *Nueva Poesía Uruguaya* [*New Uruguayan Poetry*], (Madrid, 1958), agree, among others, on S. de I's birth date to be the year 1910. Helen Ferró, *Historia de la Poesía Hispanoamericana* [*History of Hispanic American Poetry*], (N.Y.: (Las Américas, 1964), probably impressed by Sara's serene beauty that distinguished her until the age of sixty, gives the year 1918 (?) as her possible birth date. She intends to place her among the members of the Feminine Religious Poetry - to which S. de I. only belongs in a marginal and secondary way - and acknowledges "mystical signs" in *Canto* at the time when Neruda was not "so much a communist" and Sara was not "so dogmatic". The *Homenaje a Sara de Ibáñez* [*Homage to Sara de Ibáñez*], (Montevideo: Fundación de Cultura Universitaria, 1971), sets her birth date to be January 11, 1901. The same information can be found in *Canto Póstumo*, op. cit., published in 1973. (Printing was finished on June 18, 1973.)

[3] Sara de Ibáñez, *Canto* with Pablo Neruda's Prologue, first edition, Buenos Aires, 1940, p. 7. We shall quote from this edition giving the page number at the foot of every poem quoted from *Canto* in this essay.

[4] Manuel Durán, "El drama intelectual de Sor Juana y el antiintelectualismo hispánico" ["The Intellectual Drama of Sor Juana and Hispanic Anti-Intellectualism"], (México), Año XXII (julio-agosto, 1963), *Cuadernos Americanos*, pp. 238-258.

[5] *Canto*, with Pablo Neruda's Prologue, op. cit., p. 8.

[6] "The incomparable poetry of S. de I. takes its forms and transferences from the air and light...reaching its excelsitude under the advocation of the patrons of the Golden Age and from that tendency which we call on occasion *Neo-Culteranismo Surrealista*" [*Surrealist Neo-Culturanism*] (Jorge Carrera Andrade, *Rostros y Climas* [*Faces and Climates*], Paris, Maison de l'Amérique Latine, 1948, p. 175) *Homenaje a S. de I.*, op. cit., p. 24.

[7] Angel Battistessa's *El poeta en su poema* [*The Poet and His Poem*], Buenos Aires, 1965, establishes that the Chacón manuscript is the only index which registers dated the compositions of Góngora by Foulché-Delbose in 1900 and that said production is next to that of Lope de Vega in quantity and is constituted in sonnets - somewhat less than a third - composition which Góngora cultivated with preference during his life (p. 42). We ought to point out, likewise, the preference of Sor Juana and of Sara de Ibáñez for the sonnet.

[8] She publishes the following works in chronological order: *Canto* (1940); *Canto a Montevideo* [*Song to Montevideo*] (1941); *Hora Ciega* [*Blind Hour*] (1943); *Pastoral* (1948); *Artigas* [*Burning Fields*] (1952); *Las estaciones y otros poemas* [*Seasons and Other Poems*] (1957); La Batalla (1967); *Apocalipsis* [*Apocalypse*] (1970); *Canto Póstumo* (1973).

[9] S. de I. shares with Góngora the playful Baroque transposition of establishing an indirect

relation between meaning and form. The process becomes complicated when the referent leads us to another referent thus requiring a subtle and ingenious game of imagination which characterizes the *culterano* poem as well as the *conceptista* and obstructs immediate apprehension.

[10] Sor Juana Inés de la Cruz, *Obras Completas,* [*Complete Works*] *El sueño* [*The Dream*], (Mexico: Editorial Porrúa , 1972, 1972), p. 184.

[11] Sara de Ibáñez, *Las estaciones y otros poemas* (México, 1957), pp. 35-7.

[12] Sara de Ibáñez, *Canto Póstumo* , op. cit., p. XIX.

[13] Sara de Ibáñez, *Las estaciones y otros poemas*, op. cit., pp. 42-3.

[14] Ibid, p. 53.

[15] Sara de Ibáñez, *Las estaciones...*, op. cit., pp. 73-82.

The Phenomenology of Nothingness in the Poetry of Julia de Burgos

ELPIDIO LAGUNA-DIAZ

Rutgers University

Any approach to the poetical works of Julia de Burgos should begin by bearing in mind that she never belonged nor should be adscribed to any definite or particular literary trend, movement or school. Needless to say that her cultural background was far-ranging and varied in all aspects including classical and contemporary literature. Yet, her literary activity was not oriented as an aesthetic endeavor *per se*; the literary work was there but to be a means of expression, a channel of communication between her and the world she carried within. These are some of the considerations we must take up before pronouncing a verdict of "sentimentalism" for Julia de Burgos and, for that matter, for other Latin American women writers as well. A critical approach, besides the technical and stylistic probes into Julia's poetry, must not set aside or neglect her solid philosophical education for in her work as a poet what we may term the "poetical word" not only acquires the hues of emotion and experience, the selective processes of conscious literary creation, but is extended in meaning through its philosophical implications and suggestions. This does not mean that Julia's treatment of the poetic word is subordinate to philosophy as vocabulary pertaining to any particular system. Hers is not a poetry of definitions. It does point to the fact that to obviate or underestimate the poetical and aesthetic treatment of the "philosophical word" in her poetry is to lose sight of her themes, symbols and ultimate "cosmovisión".

The consideration of what we have termed "phenomenology of nothingness" in the poetic works of Julia de Burgos is not a philosophical one. We are not concerned with the ontological problems or metaphysical import of a particular school or trend in philosophy as applied to the ideas and references to nothingness permeating the poems of the Puerto Rican poet. Yet, her poems are imbued with a kind of existential stoicism that always points out to both, the mentioning of nothingness as a philosophical concept related to certain aspects of her life-circumstance and, also, as a feeling of multiple projections, what we may call a product of the interaction between the inner forces of the poet and the obstacles encountered by those forces as they tend to become expression.

Nothingness in the poetry of Julia de Burgos, thus, is sometimes a concept, an idea that Julia mentions not without a note of bitterness and irony. It is in these instances when she comes the nearest to a philosophical consideration of nothingness. Nothingness, then, is related to the concepts of time, life, death, the transcendence of the human person or its permanence beyond the limits raised to existence. Nothingness, its idea or purely speculative inceptions do not form a part of Julia's poetry. Nothingness does not come to her verses as an objectless concept, as an ''ens rationes''. For the same reason, it is not something that is apprehended intellectually and then carried over to her poetry.

On the other hand, little would we have to say about the "phenomenology of nothingness" in Julia de Burgos' poetry if we were simply to look for a word, the recurrence of a term here and there as poetic or as poetically treated as it may be; if we were to neglect the embodiment of existence in which all her poetry is immersed. From the first poem of her collected works, in *A Julia de Burgos* [*To Julia de Burgos*], Julia establishes her poetical and existential stand when she speaks to that part of her own self which is the Julia of social convention, of compromise, the "other" Julia, the one people see, hear, touch:

> People murmur - she says - that I am your enemy
> for I give your own self, in a verse, to the world.

> They lie Julia de Burgos. They lie, Julia de Burgos.
> What raises from my verses is not your voice: but my voice;
> while you are but a mere clothing, the essence is I;
> and the most profound abyss lies between us both. [1]

The "other" Julia is the Julia that capitulates with every hour and action lived in the world of society and customs. The "essential" Julia claims the liberty of being herself. The need and the right of being the center and voice of the Julia that is. The essential Julia has lived in the shadows, the Julia of convention has been her refuge, her camouflage: "everything you have - says the essential Julia - is your own self, which you owe to everyone,/while I, I do not owe my nothingness to anyone''. [2] Nothingness here is synonymous with "hiddenness". From now on her poetry will be the means, the grounds where the real, essential Julia will make her abode. Thus, if nothingness was before the hiding place of the essential Julia - and for this very reason just an "appearance" of nothingness - when she takes over

the total expression of her own self, she casts away the "conventional" Julia
to the realm where most people live, the realm of shadows, where light is
cancelled out: "I felt myself to be as another life behind a surface of colors
and forms./And I saw myself as clarity, making the shadow cast on earth by
man, to flee" (*Intima*) [*Intimate*].

Yet, "nothingness" has no phenomenology properly speaking, up to
now. What we have is an affirmation of her most genuine self, and its seizure
of a world that will have no other interpretations than those that will be given
by her. She is the center of that world and she begins to live, to operate from
her own self. Her existence, her presence throughout the world of her poetry
will be all we see and perceive. We will see through her eyes and through her
feelings as she feels and sees. Whatever the essential Julia experiences, at
whatever level of perception or intensity, will not only be what we will know
of her world, but *all* we will know of that world. She is not a mere interpreter
of a given world. On the contrary, that world will be "what she lives in it".
an extension of herself. Her poetry is not merely "Julia's world" or its
elements. A thematic inquiry into her poetry will soon enough find itself
rotating around a series of constants; an inquiry into the elements of her
poetic world will have us toiling through a rather simple and recurrent
succession of symbols, images and relations. Within the ambience of her
poetry, criticism is bound for a "participated experience", not for an intricate
aesthetic or "avant garde" literary display. All we will come to experience
through her poetry is what she discovers, unveils for us. It is then that
"nothingness" acquires a phenomenology of modes and manifestations; it is
then that the rest of the elements of her world, symbols, motives, concepts,
experiences, etc., acquire such a phenomenological import too. Julia sets
herself on the reason of her own being. Thus, freedom will be her lot. It will
be her, the fullness of her presence, her love, her passion, her thoughts, her
senses, that will imprint on the succession of time, things, happenings, the
changes, the alterations, the phenomenology of modes of being that they will
undergo as they become objects of the poet's attention or witnesses of her path
through experience. Because she founds all this world on her own genuine
life, she is free. That freedom leaves far behind what we may understand,
even sometimes recognize, as "liberation" from contingencies. That
freedom she has reached is a *state of being* in her world, not a "moment" of
action or thought.

This places us, at last, on the track of a "phenomenology of
nothingness" in her poetry. Nothingness is not a concept in her; it has no
ontological imminence either. The phenomenology of a "Nothingness" that
would be beyond her, alien from her world, is not present in her poetry. And
Julia is the "All", the demiurge of that world. Nothingness will neither be
the absence of that world nor its possible or expected evanescence, nor its
future destruction. Nothingness is in the poetry of Julia de Burgos everything

the world (people as well as circumstances) lacks as related to herself, everything that has no co-incidence with her being, her way of being; everything that when she loves, needs, discovers, gives, creates, is not there to meet her. Be it social injustice, be it her lover; be it vulgarity or misunderstanding; be it shallowness of heart or mind.

In *Dame tu hora perdida* [*Give Me Your Lost Hour*], to the "lost hour", to the "emptiness" of life, of desires, of love, of tenderness, of purpose in her lover's life, she offers the reality of her own self, in life, in desires, in love, in tenderness, in purpose. Yet, that lack of coincidence which manifests itself like a void, like an emptiness between her and the rest of the world, like a gap ("distance" she will often call it) that she wants to close and thus keeps her soul in a constant outward and inward tension, will be like a pathetic destiny, like a condition of her own existence in its relation to the rest of the world. Perhaps this lack of coincidence, in the aspect of love, is best exemplified in her poem *Nada* [*Nothing*], where an ironical tone only serves to disclose the bitterness left by the patent and insurmountable "distance" between their two lives:

> As life is nothingness in your philosophy,
> let's toast to the certain non-being of our bodies.
>
> Let's toast to the nothingness of your sensuous lips
> which are sensuous zeros round your blue kisses;
> and, as everything blue is, they are a chimerical lie
> of colorless oceans and colorless skies.
> . . . .
> Let's toast to the nothingness, oh so nothingness, of your soul,
> galloping its lie on a loose stallion;
> . . . .
> Let's toast to us, to them, to no one;
> to this ever-nothingness of our never-bodies;
> to all, to the few; to everyone and nothingness;
> to those hollow shadows of living which are dead.
>
> If we come from non-being and we drift to non-being,
> nothing between nothingness and nothingness, /
>   zero between zero and zero,
> and if between nothingness and nothingness nothing can exist,
> let's toast to the beautiful non-being of our bodies.

As nothingness is, rather than a conceptual reality of the void, that which we confront when an action of ours is not corresponded by an equal and adequate action, its phenomenology pertains to the inner world of the poet. When our soul reaches for completion of its movements in the "other", and when that movement is left unfulfilled, a thirst, an unsatisfaction, a feeling of incompletion, of nothingness, is felt. We *expect* a correspondence to the movements of our soul from the object, from that which constitutes the "end" of those movements. That expectancy is an opening, a state of openness of ourselves to the reception of what we expect. In the movements of our souls the moment of expectancy is an anticipation of what we are expecting; the tension of our being is a reclamation of what should be there or, at least, of what could be there were it to exist. Its inocurrence, its not being there, leaves us with the emptiness we created just for its coming. That is the closest and most immediate "impression" or experience of what we may call nothingness that we are given to receive. The phenomenology of nothingness as experienced in this manner will be the phenomenology of the poet's inner self in all its tensions and by reason of its particular qualities. In other words, nothingness will have or, better, will be the "other" part of the phenomenology of the person. This Julia portrays in *Momentos* [*Moments.*]

> I, a fatalist,
> watching the lives of my fellow men
> coming, going.
>
> I, within myself,
> always in the expectancy of something
> my mind cannot foresee.
>
> I, multiple,
> as if in contradiction,
> tied to a borderless feeling that,
> alternatively,
> ties me and unties me
> to the world.
>
> I, universal,
> drinking life
> in every plummeting star,
> in every sterile scream,
> in every borderless feeling.
>
> And all this for what?
> -To go on being the same.

A *fatalist*, Julia does not necessarily look at life with pessimism. Her fatalism is not so much an attitude of life, as it is a standstill of her judgement of that life. And not *her* life, but the life of others, the everyday life of people in the streets, at home. Because there is senselessness and frivolity in the lives of individuals, because there are purposeless lives, vain lives, they all contrast, clash, with the ever-present vital tension in which she lives. Fatalism is a standstill of all her inner tensions, when she realizes that they cannot be reciprocated by others. Fatalism is that standstill of emotions and feelings, of ideas and actions which cannot be. It is, then, a phenomenon, a partial taste, a "kind" of nothingness.

Expecting, within herself, something her mind cannot foresee, Julia stands at the fringe of a world that has no "someone else" like herself. That world, that outer world which is *reality*, is a world where people are not. They just "are there". It is the world of "estar y no ser". Another stage of something we may call nothingness.

Multiple, as if in contradiction with herself, she approaches all the particular realities of the outer world. To force upon persons and things concepts with which to frame them, would be to live a lie. All the more pathetic as it would be a conscientious self-deception. Both, the objects of that world (persons, things, events) and their possible concepts, remain empty as they can only be filled or defined by what they are in reality. Any other attempt to see them differently, would be a falsification.

So she remains tied to that "borderless feeling", that "limitless tension". Neither the term "borderless" nor "limitless" mean for her a thrust towards infinity. They just represent an image of her Will to wait. To wait for what she needs in order to be filled, corresponded, completed. Not even in the realm of her love - her greatest tension, rather than passion - will she find fulfillment. As happens with "nothingness", in her poetry there is a phenomenology of love, not real fruition.

Nothingness can be the refuge of what is forgotten, of what is remembered, for in the phenomenology of nothingness memory reduces that confrontation of what is not in some extent and what is to a certain extent. But to reach that frontier one must reach a state in which immediate reality is rendered inoperant: by modifying the time-consciousness of the mind, by rendering idle the evolution and impressions of the present. This state of mind will bring us to that realm of memory in which memory itself renders its contents not as an operative faculty, but as a spontaneous , "existential" reproduction. In *Vaciedad* [*Emptiness*] Julia says:

> I have let myself down unto where dust
> has the color of nothingness,
> to the timeless instant where my shadow dies.
> There where my dream only hears itself
> from his mute song,
> and the idea comes forward, soundless, to the parting point.
> ·
> I am blank
> just over the impulse that travels my life,
> between the minute that has just passed
> and the port of nothingness...

If the phenomenology of nothingness depends on the feelings, perceptions, tensions of the poet it will go on appearing and reappearing here and there all through the poet's work as long as she Wills to live her life fully, as long as life itself is a tension projected into the future. But the moment that Will conforms to the nothingness it evidences by willing continously, then, what has been a phenomenological manifestation of what we called "nothingness" comes to a halt, becomes a *state* of the mind and the soul; it becomes the most pressing and absolute experience of nothingness: solitude. In *Poema con la tonada última* [*Poem With the Last Tune*] Julia says:

> I am going to remain alone,
> without songs or skin,
> like a tunnel, inside, where even silence
> maddens and kills itself.(p. 245)

And lastly, in *The Sun in Welfare Island* the total collapse:

> For my soul asks just
>   solitude,
> my smile depends on
>   solitude,
> my eyes are full of
>   solitude
> and all of me is loneliness
>   in a rebellious heart.(p. 322)

NOTES

[1] The English renditions of Julia de Burgos' poetry—with exception of the last one, *The Sun in Welfare Island*, originally written in English by the poet—are ours. The corresponding Spanish texts can be found in: Julia de Burgos, *Obra Poética*. (San Juan: Instituto de Cultura Puertorriqueña, 1961).

[2] "Intima", p. 67.

Love and Death: The Thematic Journey of Julia de Burgos

by

NELLY E. SANTOS

Baruch College of CUNY

The poetic works of Julia de Burgos[1] introduce us to the deeply personal, intimate voice of an artist who, in her unflagging pursuit of essence, was content to disclose nothing less than the bare essential fabric of her existence. Her poetry's deep-rooted lyricism heralds a Neo-Romanticism whose principal characteristics are the full expression of love's agonizing desolation and a petition to death for deliverance from loneliness and despair.

Her work in verse consists of lyric poetry and poems with a socio-political emphasis. In this study we will deal solely with her lyric poetry, which we consider to be her major contribution to the contemporary poetry of Latin America.

We will analyze two of her books: *Canción de la verdad sencilla* [*Song of Simple Truth*], which marks the pinnacle of her amorous expression; and *El mar y tú* [*The Sea and You*], the agonizing testimony of her courtship with imminent death dominated by the sea conceived symbolically as a bed, or resting place.

Access to the poet's personal correspondence, moreover, makes it possible for us to examine both the autobiographical material which eventually was channeled into her lyric poetry and statements she herself made concerning the origin of the poetic works under consideration.

The fundamental dialectic of her poetic compositions confers double-edged significance on the allusive symbolic components of her thematic itinerary. The latter converges in two major themes, love and death. These are explored in poems which record the inward progression from self-discovery to love; and from love, through suffering, to the atomization of death.

Wherever Julia de Burgos treats these themes, we encounter an intensity of living comparable to that which she expresses in one of her letters when she writes:

> Esta vida partida en dos que estoy viviendo, entre la esencia y la forma, entre el golpe implacable de las circunstancias, y el eco tibio y suave del amor que me llama.
>
> (New York, March 1, 1940)

[This life split in two that I am living, between form and essence, between the relentless blow of circumstances and the soft, warm echo of love which calls me.] Personal narratives such as this help us establish the circumstances of the poet's life during the period when she conceived, elaborated and published her work.

The total production of Julia de Burgos includes the following three books: *Poema en veinte surcos* [*Poem in Twenty Furrows*], *Canción de la verdad sencilla* and *El mar y tú*. The first two of these were published in 1938 and 1939, respectively, and the third in 1954, posthumously.

Canción de la verdad sencilla and *El mar y tú* mark a major step forward in Julia's poetic creativity, not only because of the extraordinary command of language these works display but, above all, because the poet succeeds in fully interpreting and expressing the nuances and tone of her romantic sentiment. The significance of her work for posterity resides precisely in the uniqueness of this expression.

Poema en veinte surcos, her first book, establishes her search for self-definition and places her on the path of self-awareness, the antechamber of love:

> Yo, múltiple
> como en contradicción,
> atada a un sentimiento sin orillas
> que me une y me desune,
> alternativamente,
> al mundo.
>
> ("Momentos," p. 73)

[Me, multiple with the nature of contradiction, bound to a feeling without any shores which joins and disjoins me, intermittently, to the world. —"Moments"] The symbols of her poetry frequently represent and allude to the struggle between time and eternity, matter and spirit.

An intense peak of emotional expression is reached in *Canción de la verdad sencilla*. This collection, a prime example of the poet's incipient romanticism, offers a moving testimonial of love. The fundamental subject matter of these poems is an all-consuming passion which leads irreversibly to the presentiment of death both close at hand and inescapable:

> Me veo equidistante del amor y el dolor.
> . . . .
> ¿Quién soy?
> . . . .
>   ¿A dónde voy?
>   A donde tú caminas esperándome.
>   ("Soy hacia ti," p. 134)

[I am equidistant from love and sorrow.... Who am I?... Where am I going? To where you roam awaiting me. — "I Live towards You"]

The fundamental attitude of this poetry is one of profound vitalism with respect to the reality of love and death. A lyric quality of deeply earnest and impassioned intimacy pervades the poetic expression as the running account of her learning to die of love:

> En ti me he silenciado...
> El corazón del mundo está en tus ojos, que se vuelan
> mirándome.
> . . . .
> (La hora más sencilla para amarte es ésta
> en que voy por la vida dolida de alba.)
>   ("Alba de mi silencio," p. 107)

[In you I've become still... The heart of the world is in your eyes, which soar aloft bearing me in their gaze.... (The easiest time to love you is now, as I wander through the wounded life of dawn.) — "Dawn of My Silence"]

Canción is a work we could justly consider the intimate confession of a woman fully acquainted with life's many uncertainties and disappointments. It is also a work which illustrates what Diana Ramírez has called the "curva evolutiva de su Eros" [evolutionary curve of her Eros], meaning by this an eroticism that never emphasizes "el morboso deleite sensual, sino la cálida respuesta que la vida da a la vida" [crazed sensual delight, but rather the warm response which life makes to life].

If we abide by the evidence of her letters, we could conclude that the poet actually lived the spiritual adventure reflected in her poetry. In a letter dated from Havana, she writes of how the book of poems originated:

...cuando recibí tu carta (X) estaba a mi lado. Tembló de alegría pues el triunfo no había sido sólo mío, sino también de él que lo inspiró desde la primera emoción hasta la última. En realidad si él no llega a

Puerto Rico y enciende como nunca mi vida en amor cósmico y
eterno, no hubiera salido ese libro...

(Havana, July 17, 1940)

[...when I received your letter (X) was by my side. He was overwhelmed with
joy, because the success was not just mine but his as well, since he had been
its inspiration from the first stir of emotion to the last. Really, if he hadn't
come to Puerto Rico and kindled my life like never before with cosmic and
eternal love, that book would never have been published...]

The theme of love can be conceptualized and expressed from two different
perspectives, one promoting a return to love's primitive sensual expression
and another which seeks to explore and communicate the constant duality of
life shattered by a disheartening experience and equally distant from suffering
and death.

The first approach to the treatment of this theme presents us with a
personal perspective, concerned little or not at all with any universal value it
might have, which commonly centers upon the psychological moment that
produced it:

> ¡Cómo suena en mi alma la idea
> de una noche completa en tus brazos
> diluyéndome toda en caricias
> mientras tú te me das extasiado!

("Noche de amor en tres cantos," p. 120)

[How my soul thrills to the thought of an entire night in your embrace,
draining myself of so many caresses as you surrender to me in ecstasy!
—"Night of Love in Three Cantos"]

On other occasions, she uses the poem as a vehicle to communicate to us
the circumstances of her personal drama, a very intimate drama which
nevertheless manages to touch upon a tender and sensitive area shared by us
all, namely, our common dread of loneliness:

> Nadie.
> Iba yo sola.
> Nadie.
> Pintando las auroras con mi único color de soledad.
> Nadie.

("Poema detenido en un amanecer," p. 105)

[No one. I was alone. No one. Painting the daybreaks with the single color
of my loneliness. No one. —"Poem Detained in a Sunrise"]

In still other examples, she describes an experience of love beyond the
body which recalls the cosmic and eternal love alluded to in the letter cited
earlier:

¡Se unen en el espacio nuestras vidas
fugadas de sí mismas!
. . . .
Hasta el poema rueda ahora sin palabras
desde mi voz
hacia tu alma...
¡Y pensar que allá abajo nos espera la forma!
(''Principio de un poema sin palabras,'' p. 112)

[Our lives unite in space escaping themselves!... Even the poem flows un-
spoken now from my voice towards your soul... And to think that form awaits
us in the depths! —''Beginning of a Poem without Words'']

The flight from reality evidenced in this poem is a constant throughout
the poetry of Julia de Burgos. We can substantiate it in three prevailing
moods or tendencies: the yearning for transcendence, the pursuit of essentiality and the desire to become lost in love's rapture.

She alludes to a hierarchy of elements to give symbolic expression to the
first of the moods indicated above. Air and water predominate and are
represented in wings, voices, butterflies, birds, flight, swallows and doves:

Hoy me acerco a tu alma
con las manos amarillas de pájaros...

. . . .
Saltando claridades
he recogido el sol en los tejados,
y una nube ligera que pasaba
me prestó sus sandalias de aire blando.
(''Viaje alado,'' p. 113)

[Today I verge upon your soul with hands full yellow with birds... Leaping
simple truths, I have gathered sunlight on the rooftops, and a light-footed
passing cloud lent me sandals of gentle breezes. —''Winged Journey''] Light
and the idea of flight often appear closely allied with the general symbolism of
air. In ''Poema perdido en pocos versos''[8] [''Poem Lost in a Few Verses'']
we read: ''Oh amor entretenido en astros y palomas'' [Oh love dallying in
doves and stars], and in ''Unidad'' [''Unity''] she declares: ''...a veces te
me acercas en la sombra, en el aire,/y en los dedos celestes de la estrella
lejana''[9] [sometimes you draw near me in a shadow, in the air,/and in the
celestial fingers of a distant star].

The pursuit of essentiality places us in quite a different plane. The poet
transforms reality amid the turbulent depths of her innermost being and
prepares us to witness the total annihilation of her own individuality:

Por tu vida yo soy

alta mar y gaviota
en ella vivo y crezco.

("Alta mar y gaviota," p. 128)

[Your life has made of me an open sea where, like the gull, I can live and grow. —"Open Sea and Gull"] This marine imagery is replaced by river imagery in the book's title poem, "Canción de la verdad sencilla" :[1]

El y yo somos uno.
Uno mismo y por siempre entre las cimas;
manantial abrazando lluvia y tierra;
fundidos en un soplo ola y brisa...

[He and I are one. One and the same forever amongst the summits; flowing spring embracing earth and rain; single breath in which both wave and breeze are blended...]

Water is the most important element in Julia's poetry. We note its presence in a superabundance of nouns, adjectives, verbs, metaphors and images, the most common examples being the following: the sea, the river; gulls, ports; to anchor, to swim, to multiply. Each one of these constitutes something symbolic of creation or the renovation of vital forces and exemplifies thereby the pursuit of essentiality in water, the beginning and end of every thing on earth.

As the thematic development in *Canción* moves forward, we notice an instability of individual being in the face of love's fullness. The same mood which so often inspired her to overflow with joy now, paradoxically, brings forth pain and sorrow:

Te quiero
en el dolor sin llanto que tanta noche ha recogido
en el sueño;
en el cielo invertido en mis pupilas para mirarte cósmica;
en la voz socavada de mi ruido de siglos derrumbándose.

("Te quiero," p. 133)

[I love you in the tearless sorrow that so many nights have harvested in sleep; in the heavens transposed to my pupils so that I might gaze upon you cosmically; in the cavernous voice of my din of crumbling centuries. —"I Love You"]

Handmaiden of her own passion, she confesses:

Camino...
En puntos suspensivos de dolor
anudo tu distancia.
El aire se me pierde.

("Insomne," p. 136)

[I walk... On suspension points of pain I knot your distance. The air slips away from me. —"Sleepless"] The poem offers us a prelude of death in suffering, loneliness and indifference—three syntheses of an inexorable truth which annuls the past:

> Yo fui la más callada.
> La que saltó la tierra sin más arma que un verso.
> ¡Y aquí me veis, estrellas,
> desparramada y tierna, con su amor en mi pecho!
>
> ("Yo fui la más callada," p. 142)

[I was the more silent one. The one who sprang from earth with no weapon but a poem. So here I am, stars, open and sensitive, with his love in my heart! —"I Was the More Silent One"]

Her capacity for love is unlimited. She clings to love as her only handhold and declares:

> Estás aquí. Conmigo.
> Por mi sueño.
> ¡A dormirse se van ahora mis lágrimas
> por donde tú cruzaste entre mi verso!
>
> (Ibid., p. 147)

[You are here. With me. Throughout my slumber. My tears are going off to sleep now there where you crossed the path of my verse!]

A year after her book of poems was published, in July, 1940, Florida-bound with plans to sail on to Cuba, Julia borders on suicide. A short time before, she had summoned forth all her emotions and emptied them out in a revealing epistolary confession:

> ...¡qué malo es soñar!, ¿verdad?, para después ver despedazados nuestros sueños... Los míos han sido verdaderos ventarrones, y siempre he caído arrastrada en mis propias alas para quedar enredada en la más inamovible realidad. Tal el carruaje en sueños de mi amor. Lo he querido hacer alas, lo he querido hacer ágil para enfrentarme a realidades frías que me separan de sus brazos cuando más lo necesito.
>
> (New York, April 30, 1940)[11]

[How terrible it is to dream—don't you agree?—only to see our dreams get shattered later... Mine have been real windstorms, and I've always gotten swept away on my own wings to become entangled in the most unshakable reality. Such is the dream vehicle of my love. I've wanted to give him wings, I've wanted to make him agile the better to cope with the cold realities that separate me from his arms when I need him most.] The symbolism of abandonment corresponds to an aspect of death. This observation is borne out in her last book, *El mar y tú*, published posthumously in 1954.

Anyone who has read the poetry of Julia de Burgos knows the importance and unique significance of death in her work. In particular, death causes individual harmony with life to cease. In more general terms, however, death represents confrontation with a destiny dominated melancholically by life; hence, it is a paradoxical exercise of the act of love:

> Me he encontrado la vida
> al ascender mi castidad de impulso
> contigo en ti y en todo.
>
> ("Canción para llorar y amar," p. 151)

[I've found life since my pure inclination rose with you, in you and in everything. —"Song for Weeping and Loving"]

As we investigate the gestation of this book of peoms, we come across another helpful passage in her letters. During Christmas of 1941, Julia writes to her sister Consuelo: "Estoy agotada, muerta, aturdida... He sufrido lo que tú no puedes imaginar. ¡A qué caro precio se paga el amor!"[12] [I'm worn out, dead, bewildered... I've suffered more than you can ever imagine. What a price one pays for love!] Once the harmony of love has been broken, the relative regularity of her "unirse" and "desunirse" (see above, note 2) with the world is interrupted, and we see develop a poetry of tragic and elegiac overtones. In these poems, the poet reclaims and confirms the personal experiences that came together to produce them:

> He escrito los poemas más trágicos de mi vida, y he tenido días negros
> en los que he pensado hasta en el suicidio...
>
> (Havana, January 7, 1941)

[I have written the most tragic poems of my life, and I have spent days of utter gloom in which I've even contemplated suicide.]

El mar y tú offers the first evidence of her resignation to live alienated by suffering. Death comes to be viewed as a doorway of salvation.

In this collection, we can distinguish two distinct poetic moments, which in turn reflect the existence of two prevailing moods. "Velas sobre el pecho del mar" ["Sails on the Breast of the Sea"] charms us completely with its tender treatment of the theme of love and represents the poet's final attempt at reconciliation with life by virtue of a total metamorphosis of "reality":

> Lo saben nuestras almas,
> más allá de las islas y más allá del sol.
> El trópico, en sandalias de luz, prestó las alas,
> y tu sueño y mi sueño se encendieron.
>
> ("Poema de la cita eterna," p. 191)

[Our souls know it, beyond the islands and far beyond the sun. The tropic, on sandals of light, lent its wings, and your dream and my dream took flame. —"Poem of the Eternal Reunion"]   Note the symbiotic sequence of the elements earth, air and fire and the surreal treatment of the two dreams. Observe also how every turn of speech is charged with allusions to the cyclical journey, as if emphasizing its experiential reality: nothingness — life — love — death — nothingness; a longing to die in what is longed for, to dissolve in the dissolved:

> Sobre el mar, sobre el tiempo
> la tonada, la vela...
> La cita eterna, amado,
> más allá de los rostros de las islas que sueñan.
>
> En el pecho del viento van diciendo los lirios,
> que en el pecho del mar dos auroras se besan.

(Ibid., p. 192)

[Upon the sea, upon time, the melody, the sail... The eternal reunion, beloved, beyond the faces of islands that dream. In the bosom of the wind the lilies spread rumors about two dawns that kiss in the heart of the sea.]

On the other hand, the referent of the synecdoche "velas" [sails] refashions for us the ship which, by virtue of its indeterminate symbolism, serves as a vessel of transcendence. By analogy, ploughing through the waters is an impetus to action which denotes a constant process of involution, paralleling that moment when Julia perceives a closed universe even as she envisions an inexorable order leading back to existence:

> Todo el color de aurora despertada
> el mar y tú lo nadan a mi encuentro,
> y en locura de amarme hasta el naufragio
> van rompiendo los puertos y los remos.

("El mar y tú," p. 193)

[Through all the color of freshly awakened dawn the sea and you come swimming to meet me, and crazed with love for me to the point of shipwreck go smashing ports and splintering oars. — "The Sea and You"]

The sea voyage, therefore, is nothing but the arrival at the point of departure, the sea. Symbolically, the sea is transformed into the mediating agent between life and death; the sea is both cradle and tomb:

> Mar mío,
> mar lecho,
> mar sin nombre,
> mar a deshoras,
> mar en la espuma del sueño,

mar en la soledad desposando crepúsculos,
mar viento descalzando mis últimos revuelos,
mar tú.
mar universo...

                              ("Letanía del mar," p. 244)

[My sea, sea-bed, sea without a name, ill-fated sea, sea in the foam of sleep, sea-solitude joining twilights in marriage, sea-wind baring the feet of my most recent torments, sea you, sea the universe... — "Litany of the Sea"]

As we continue through this book of poems, the transfigurations and impossibilities follow one after another in rapid succession. The sea sometimes ceases to be water to become a "mar etéreo" [ethereal sea], and birds no longer fly but instead can be seen "nadando cielo" [swimming through the sky]. Although Julia was never able to surrender to death by suicide, by removing herself to the transmutable plane of "her reality" she demonstrates the process of her definitive isolation from the world via the involution towards Nothingness. The process is suggested in these introspective lines:

¡Oh día de sueño y ola...!
Nuestras dos juventudes hacia el viento estallaron.
. . . .
Recuerdo que al mirarme con la voz derrotada,
las dos manos del cielo me cerraron los párpados.
. . . .
¡Amante, la ternura desgaja mis sentidos...
yo misma soy un sueño remando por tus aguas!

                        ("Donde comienzas tú," pp. 203-4)

[Oh day of slumber and ocean wave...! The days of our youth scattered to the wind.... I recall how, seeing me with my voice in ruins, both hands of heaven closed my eyelids for me.... Lover, tenderness uproots my senses... I myself am but a dream rowing upon your waters! — "Where You Begin"]

The process of introspection yields a series of tortured poems in which the poet tries to effect her transference into that cosmic infinity which has been the subject of so many of her poems:[15]

Mi senda es el espacio.
Recorrerme es huirse de todos los senderos...
Soy el desequilibrio danzante de los astros.

                        ("Mi senda es el espacio," p. 216)

[Space is my only path. To traverse me you must flee all paths... I am the dancing instability of the stars. — "My Path is Space"] This poem offers a vivid portrayal of the "naufragio" [shipwreck] of her conscience in a peaceful acceptance of death.

In the second part of the collection, entitled "Poemas para un naufragio" ["Poems for a Shipwreck"], we find profoundly dramatized the funeral premonition set forth in the final poems of "Velas sobre el pecho del mar" ["Sails on the Breast of the Sea"].

The very notion of "naufragio" [shipwreck] is contrary to "velas" [sails], since it represents a voluntary, or involuntary, negation of action. Death by immersion brings us face to face with her conscious denial to live in continual anguish:

> He tenido que dar, multiplicarme,
> despedazarme en órbitas complejas...
> Aquí en la intimidad, conmigo misma,
> ¡Qué sencillez me rompe la conciencia!
> . . . .
> ¿Qué me queda del mundo? ¿Qué me queda...?
> ("¡Oh lentitud del mar!", p. 238)

[I have had to give, to multiply myself, to shatter into complex orbits... Here in my innermost being, alone with myself, what simplicity breaks through my awareness!... What remains of the world? What remains...? —"Oh Slow-moving Sea"]

"Intimidad" [intimacy], "sencillez" [simplicity] and "conciencia" [awareness] represent three stages of involution, or that process already declared in the noun "naufragio." The water symbolism underscores the idea of the sea's softness and repose, while at the same time it offers us a fascinating duality of the abyss. The bottom of the sea takes on the character of the "país de los muertos" [land of the dead], commonly associated with the ocean depths.

Dazed and blinded by her own awareness, "En la ribera de la muerte,/tan cerca!... [On the shore of death, so close!], she wonders:

> ¿Seré yo el puente entre el sueño y la muerte?
> ¡Presente...!
> ¿De qué lado del mundo me llaman, de qué frente?
> Estoy en alta mar...
> . . . .
> ¿Estoy viva?
> ¿Estoy muerta?
> ("Entre mi voz y el tiempo," p. 232)

[Might I be the bridge between sleep and death? Here...! From what part of the world do they call me, from what battlefront? I'm on the open sea... Am I alive? Am I dead? — "Between my Voice and Time"]

From this point forward, we sense a growing fascination with the idea of "naufragio." It suffices merely to scan the titles of the poems in the last section to fully grasp her vision of the irreversible course of her life: ''Poema para la estrella integrada'' [''Poem for the Integrated Star''] , ''Oh mar no esperes más'' [''Oh Sea, Wait No Longer''] , ''Ruta de sangre al viento'' [''March of Blood to the Wind''] , ''Letanía del mar'' [''Litany of the Sea''] and ''Poema con la tonada final'' [''Poem with the Final Melody''].

Throughout this section, a highly compressed richness of emotional expression causes us to plunge forward at a dizzying pace into the very essence of her inner world. Here she draws upon the very best of her poetic talent and offers a sort of selected anthology. The personal perspective, which in a lesser poet would have produced a work both weak in style and lacking in literary ingenuity, for Julia is a source of strength; in fact, it constitutes the vital axis which gives meaning as well as stylistic and thematic unity to the reality represented in her poems.

Her tendency to employ a verbal simplicity bordering on the barest essential makes it possible for her to sustain a dialogue with herself by virtue of the powerful symbols of her poetry. As her style grows progressively more refined, her poetry acquires a' more accentuated confessional tone, increasingly availing itself of her own inner resources.

Like Alfonsina, Julia wrote her epitaph in the premonition of her own verses:

> ¿Cómo habré de llamarme cuando sólo me quede
> recordarme, en la roca de una isla desierta?
> Un clavel interpuesto entre el viento y mi sombra,
> hijo mío, y de la muerte, me llamarán poeta.
>
> (''Poema para mi muerte,'' p. 275)

[Whatever shall I call myself when all that is left for me is to remember myself, on the rock slab of a deserted island? A carnation placed between the wind and my shadow, my son, and death's, they'll call me a Poet. —''Poem for My Death'']

In these lines, as in the entire last part of the collection, the dramatic note acquires great significance, echoing the anguish of her personal life.

The ''yo'' of her poetry is no mere stylistic recourse but rather the real, true voice with which she records the evocation of actual events, without recourse to literary fabrication. As we have seen, a fatalistic view of the world pervades her lyric poetry, and this world view must be taken into account if one is to fully understand and appreciate the aesthetic qualities of her work. Julia de Burgos is pre-eminently a lyric poet, and the poetry of all great lyric poets is the verbal incarnation of their most intimate life and feelings. In ''Poema con la tonada final,'' the poet sums up her vision of the external world in an emotional statement, saying:

> Voy a quedarme sola

sin canciones, ni piel,
como un túnel por dentro, donde el mismo silencio
se enloquece y se mata.

(Ibid., p. 245)

[I'm going to remain alone without songs nor skin, like a tunnel inside, where even silence itself goes crazy and kills itself.] We have seen that her relation to the world is determined primarily by her subjective feelings with particular regard to her experiences and the values that surround her. It is not surprising that this relationship is established and sustained in her poetic world by use of the symbol. The symbol affords her a dynamic and universal means of establishing the necessary communication between her inner self and the outer world; at the same time, it unfolds a poetic universe that is both subjective and unitary with regard to form and content.

The symbolic elements of this lyrical world—river, sea, waves, furrows; bird, wings, abandon; sails, shipwreck—effectively promote the major themes of love and death. These, in turn, are determined by the poet's complex attitude toward external "reality." Alfonso Reyes defined this attitude when he stated that art is a continual victory of consciousness over the chaos of external realities. The intuitive character responsible for such an essential part of the poetic vision of Julia de Burgos repeatedly vouches for the accuracy of Reyes' statement:

Casi voy por la vida como gruta de escombros.
Ya ni el mismo silencio se detiene en mi nombre.
Inútilmente estiro mi camino sin luces.
Como muertos sin sitio se sublevan mis voces.

("Oh mar, no esperes más," p. 239)

[I go through life almost like a wreckage heap. Not even silence takes notice of my name any more. My unlit path drags on to no avail.] Like restless corpses my cries rise up in defiance. —"Oh Sea, Wait No Longer"

As essential counterparts of the human condition, common to every age, the themes are well-trodden and even commonplace, differing only in the manner of focusing on them. The uniquely expressive form and mythical elaboration with which Julia de Burgos wrested her images from language assign to her poetic work a place of eminent distinction for posterity.

Translated by FRED R. WORTH

NOTES

[1]She was born on February 17, 1917, in Santa Cruz near Carolina, Puerto Rico. She died on July 16, 1953, in New York.

[2]Quoted by Yvette Jiménez de Báez in *Julia de Burgos, Vida y poesía* [*Julia de Burgos, Life and Poetry*] (San Juan, Puerto Rico: Ediciones Borinqen, 1966), p. 37.

[3]All poems cited are from *Obra poética* [*Poetic Works*], ed. Consuelo Burgos and Juan Bautista Pagán (San Juan, Puerto Rico: Instituto de Cultura Puertorriqueña, 1961).

[4]See examples of these symbols of conflict in the following poems from *Canción*: "Trans mutación" ["Transmutation"], p. 109, "Armonía de la palabra y el instinto" ["Harmony of Word and Instinct"], p. 122, "Canción sublevada" ["Song of Rebellion"], p. 143, "Canción para llorar y amar" ["Song for Weeping and Loving"], p. 150, "Confesión del sí y del no" ["Confession of Yes and No"], p. 184.

[5]Diana Ramírez de Arellano, *Poesía contemporánea en lengua española* [*Contemporary Poetry in the Spanish Language*] (Madrid:Colección Aristarco, 1961), p. 308.

[6]José Emilio González, prol. *Obra poética, op. cit.*, p. 15.

[7]Yvette Jiménez de Báez, *op. cit.*, p. 29.

[8]*Obra poética, op. cit.*, p. 116.

[9]*Ibid.*, p. 133.

[10]*Ibid.*, p. 155.

[11]Yvette Jiménez de Báez, *op. cit.*, p. 38.

[12]*Ibid.*, p. 50.

[13]*Ibid.*

[14]See also certain poems from *Canción* in which these kinds of transfigurations and im possibilities appear: "Desvelos sin sollozo" ["Sleepless Nights without Sobbing"], p. 145, "Regreso a mí" ["Return to Me"], p. 146; and for the best example, the third canto of "Noche de amor en tres cantos" ["Night of Love in Three Cantos"], p. 120.

[15]Here are two:

> Como si entre mis pasos se paseara la muerte,
> desde el cielo me miran consternados los astros.

> ("Es un algo de sombra," p. 220)

[As if death were strolling among my footsteps, from heaven the stars gaze down at me in consternation. — "It's a Little Bit of Shadow"]

> ¡Qué mundo forjaríamos del mundo!
> ¡Qué azul nuestro secreto!
> ¡Hijos de claridad!
> ¡Flores de viento!
> ¡Tierra y agua de amor!
> ¡Aire de sueño!

[What a world we could create from the world! How blue is our secret! Children of clarity! Flowers of wind! Earth and water of love! Air of dreams!]

The Short Stories
of Lydia Cabrera:
Transpositions or Creations?

by

ROSA VALDES-CRUZ

Northern Illinois University

In the prologue to her book *Ayapá: Cuentos de Jicotea,*[1] Lydia Cabrera calls her short stories "'transpositions.'" If we take "'transposition'" to mean the act of simply moving an object (in this case, a story) from one place to another, then we believe the author has defined her work very modestly indeed. Her statement would give one the impression that she was merely a compiler of the tales, myths, legends, rites, superstitions, and customs brought to Cuba from Africa and that some of her compilations had come into her possession in their original form while others had been amplified or altered as a result of Cuban influences before she received them.

The short stories of Lydia Cabrera are much more than transpositions. In them she recreates and reelaborates the material of African and universal folklore. She utilizes formal elements, characters, themes, and motifs of this folklore, but she also amplifies or deletes the material to suit her own purposes. In juxtaposition with cosmogonical myths are descriptions of a markedly surrealistic nature. Details of Cuban customs of the 19th century and the first third of the 20th century are present. The stories have been modified by infusing them with local color and different types of episodes and experiences. Finally, it must be noted that Lydia Cabrera penetrates into the inner thoughts of her characters and artistically elaborates her style in such a manner that her short stories are truly unique from those simply gathered by a compiler. Her short stories therefore must be considered literary creations.

In order to demonstrate their literary creativeness, and taking into account the limitations of space, we will concentrate on only one aspect: the special treatment the author gives to well-known folkloric themes by viewing them from a different perspective and reelaborating their various motifs.

Many examples can be found in the sixty-nine narratives of Lydia Cabrera's three collections to prove that a well-known folkloric theme merely serves as a springboard for her literary creativity. This is evidenced in the short story "El Sapo Guardiero" ["The Guardian Toad"] [2]where she develops the ancient theme of the lost children who are devoured by a monster. The author creates a tender account full of poetic suggestion in which she makes us see the psychological evolution of a cold, lonely toad who is the guardian of a forest "without the music of the birds or the sweetness of the frogs." The indifferent and unloving toad suddenly softens when weeping, terror-stricken twins—small as canary seed grains—embrace him for protection. Because of him the twins are saved from the witch-owner of the forest when the toad hides them inside of his stomach even he knows this action will cost him his life.

Another very popular theme of universal folklore is that of the magic object—a tablecloth, pocketbook, salt shaker, etc.—that provides for its owner.[3] In "La Loma de Mambiala" ["The Slope of Mambiala"]a variation on the theme is inserted with the appearance of the gracious and youthful Cazuelita Cocina-Bueno who is found by the Negro Serapio in a pumpkin field. She gives him enough food for everyone in his village. This theme provides the author with an opportunity to present, with a display of ironic humor, certain types of characters whose counterparts could be found in the population of colonial Cuba: the owner of the Naviera Shipping Company is "a very honorable slave dealer" who would exchange his schooner "Gaviota" loaded with slaves for "Cazuelita." The wealthy lender Marqués de Zarralarraga offered Serapio a million pesos in order to own her because he would then have a "monopoly on the world's food."

One of the themes of universal folklore which is treated most frequently is that of the magic fish who is caught by a fisherman and promises to grant the fisherman three wishes if he will let him go free. However, the excessive ambition of the fisherman's wife ruins everything and the two remain as they were in the beginning.[4] Lydia Cabrera develops the theme in two of her short stories. In "Ellá" (*C.N.*, 46), without departing too much from the original African theme, she has the remains of a fish give birth to two characters who are very typical of this folklore, the Ibelles or twins named Taewo and Kaínde. Many years later in *Cuentos de Jicotea* she again develops the theme in "The Devil's Treasurer." This short story has a much more elaborate technique and a marked satirical intention. The only detail of the traditional theme conserved by the author is a miraculous animal who grants wishes to his captors. In this case the miraculous animal is Jicotea de Oro[Golden Turtle], "the devil's treasurer who helps people climb the social ladder or knocks them down" and who enriches the Negroes Francisco, María Francisca, and Francisquillo.

The setting for "The Devil's Treasurer" is Cuba. Although Lydia Cabrera intentionally alludes to a much earlier epoch—that of the fabulous tales of Nana Siré—it is clear that in any epoch or place sudden changes of fortune similar to those experienced by the main characters or of attitudes of submissiveness to the powerful on the part of society can occur. It is also made clear that these sudden changes are not due precisely to sacrifices or personal effort.

The story shows the various stages of enrichment of the Negroes. The richer they become the more they demand from their protector until they aspire to equate themselves with God. Then they lose Jicotea's help and return to the poor hut from whence they came originally.

Lydia Cabrera uses these stages to create humorous sketches of local customs and to make acute observations about different segments of the Cuban population. We attend a party of the grand world of black society which consists of reputable tailors, elegant coachmen, famous chefs, and "aristocratic maids of aristocratic ladies." With her accustomed wit the author describes that ball to us where "the white aristocracy's counterpart in ebony and cinnamon wiggled proudly without losing a beat." (*C. de J.*, 149) We laugh at her description of the protagonist María Francisca, bound in a corset and tight shoes for the first time in her life; and at Francisco, "paralytic with elegance, wearing white gloves"; and at both "suffocating on account of their feet" and "choking because of their hands."

Following the blacks on their climb up the social ladder, the author achieves a coup in her subtle satire of the upper layers of Cuban society and the ruling class. Everyone falls for those who are ill-equipped by the grace of the devil, even the Captain-General, who eventually falls victim to the charms of the "by no means strait-laced" doña Francisca. With a mere display of grandeur they conquer the most renown windbags and chatterboxes of the speaker's platform and the press, the philanthropic ladies, the Army and the Navy, and finally even the poets who compose verses in their honor.

However, we find one of Lydia Cabrera's most original elaborations in "The Sweet Potato Thief" (*C. de J.*, 78) where she recreates and gives an artistic twist to the well-known theme of the tar baby.

There are numerous versions of the tar baby theme which have been studied in depth by Aurelio Espinosa, who traces the theme itself to the *Jataka* of India. The *Jataka* alludes to a devil with sticky hair who traps the Buddha at five different points of his body.[5] From this remote origin the theme spread throughout the world and conserved more or less the same principal characteristics which can be summarized as follows: a man has a garden or planted field which is robbed periodically. In an attempt to find out who the thief is, he places a human-like figure smeared with tar or any sticky substance in the field. The thief comes to do his pilfering, greets the dummy and, not receiving a reply, initiates a monologue and begins to beat the figure, ending up by having his hands and feet and sometimes his head and stomach stuck to the dummy. There the owner finds and punishes him, but sometimes he succeeds in escaping with the aid of a friend who frees him.

In Lydia Cabrera's embellished version the majority of the fundamental elements of the theme are present: Jicotea [Turtle] steals sweet potatoes at night until he is caught by a tarred scarecrow whom he hits because it has not replied to his questions. When the basic plot of Cabrera's version is outlined, her story does not appear to depart greatly from any of the existing versions. But upon reading the story, we become aware of the author's rich elaboration which we shall now point out.

Lydia Cabrera's story begins with a young Jicotea on whom "a mustache was just beginning to appear," and therefore the time for him to make a decision about his future had arrived. His worried mother suggests a series of trades in a dialogue replete with humor and subtle irony:

—"Son, do you want to be a cook? a baker? a candymaker?"
—"No, mother."
—"or, how about a tailor? Coats and jackets fetch a high price here."
—"No, mother."
. . . .
—"Son, do you want to be a scoundrel?"
—"Yes, mother!"
Mother and son smiled. "God is great: a chip off the old block," said the old woman to herself." (*C. de J.*, 69)

This introduction gives us the background and personality of the central figure, a character who is very different from the one in the traditional folk tale.

The author then brings us to the central episode in which Jicotea steals a sweet potato every night. Jicotea's pilfering is skillfully done because he always keeps his mother's advice in mind that "caution is a quality that is useful and honorable to a thief." He continues to gain confidence and eventually steals as many as six sweet potatoes every night in spite of another bit of advice from his mother, who warns him that "gluttony will hinder you from acquiring things and prevent you from keeping those you have." (p. 80) Meanwhile, the alarmed farmer calls in "La Guardia Civil" [the civil guards] who, after two long nights of vigil are able to spot nothing more than the thief's tracks on the ground. This makes them think that the thief is a spirit from the other world. However, the shrewd farmer thinks otherwise and makes a tarred scarecrow. That very night Jicotea spots the scarecrow and greets him in his nasal falsetto voice but recieves no response from the man who with "arms spread wide...had his absurd head turned toward the sky. He was engrossed, lost in contemplation of the continual swarm of twinkling stars on the black walls of the heavens." (p. 81) The impassiveness of the great gentleman enrages Jicotea but his violent anger is followed by a state of depression when he finds that his hands and feet are stuck to the mysterious person. In the following passage Lydía Cabrera describes the prisoner's inner thoughts as he awaits his fate:

> He thought about death...it seemed to him that it was too late and useless to repent for his sins. He bitterly made fun of his insolence, of his daring. He heaped insults upon himself and a thousand times he shouted, ''Stupid!'' Finally, he cried inconsolably for himself a long time with that infinite compassion of one who does not deserve such misfortune...(p. 82)

The arrival of a trembling and panting Venado [Deer], fleeing from his eternal enemies the dogs, rescues Jicotea from his terrible   predicament. Venado frees him by grasping the protuberances of Jicotea's shell with his mouth and pulling him away from the scarecrow.   However, the sly, deceitful, mischievous Jicotea decides to reward his rescuer with treachery. He begs Venado to hit the scarecrow, and when he does he gets stuck to it. In spite of Venado's pleas Jicotea does not help him. Instead he goes to the farmer and denounces Venado. The farmer returns to the field armed, takes aim at the unfortunate victim's forehead, and skillfully fires a bullet ''between the beautiful, huge, tear-filled eyes of the innocent Venado.'' (p. 84)

''The Sweet Potato Thief'' lacks the customary tone of other folklore tales and it is presented in a different manner from them. There is no Venado in traditional folklore tales whose eyes are filled with tears upon seeing the reward of a friend for his good deed. Nor is there a Jicotea who becomes introspective upon seeing himself near death.

The denouement of Cabrera's story does not conform to any previous versions of the original tale. Generally, in the other versions the thief is punished although he does manage to escape sometimes by tricking his captors. The thief's trickery usually consists of making his captors believe that the method of punishment they have selected for him is dreadful when it actually will not punish him at all. Aurelio Espinosa, in his works on this folkloric theme, refers to the captive's trickery as a ''mock plea.'' The mock plea consists of certain shrewd sentences that the culprit says in order to confuse those who are going to punish him. In traditional folklore it is usually Liebre [Rabbit] who suggests to the rest of the animals that they throw him into the briar patch since this would be the worst kind of punishment for him. And, of course, this is exactly what he wants the animals to do.[6]

Lydia Cabrera does not use the mock plea in ''The Sweet Potato Thief.'' Rather, she employs it in another story dealing with the judgment passed on Jicotea by the other animals because he had deceived Elefante [Elephant] in order to steal his food. The ''legal'' proceedings take place with the animals seated, encircling the guilty ''defendant'' who cries hypocritically ''with only one eye.'' Each animal suggests a horrible punishment while Jicotea listens in silence because, as he says, ''Flies never enter a closed mouth.'' (C.

de J., 252)

The author takes advantage of the ''trial'' to give us a somewhat ironical sketch of life-like characters who could represent examples from any society, but especially Cuban society at the beginning of the republic, and she satirizes them humorously. In Loro [Parrot] we discover the orator and politician who uses his eloquence to gain popularity while saying absolutely nothing of substance in his long-winded speeches. This orator, who demands that Jicotea be flung into the deepest part of the sea and drowned, is described in a vivid passage as ''breathless, rasping, and plucking himself, as is typical of orators in these latitudes.''

Upon hearing the word ''water,'' which is precisely his milieu, Jicotea reacts with an impressive wail: ''Oh Lordy, now I'm gonna die!'' thereby convincing everyone that this must be the most terrible punishment in the world for him. With the intention of drowning Jicotea, the animals take him to the lagoon, because the ocean is too far away. Lydia Cabrera describes the carrying out of sentence thus:

> It was Elefante who with his trunk launched Jicotea on his death flight, making him describe a serene and beautiful curve in the brilliant afternoon air....Jicotea remained happy with his mother and wife Guadimamba in his quiet home of sweet water that holds the sky to its bosom. (p. 256)

The story ends with Jicotea singing the following refrain to his captors to make fun of them:

¡Karima ya ayá karima
Karima buka Kambike
Karima ya ayá karima...!

This rhythmical refrain adds African touches to the delicate grace and subtle irony which pervades the story. These three elements are always present in Lydia Cabrera's style.

NOTES

[1] Lydia Cabrera, *Ayapá: Cuentos de Jicotea* [*Ayapá: Stories of Jicotea*] (Miami: Ediciones Univeisal, 1971), p. 18. (Hereafter cited in the text as *C. de J.* with page number given.)

[2] Lydia Cabrera, *Cuentos negros de Cuba* [*Black Stories from Cuba*] (La Habana: La Verónica, 1940), p. 272. (Hereafter cited in the text as *C.N.* with page number.)

[3] The theme of the magic object that provides for its owner has been classified by Stith

Thompson in *Motif Index of Folk Literature* (6 vols, in 3; Bloomington: Indiana University Press, 1932-36) as belonging to Type 563 in which there are three objects—usually a cloth, a horse, and a stick—and to Type 564 when only two objects are mentioned. In both instances a man receives the first object and loses it or it is stolen, but with the help of the remaining object he recovers the lost one. A third version, classified as Type 565, has only one object which may be a magic salt shaker that produces salt or a pot that provides cooked food for its owner. This version always ends with the production of too much salt or cooked food which brings fatal consequences.

[4] The story of the miraculous fish (Type 555) is very well-known in Europe, with almost the same diversity of motifs being introduced. In the Italian version—and sometimes in the French— climbs up to heaven on a bean stalk and obtains concessions from God or heaven's gatekeeper. But in all versions of the story the growing extravagances of the wife and their consequences are emphasized.

[5] Aurelio M. Espinosa has analyzed the tar baby theme in 267 versions collected throughout the world. From his study he concludes that the story is of Hindu origin, despite the fact that many believe it had its origin in Africa from whence the slaves brought it to the New World. It was also brought to many areas by the Spaniards who already knew it, as is proved by various versions collected in Spain. For more detailed information on the tar baby theme, the reader is referred to two of Espinosa's articles: ''The Tar-Baby Story,'' *Journal of American Folklore*, XLII (1930), 129-209; and ''The Tar-Baby Story: A New Classification of Two Hundred and Sixty-Seven Versions,'' *Journal of American Folklore*, LVI (1943), pp. 31-37.

[6] Joel Chandler Harris' ''The Wonderful Tar Baby,'' which appeared in the first edition of *Uncle Remus* (1880), has Brer Rabbit mock pleading that he not be thrown into the briar patch.

An Interview with

Women Writers in Colombia

By

RAYMOND L. WILLIAMS

University of Kansas

The International Women's Year was precisely that, the year of the woman, in reference to recent Colombian fiction. The young Colombian novelist Albalucia Angel gained national attention in the land of García Márquez and Mejía Vallejo by winning the award sponsored by the magazine *Vivencias* for the best Colombian novel in 1975 with *Estaba la pájara pinta sentada en el verde limón*. The title is based on a well known nursery rhyme, translated into English as *The Colored Bird Was Sitting on the Green Lemon Tree*. On the other hand, her young compatriot Fanny Buitrago had just won the national context for short story sponsored by *El Tiempo*.

These two writers form part of a new generation of young writers that follows García Márquez, which includes Gustavo Alvarez Gardeazabal, Hector Sánchez, Benhur Sánchez, Oscar Collazos and Marco Tulio Aguilera Garramuño, among others. Fanny Buitrago was the most precocious of all, having published at the age of eighteen a novel about the youth of her generation *El hostigante verano de los dioses* [*The Harrassing Summer of the Gods*] in 1963, which scandalized a conservative reading public in Colombia with its decadence and sexual candidness. Her second novel, *Cola de zorro* [*The Fox's Tail*], 1970, was a finalist for the Seix Barral Prize in 1968, and in it she exercises a now mature manipulation of narrative technique in a study of a family from various tempo-spatial levels. Albalucia Angel's fiction is also characterized by a progressive maturity from her first experiment, *Los girasoles en invierno* [*Sunflowers in Winter*], 1970, to the more accomplished *Dos veces Alicia* [*Alice Twice Over*], 1972, a game at several levels—with narrative technique, with distinct planes of reality, with the reader himself. Her most recent prize-winning novel is a study of the period of "the

Violence'' in Colombia which features the innovation that typifies this young generation of novelists.

Here the two foremost women writers in Colombia discuss their fiction, their "demons" as Mario Vargas Llosa calls them, and their situation in Colombia—problems like the "myth" of García Márquez in their country, and the fact that they are now influential intellectuals in a country where men have always dominated.

RLW: Why don't we start with this common interest in Lewis Carroll? I've noticed you both quote Carroll in your novels.

Angel: Lewis Carroll is an unforgettable childhood fantasy because *Alice in Wonderland* is one of the most fascinating aspects of childhood. When talking with people of my generation they have told me they were even afraid of *Alice in Wonderland.* I certainly wasn't afraid of it, but was fascinated, and when I went to England it happened to be the centennial of the publication of *Alice Through the Looking Glass* so I relived this English world of Lewis Carroll. They did a lot of publications and presented a beautiful special on T.V. with an extraordinary version of *Alice* and I was writing a novel at the time, so I included her as an element, once again: it was something fascinating, newly discovered.

Buitrago: I've always been a great reader of children's stories, not only when I was young, but they still entertain me a lot. There are certain books I always turn to when I'm bored; one of them is *Alice in Wonderland* which I always have at hand. I really like it because it's a model to get away from the daily routine of writing.

RLW: But couldn't all this be considered a matter of simple escapism?

Angel: Lewis Carroll was a master of logic, and the escapism of Alice to the world of the illogical, the world of the mirror, was a totally real reflection for me. I didn't consider it escapism, but rather a "real invention" as Mario Vargas Llosa would say. It was my childhood truth; a reality. As Fanny says, it has served as a model and example for me, within this children's literature. *Alice in Wonderland* (or *The Little Prince,* also one of the first-rate books) just wasn't an escape from reality. I considered it very serious. That's why I consider my novel *Alice Twice Over* a very serious game, emulating Carroll's system quite openly. I'm not so sure it's strictly for children.

Buitrago: Well, I do consider it a little escapist because *Alice in Wonderland* confronts me with my own childhood. I lied a lot as a child because, of course, I had a lot of imagination. I lived in a boarding school in a boring world, surrounded by boring people whom I didn't like, so most of the time I really lived in a fabricated world in which I liked to think I was Alice, living more in Wonderland than in the real world.

RLW: Would you call the youth in *The Fox's Tail* escapists?

Buitrago: The youth in *The Fox's Tail* are more than anything young Colombians. They live with one foot in reality and the other in escapism. They are in general a very tortured and very solitary youth.

RLW: Considering more of these "demons" of the past—we just can't discuss "demons" in Colombia without necessarily bringing up the subject of García Márquez. Everyone here talks a great deal about the "big dark shadow" he has left for the young writers who are attempting to write in this country after the overwhelming popularity and success of *One Hundred Years of Solitude.* How do you confront this supposed problem?

Angel: It's indisputable that the world of Gabriel García Márquez, being clearly Colombian (and as Fanny says, this escape from reality that Colombia lives, with one foot in one part and the other in another) makes it almost impossible for a writer in this country to avoid being behind this fantastic universe. But it is reality too. I think a lot of writers have suffered Gabo's impact, not only in Colombia, but the rest of the world. Gabo's themes are both hallucinating and hallucinative. For us, the hallucinated, it all seems more normal. All of these stories are the ones we call "ol' ladies' stories," so fabulously transcribed with Gabo's technique. The interesting part is the literary procedure with which Gabo armed this unreality that is so much ours. Inevitably each of us has a part of this history that is quite similar. In my own case, the history of Pereira (Colombia) and the founding of my town could be classified a Macondian saga. Each of us must translate this saga, each in his own language and his own style, which is difficult too, since each of us is vulnerable to those "demons." First is the problem of the history, which is ours and we all have in common, and second, the problem of copying the style and this irrefutable mastery with which Gabo was able to arm his story. A lot of writers don't make it, but I think that by starting from this base, the style of García Márquez, we can fabricate stories that are also Colombian, but with other styles and in other ways we'll start finding new outlooks. It's difficult, because a master is a master, and I consider the influence of Gabo very beneficiary, although many of us have had to work hard to go beyond it.

Buitrago: I think this "shadow" of Gabo, as Ray says, isn't so ominous except as seen by the critics and pseudocritics here in Colombia that before reading a book, start with the prejudice that the writer must necessarily be domesticated beforehand by the style of García Márquez. So what happens is that before a new writer even has time to get off the ground they immediately pigeonhole him as copying García Márquez's style, which in the majority of the cases is foolish because all of us in Colombia and America have the same roots, the same ancestors, the same history, and besides that, the same "demons." Gabo's technique is very Gabo, but nevertheless, one can appreciate the beginnings of this type of writing in writers like Fuenmayor and Rojas Herazo. It might be more valid to use the environment as a point of departure, not García Márquez. In my personal case these pseudocritics have done me great harm because now I don't dare read García Márquez. I irrevocably no longer read him because I'm scared to death tomorrow or the day after I'll mix in some paragraph from García Márquez. So it upsets me terribly because I like reading him a lot.

RLW: I suppose that being women and at the same time being intellectuals in this country— and successful intellectuals—you have confronted problems. Have you had, might we say, any reaction?

Angel: Yes. I've had a personal reaction of fear because the title here becomes quite grandiose and grandiose titles probably don't fit me very well. I would prefer being a writer, nothing more. That is, an intellectual to the extent that one is conscious of truly having a broad knowledge of history, life, and the profession—a broad knowledge that might help others.

Buitrago: Yes, I've confronted violent reactions, not only against my books, but against myself as a person. Everyone expects extraordinary things of a writer. They expect you to know about philosophy, about new literary tendencies, about gymnastics, economics, didacticism. All of this is completely absurd. Besides, in this case, one sees the tendency to think the writer has to be a kind of walking library, and in this country no one has been able to distinguish literature from reality. So they think you must necessarily have experienced what you write. If I write a violent love scene in a book, it is assumed I've experienced all this, and it happens I just haven't had time yet. What can we do? I haven't lived all these experiences—if I'm writing about an assassination, then supposedly I must have seen who knows how many assassinations. So everybody demands explanations. Everyone feels superior: a complete stranger on the street will harrass you, or insult you, or perhaps become overly friendly to you. Well, in the final analysis it's a little unpleasant being a woman writer in this country. It's best to go out only from time to time because otherwise they'll eat you alive.

RLW: Have you been particularly interested in women writers? Who are your feminine "demons"?

Angel: A lot. As far as the great demons of women's literature, the first and foremost one that has affected me is Virginia Woolf. After that come Natalie Sarraute, Christiane Rochefort and Ana María Matute. When I was young the stories of Ana María Matute and Carmen Laforet impressed me a lot. I follow them; I follow them a lot. Also Susan Hill and Doris Lessing in England, and Elena Poniatowska and Silvina Bullrich. Yes, I have great feminine demons and I've always been interested in following this literature. I think it has a great strength. It is called feminine literature, that is, written by women, but it doesn't have sex. Virginia Woolf, for example, demonstrated this great duality in her masterpiece *Orlando.*

Buitrago: Well, Abalucia's answer has left me stunned because although I am acquainted with most of those names, the only ones I really read are Virginia Woolf and Silvina Bullrich. I suppose I just haven't run across the others because my favorite writers are men.

RLW: Why haven't there been any women writers in the "boom"?

Angel: There haven't been any women writers in the boom because it hasn't occurred yet to any editor: they just haven't hit upon the idea.

Buitrago: I think it's more a problem of a mafia. Among the writers there is a kind of very tight cord, not only abroad, but also in Colombia. These solid groups are formed that are always willing to support each other, but they don't consider it necessary to include women because of their *machismo*, because they still operate on the basis that women are still just a little inferior. However, among other curiosities, Albalucia Angel, sitting there, and Fanny Buitrago, sitting here, dispelled this myth in Colombia because the two most important recent literary prizes were won my women: last year I won the short story prize and now Albalucia has won the novel prize, defying all those who call themselves writers in this country. So I think we can begin to fight the myth now. We just have to start breaking it down, just as we broke down the idea that masculine writers had to win the literary prizes because they were the only ones that knew about literature, because they were the big names, because they were "heavy", without realizing that the writer doesn't have a sex.

RLW: Is Colombia *machista?*

Angel: I think so.

RLW: How is it expressed?

Angel: On numerous levels. Colombia is *machista*, but in the last few years I've been surprised to see the women occupying key posts in several areas. She can now be a minister, a governor, or a director of a museum. I've seen a great advance in the last ten years. So despite the fact that men continue being *machista*, and despite the fact that they continue laughing at all these old ladies who should be knitting socks instead of trying to work in literature (as one critic said recently), well, the old ladies continue. The Colombian woman has an admirable strength and stubbornness. And besides that, and this is very essential, they are very intelligent. We have La Tertulia organized by women in Cali; we have Gloria Zea managing Colcultura; there are many women in politics, doing things and manipulating things. Now we even have a woman as minister of the Department of Labor, a post that was apparently strictly for men, and at first they retaliated. The men said "no," these old ladies just think they have the power, what do they know about politics? But our actions have proven us to be capable. The *machismo* continues, as do the attacks, and the criticism is always at the personal level, always aimed at the feminine part of the personality. But women here just haven't given up. Nevertheless, men continue being *machista* in many respects—even from the way they handle marriage, this pairing that should be so balanced. At all social levels the man is the head, the man dominates. And today in Western European civilizations the man *isn't* the one who dominates. The woman is equal and a value in the home and at the same time enjoys a balanced responsibility at work. Yes, it is definitely very *machista* here. And all Latin America is very *machista*.

Buitrago: Albalucia has given a fairly complete explanation, so I'm going to give a little more detail concerning *machismo* in Colombia. I think men here are *machista* more because of their education than from pure conviction. Mothers here inculcate *machismo*—it's strange, the mothers themselves—in their sons from when they are very young. Usually a boy is served by his sisters so he is practically a useless little beauty for whom absolutely everything is done; from choosing his socks and clothes to having his meals hot at the time he happens to come home. So our men are raised with the idea that women are objects to serve them and praise them, only to find out later that the women in their homes are not only capable of thinking, but are also from time to time as intelligent as they are. So the breakdown between this education and the reality that has come upon them recently, as Albalucia has explained, was a rude awakening, but it is something they have accepted with courage, although of course, fighting all the way. But we're fighting too. Their defense is always the same: women are made to have children; women are made to cook; women are made to show off. But in the end, they always prefer an intelligent woman at their side.

RLW: Is there a feminist movement in Colombia?

Buitrago: I would say there is more an uneasiness, a feeling of the necessity to move forward. Colombian women have shown they can move ahead in many fields so there's no use repeating what we've already said. But there isn't a feminist's *feminist* movement because Colombian women are very self-indulgent—perhaps the most self-indulgent women in Latin America. And the Colombian woman, despite her screaming and shouting that it isn't true, is fascinated not only having a man at her side, but also in having that all-important prestigious last name her husband will give her. And especially within the middle class they love to have a man who will maintain them with the very best of everything. This is so much the case that quite often marriage is determined by who can pay all these expenses. There are also cases in which women with a career background forget their career the moment they marry. They simply contract a man to work for them. So we return to the story of *machismo*—they nourish *machismo*, but they live beautifully from it.

Angel: I agree with Fanny. Although I haven't lived in Colombia the last few years, I see things the same, and just wanted to add that I hope there isn't ever a feminist movement in Colombia, with all this screaming, but rather simply a study of vindication for the woman, and then to continue, as Fanny says, in a balanced way. Man is really the complement, man is the great friend, the antipode, the antagonist. So how are we going to live without him? I don't think we can make an Amazon society. Never! May God free us from that, as my grandmother always said.

WOMEN POETS

SILVIA BARROS

Silvia A. Barros was born at the Washington sugar refinery, Las Villas, Cuba, in 1939, and graduated as a Kindergarten teacher in Santa Clara, Cuba, in 1958. While working as a teacher she finished and published her first book of poems, *Veintisiete pulgadas de vacío* [*Twenty seven Inches of Emptiness*](La Habana: Editorial El Puente, 1961). From that date to 1962 she worked first with the Guanabacoa Guinol Group and later with the Guinol de Cuba, doing all kinds of activities in theater for children. "Copito", her first play for children, was staged in 1962 by that group. From 1962 to 1966 she was a writer of children's plays for the Consejo Nacional de Cultura, while working also as a consultant in children's literature and a teacher of puppetry for the teachers of Círculos Infantiles. In 1965 she published her second book, *Teatro Infantil* [*Children's Theater*](La Habana: Editorial El Puente), and finished an unpublished book of stories for children, "La pajarita de papel" ["The Little Paper Bird"]. That year she also staged a version of a Cuban negro folktale, "La loma de Mambiala" ["Mambiala's Hill"] for adult audiences. In 1967 she moved to Spain where she worked as a teacher of creative dramatics and puppetry with children of several schools. In 1968 she moved to the United States where she obtained her Bachelors Degree at Hunter College in 1971, and her Master of Arts in 1973 from The Graduate School of The City University of New York where she is currently enrolled as a Ph.D. Candidate in Comparative Literature. She has worked as Lecturer at Hunter College, CUNY for two years and also at Mercy College at Dobbs Ferry in the Department of Romance Languages. Her essay "La literatura para niños de José Martí en su época" [' 'Children's Literature of José Martí' '] appears in *Estudios críticos sobre la prosa modernista hispanoamericana* [*Critical Studies on Hispanic American Modernist Prose*], edited by J. O. Jiménez (New York: Eliseo Torres and Sons, 1975). She has two unpublished books of poems: "Maromas y musarañas," N.Y. 1973, and "Escrito con la uña" ["Written with my nail"], N.Y. 1974, to which the two poems included in this anthology belong.

Cuando adivinas el por qué cae el parpado
y lo insoportable del esfuerzo
eres más yo que tú
y te quiero...
Este volverme tú
(el doble pincho del ancla del barco)
va en círculos que se salen por las ventanas
va en bufidos
que saltan dimensiones en lo aglomerado del espacio
alcanza allá
y trasciende
y se muda de un elemento a otro
y se hace anices...

Y luego todo vuelve
ya pequeño
ya gastado
y se mete en la manchita parda de tu seno
como aguja en el blanco

Silvia Barros

When you guess why the eyelid falls
and how unbearable is the effort
you are more me than you
and I love you...
This becoming you
(dual prong of ship's anchor)
goes in circles that exit through windows
in bellows
that leap dimensions in the conglomeration of space
reaches there
and transcends
and changes from one element to another
and shatters...

And later all returns
already diminished
already wasted
and crawls into the small, dark stain of your breast
like a needle in the target

(English version by Robert Lima)

Son tiernos los oídos de las palomas
y cuando gritas
y revientas la puerta contra el marco
ellas escuchan el pistoletazo del silencio

Por mí no temas
yo solo tengo oídos para la brisa
cuando está en calma

Silvia Barros

The ears of doves are tender
and when you scream
and shatter the door against its frame
they hear the pistol-shot of silence

No matter to me
I have ears only for the breeze
when it is stilled.

(English version by Robert Lima)

Angela de Hoyos

Angela de Hoyos, painter and poet, was born in Coahuila, Mexico, of predominantly Spanish parents, but she has lived since childhood in San Antonio, Texas, where she maintains an art studio. She attended San Antonio College and also received private instruction. She has received various art and literary awards. Most recent is the 2nd Prize for Poetry, CSSI International Competition, Italy. For the past five years she has served on the Board of Translators of World Poetry Society, translating the works of contemporary Spanish-speaking writers. Her poems and translations have appeared in: *Modern Poetry in Translation, Orbis* (England): *Poema Convidado* (in Portuguese translation); *Revista Chicano-Riqueña* (Indiana University, Northwest); *Mele* (University of Hawaii); *Cauce* (Peru); *Ediciones Cosmos* (Universidad Veracruzana, Mexico); *Poésie Sonore Genève*(Switzerland) in French translation; *Esparavel* (Colombia) in Spanish translation; etc.

Books published: *Arise, Chicano and Other Poems* (Indiana: Backstage Books, 1975) - (bilingual edition, Spanish translation by Mireya Robles); *Chicano Poems: For the Barrio* (Indiana: Backstage Books, 1975); *Time, The Artisan|Tiempo artesano* (translation from the Spanish) bilingual edition, (Austin, Texas: Dissemination Center For Bilingual Bicultural Education, 1975); *While Springtime Sleeps* (translation from the Spanish *Mientras Duerme la Primavera*: Teresinha Pereira) (Texas: Editorial Azteca, 1975); *Help, I'm Drowning!* - (translation of five short stories from the works of Teresinha Pereira) (Chicago: Palos Heights Press, 1975).

Plaquettes: *La risa final* - poetry (in Spanish translation by Mireya Robles) (Universidad Veracruzana, Mexico: Ediciones Cosmos, 1974); *Poems| Poemas* - (Bilingual Edition, Spanish translations by Marta Milesi) (Buenos Aires, Argentina: Ediciones La Rosa Blanca, 1975).

THE MISSING INGREDIENT

Geared to the sterility
of machine-made symbols,
out of his element he was
—victim of a daily trauma.

Become maladroit
at calling his own cards
robot-like, he was seeking

(lost in a ticker-tape mountain
of mundane ideas:
love-thine-enemy policies
hypocritical handshakes
social-science amenities
and e pluribus unum)

a formula infallible
for painless living.

When before him there appeared
the guardian-ghost of alchemy
who—surveying the situation—
transmuted life's baser metals,
extracting the gold of Wisdom
from the heap.

ANGELA DE HOYOS
(2nd Prize - CSSI International Poetry Competition-1974)

EL INGREDIENTE AUSENTE

Atado a la esterilidad
de símbolos fabricados
permanecía fuera de su circunstancia
—víctima de un trauma cotidiano.

Sin destreza
para poner sus cartas sobre la mesa,
como un robot, buscaba

(perdido en una montaña de cintas magnéticas
de ideas mundanas:
el sistema de ''ama a tu enemigo''
hipócritas apretones de mano
amenidades de la ciencia social
y e pluribus unum)

infalible fórmula
para una vida sin dolor.

Cuando delante de él apareció
el ángel guardián de la alquimia
quien—midiendo la situación—
transmutó los metales inferiores de la vida,
extrayendo el oro de la Sabiduría
de entre el montón.

ANGELA DE HOYOS
(Translated from the English by Mireya Robles)

THE FINAL LAUGH

On an empty stomach,
with the pang of mendicant yesterdays,
I greet my reflection
in the dark mirror of dusk.

What do the entrails know
about the necessity of being white
- the advisability of mail-order parents?

Or this wearing in mock defiance
the thin rag of ethnic pride,
saying to shivering flesh and grumbling belly:
Patience, O companions of my dignity?

Perhaps someday I shall accustom myself
to this: my hand held out
in eternal supplication, being content
with the left-overs of a greedy establishment.

Or - who knows? - perhaps tomorrow
I shall burst these shackles
and rising to my natural full height
fling the final parting laugh
O gluttonous omnipotent alien white world.

ANGELA DE HOYOS

LA RISA FINAL

El estómago vacío,
con espasmo de mendigos ayeres,
me enfrento a mi reflejo
en el oscuro espejo del atardecer.

Qué saben las entrañas
de la necesidad de ser blanco
—de la ventaja de padres escogidos?

O de llevar, en escarnecido desafío
el fino trapo de orgullo étnico
diciéndole a la carne estremecida y al rugiente estómago:
Paciencia, compañeros de mi dignidad?

Tal vez un día me acostumbre
a esto: mis mano extendidas
en eterna súplica, contentándose
con las sobras del avaricioso dueño del poder.

O— quién sabe? - tal vez mañana
rompa las cadenas
y me eleve a mi talla auténtica
y lance en mi partida, mi risa final
al vorazmente insaciable, omnipotente, ajeno mundo de los blancos

ANGELA DE HOYOS

(Translated from the English by Mireya Robles)

PROBLEMS OF ETIQUETTE

The mail-order houses
do a healthy business
along with newspapers, magazines,
and sundry publications
advertising all manner
of delightful inducements:

The All-American game.
A vacation-for-two in Acapulco.
The 'fly now-pay later' plan.
Typewriter ribbons, cheaper
by the dozen. Prompt delivery.
Etceteras. Millions of
happy customers. Satisfaction
guaranteed.

You name it: your happiness awaits you
like a friendly diamond
ready to be tried on for size.

I shall order me
a king-size platter of happiness
-and when it finally arrives
like an Epicurean delight
placed before me

by a smiling waitress
I will probably sprout
a nervous fit
wondering which fork
to use first.

                          ANGELA DE HOYOS

PROBLEMAS DE ETIQUETA

Las casas encargadas por correo
producen saludables ganancias
conjuntamente con los periódicos, revistas,
y un surtido de publicaciones
anunciando toda clase
de atractivas seducciones:

El calculado 'modus vivendi' americano.
Vacaciones para dos en Acapulco.
"Viaja ahora y paga después".
Cintas de máquinas de escribir, más baratas
por docena. Entrega inmediata.
Etcéteras. Millones de
clientes satisfechos. Satisfacción
garantizada.

Menciona lo que se te ocurra: la felicidad te espera
como una amistosa sortija de diamantes
que se prueba para calcular la medida exacta.

Ordenaré
una enorme bandeja de felicidad
-y cuando llegue, al fin,
como una exquisitez epicúrea
presentada
por una sontiente camarera
probablemente me convulsione
un ataque de nervios
ante el dilema de escoger el tenedor
que habré de usar primero.

                          ANGELA DE HOYOS
            (Translated from the English by Mireya Robles)

BRINDIS: FOR THE BARRIO

"Y cuándo nos veremos con los demás, al borde
de una mañana eterna, desayunados todos."
LA CENA MISERABLE: César Vallejo

Brothers, today we drink
the fresh milk of dawn
-for once, not tasting
of sourness.

For once,
the table is set
with plates full of hope,
and in our illiterate hands
some kind fate has placed
a promise of gold for tomorrow.

Not that the hollows
in your sad face of death
will ever be filled
-or the seedy, stale figure
of the poor
feel at ease in fine clothes-

but today we eat
to soothe a pain
-a pain of alien-hungers
Vallejo never knew...

ANGELA DE HOYOS

BRINDIS: POR EL BARRIO

"Y cuándo nos veremos con los demás, al borde
de una mañana eterna, desayunados todos."
LA CENA MISERABLE: César Vallejo

Hermanos, tomamos hoy
la fresca leche del amanecer
-por vez primera, sin sabor
a agrio.

Por vez primera
la mesa puesta
con platos llenos de esperanza,
y en nuestras manos analfabetas
algún noble destino ha depositado
una dorada promesa para el mañana.

No es que las cuencas
de vuestro triste rostro de muerte
llenarán su vacío
-ni la rasgada, rancia figura
del pobre
se acomodará entre finas vestiduras-

pero hoy cenamos
para calmar la pena
-la pena de remotas hambres
que Vallejo nunca llegó a conocer.

ANGELA DE HOYOS

(Translated from the English by Mireya Robles)

BELOW ZERO

No se puede traducir
el aullido del viento:
>   you can only feel it
>   piercing your skinny bones
>   through last year's coat
>   papel-de-China
walking to work
from deep in the barrio
una mañana de tantas
>   bajo cero.

ANGELA DE HOYOS

BLUES IN THE BARRIO

Con la mañana oscura,
en su delantal blanco,
Mama rolls out tortillas
>   paper-thin
>   as her hope.

Atiza la lumbre
warming yesterday's
left-pver beans.

"Dios mío, qué más les doy?"
it is more a reproach
than a prayer
>   on her silent lips

-a cry, inaudible
like the specter of fear
that chills her bones:
Never enough food to fill
a plate, ni hoy
ni mañana
ni después...
Tonight she will kiss
with the flame of her faith
the warm crucifix at her throat:
"...porque no le falte a mi niño."

ANGELA DE HOYOS

WHO KILLED BROWN LOVE?

I did
-dijo el hombre blanco-
with my little knife

cuchillito de palo
slowly but surely
magullando.

ANGELA DE HOYOS
(from "CHICANO POEMS: FOR THE BARRIO" by the author

MAYA ISLAS

(Maya Islas is the pen name of Omara Valdivia)

Maya Islas was born in Cabaiguan, Las Villas, Cuba on April 12, 1947. She came to the United States in 1965, and got her B.A. degree in Psychology at Fairleigh Dickinson University. Now she is working for her Master's degree at Montclair State College, New Jersey; also, she is a part-time adjunct instructor in Spanish at Elizabeth Seton College, Yonkers, New York. *Publications:*

Book "Sola, Desnuda, Sin Nombre", [Alone, Nude, Without Name] 100 poems, Editorial Mensaje, New York, 1947.

She has published articles and poems in the Spanish newspapers of New York. Selected for poetry readings at the Second Festival of Cuban Art in New York, Cathedral St. John the Divine, June 1974.

Her unpublished book "Gaviota" classified finalist in the Poetry Award Juan Boscan 1974 celebrated in Spain.

Her poem, "Kant me hablo de ti" won third prize, category C, in the *Literary Awards Sigma Delta Pi*, University of Maine, 1975.

Some of her poems have been translated into Portuguese and published in the poetry magazine *PC 5, PC 6,* from Indiana. Others have been published in *La Letra Nueva* from Argentina, *Esparavel* from Colombia, *Days of Milk and Honey* from Michigan.

She participated in poetry reading at the Conference of Women Writers from Latin America, presented by the *Latin American Literary Review* at Carnegie-Mellon University, Pittsburgh, Penna., March 1975.

Her bio-bibliography will be included in the *World Who's Who of Authors,* International Biographical Centre, Cambridge, England, and in the *Community Leaders and Noteworthy Americans.*

> Piedra de granos amargados,
> cuadriculados.....
> has limado mis uñas

con tus golpes invisibles,
mascándome en tu sátira
de naturaleza-crimen.
Abstracta yerba te transformas
rozando el primitivo de los siglos,
y te acomodas
en la herida tonta de mi necesidad.
Piedra de granos amargados,
cuadriculados.....
eres lapso en mi estómago de miedos,
perturbas mis movimientos
con tus sádicos momentos de omnipotencia;
no puedo.....piedra
cargarte del camino
y escupirte a espacios que no sean míos,
si te llevo.....
inventaré a mis manos hierros nuevos
para romperte entrañas
y con el tiempo,
que ruedes triturada
.....devuelta al origen de tu arena.

                                  Maya Islas

Stone of embittered particles,
in quadrants...
you've filed my nails
with your invisible blows,
chewing me up in your satire
of nature-crime.
Abstract grass yourself transform
barely touching origins of centuries,
yourself accommodate
in the foolish wound of my necessity.
Stone of embittered particles,
in quadrants...
you are a lapse in my stomach of fears,
perturbing my movements
with your sadistic moments of omnipotence;
stone...I can't
lift you from the path
and spit you beyond spaces that are mine,
if I bear you...
I'll invent new irons with my hands

to smash your core
so that with time,
you may tumble on pulverized
...returned to origins of sand.

(English version by Robert Lima)

Del libro inédito "Gaviota"

Estoy en la euforia de tus alas blancas
rebuscándote paisajes.....
Me enternece el doblaje de tu cielo preso,
y tu silencio.....de tan hueco, bullicioso.....
Me corro a tus libertades,
y en el aire bueno de tus días prestados
¡estoy aprendiendo a romperte las tristezas!
.....estás aprendiendo a morirte en mi.....
.....y a re-encontrarnos.....

I am in the euphoria of your white wings
searching for you landscapes,
how tender the bending of your imprisoned sky,
and your silence...being so hollow, noisy...
I run towards your liberties
and in the good air of your borrowed days
I'm learning to shatter your sorrows!
....you are learning to die within me....
....and to re-find us.

                                        Maya Islas

TERESINHA PEREIRA

Teresinha Pereira is a Brazilian poet and playwright. She has resided in the United States since 1960. She has a Ph.D. from The University of New Mexico in Spanish and she taught Luso-Brazilian Literature and Portuguese at Stanford University, at Tulane and Georgetown University. Now she is teaching at the University of Colorado at Boulder. She has published a number of books in Brazil, Portugal, Mexico and Colombia. In 1972 she was awarded the Brazilian Naitonal Playwright Prize. Several of her books, "Anti-Poem For Christmas And Other Non-Christmas Poems" (translated by Russell Tarby), "Lines Of A Broken Alphabet", "While Springtime Sleeps" (translated by Angela de Hoyos, "Alien", "The Falcons Swoop In" (translated by David Wade) "Help, I'm Drowning!" (translated by Angela de Hoyos) have been published in the United States. She has one book translated into Swedish: ("Pa Mina Landsflyktiga Vägar" (translated by Carl-Erik Sjöberg) and published in Göteborg, Sweden and another pulbished in France: "Mauvais Sang" (translated by Albert Chantraine). Teresinha Pereira is the editor of *Poema Convidado*, a poetry magazine that publishes international poetry translated to Portuguese.

AUSTIN: CIUDAD AJENA

La ciudad no se había organizado.
La veía innoble, perdida, sin tocar los intercambios
del tiempo.
Otrora verano, hoy pura nieve: cinco años pasados!
No te puedo reconocer!

En la jornada de la angustia
veo árboles que se cubren con mis ojos.
Mi palabra era un viento en la llanura

y era de mi que partían los olvidos.
Ciudad: no me recuerdes tampoco!

Una blasfemia corta y el sol se oculta.
Hay en este lugar una incapacidad para aprender
las razones del odio.
Me cogen por los gritos, tíranme en el vacío.
Ciudad, Austin. No te quiero conocer.

Teresinha Alves Pereira

AUSTIN: FOREIGN CITY

The city had not organized itself.
I beheld it motionless, lost, untouching interchanges
of time.
Once summer, now pure snow: five years lapsed!
I can't recognize you!

In the span of anguish
I see trees covering themselves with my eyes.
My word was a wind on the plain
and oblivion came out of me.
City: don't remember me either!

A brief blasphemy and the sun hides itself.
Here there's an inability to learn
the rationale of hate.
They grab me by screams, throw me into nothingness.
City, Austin. I don't want to know you.

(English version by Robert Lima)

NOTICIAS DE MI PUEBLO

Mil compañeros en la carcel.

Oración por ellos:
Señor, no habitaré la tierra que diste a mis hermanos
y de mi pueblo sacaré mis alegrías;
le entregaré en cambio mi coraje
y esta lluvia de mi loca esperanza.

Les echaré mi corazón de carne,
les entregaré en la plaza mis ojos y mi lengua
- despúes seguiré por ellos tus preceptos

para cantar el amor por la libertad del hombre,
aunque con mi sed de justicia
·sienta también, de lejos, que ellos en la carcel,
están más libres que yo en tierra ajena.

Teresinha Alves Pereira

NEWS FROM MY TOWN

A thousand companions in jail.

Prayer on their behalf:
Lord, I won't inhabit the earth you gave my brothers
and I'll withdraw my joy from my town;
in exchange I'll give my courage
and this downpour of my crazed hope.

I'll throw them my heart of flesh,
I'll turn over my eyes and tongue in the plaza
-afterwards I'll follow your precepts for their sake
to sing out love for mankind's freedom,
although with my thirst for justice
I may also feel, from afar, that in their cells
they are far freer than I in this foreign land.

(English version by Robert Lima)

Mireya Robles

Born in Guantanamo, Cuba. She has published poems, short stories and articles in literary magazines, anthologies and journals in several countries including: *Nuevos narradores cubanos*, anthology, Miami; *La última poesía cubana*, anthology, Madison; *Voces de mañana*, anthology, New York; *Poet*, India; *Norte*, Holland; *Revista de Occidente, Papeles de Son Armadans, Azor, Fablas, Tarotdequinze, Ioseph, Caracola, Nueva etapa, Base 6, La voz de Castilla, Poesía hispánica*, Spain; *Il gironale dei poeti*, Italy; *Marginals*, Belgium; *Poesie Sonore*, Switzerland; *Conjonction*, Haiti; *Abside, Cuadernos Americanos*, México; *Entre nosotros, Briarcliff Literary Review, Envíos, Cuervo Internacional, La Nueva Sangre, Nueva generación, Star-West, International Poetry Review*, USA; *Poesía de Venezuela, Arbol de Fuego*, Venezuela; *Razón y Fábula, Thesaurus, Esparavel, Esquirla, Arco,* Colombia; *Boreal*, Canada; *Crónica, S.A.L.A.C., La rosa blanca, Letra nueva,* Argentina; *Ceiba, La ventana, El Día,* Puerto Rico; *Folha Nova,* Brazil; *Days of Milk and Honey, Puerto Norte y Sur, Revista Chicano-Riqueña, Siempre, Poema Convidado,* USA; *Le journal de Poètes, Fantasmagie*, Belgium; *Profils Poétiques des Pays Latins, Cadáver dichoso,* France; *Península, Guardelave,* Perú. Selections of her works have been translated into French, Basque, Catalonian, Portuguese, English, and Italian. She has received several international awards: A gold medal for several unpublished books of poetry, short stories and essays from L'Academie Internationale de Lutèce (Paris); Silarus (Italy); Xilote (Mexico); Círculo de Poetas y Escritores Iberoamericanos de New York; Sigma Delta Pi (University of Maine); Finalist in Poetry: Ciudad de Barcelona, Diario de León (Spain); and short stories: Diario La Verdad (Spain); Finalist: Juan Boscán Poetry Award (Spain). She has published three books of poetry: *Petits Poèmes* (France); *Tiempo Artesano* (Spain); *Time, the Artisan*, bilingual edition translated by Angela de Hoyos, sponsored by Dissemination Center for Bilingual and Bicultural Education, Austin. She teaches at Briarcliff College.

Cuando sólo se llenan las horas
y la vida vacía
y en la boca el polvo
y la alegría de otro
y siempre aquél
y siempre el otro
y yo en el sudor de mi camisa
y el pan no ha llegado todavía
y nos mordemos las venas hasta sangre
y siempre el caminar del mediodía
y la cabeza baja
y en cada ceja el hambre
y siempre deshabitando pasos
siempre deshabitando
hasta mirar de frente este vacío.

                    Mireya Robles

When the hours are only being filled
and life's emptiness
and in our mouths the dust
and someone else's joy
and always that other one
and always someone else
and I in the sweat of my shirt
and bread has not yet arrived
and we bite our veins until blood
and always the treading at highnoon
and the bowed head
and the empty arms
and on every brow the hunger
and always uninhabiting the footsteps
always uninhabiting
until squarely facing this emptiness.

                    (Translated by Angela de Hoyos)

Pidámosle silencio al miedo
--tu ausencia rompe el asombro
   para doler de cerca

hiere en vuelo:
　punto tiempo horizonte madrugada
Pidámosle silencio al miedo,
que no suene en el cordón de mis zapatos
cuando digo:　niña, corre, el abecedario a cuestas
y en el plano inclinado se descarna
tu muerte
en el dos tan frágil de la tarde
Jugabas a llorar tempranamente
sin dedos para contar el aliento de los otros
y tú, tan niña, muriendo eternamente
Escucho golpe a golpe,
las horas me despiertan
y digo, muerte, Neruda,
y aun no la conoces
y sigues muriéndote hacia dentro
un poco, hacia dentro.

Mireya Robles

Let us ask fear to be silent
--your absence breaks through the dread
　to bring pain near
it wounds time in flight:
　point time horizon dawn
Let us ask fear to be silent
so it won't sound in the string of my shoes
when I say:　run, little girl, the abc's on your back
and in the inclined plane
your death scrapes flesh
in the noon's two o'clock so fragile
Prematurely you played at crying
without fingers to count the breath of others
and you, so young, eternally dying
I hear blow after blow,
the hours awake me,
and I say, death, Neruda,
and still you do not know death
and you keep on dying inwardly
a little, inwardly.

(Translated by Angela de Hoyos)

IN THE OTHER HALF OF TIME

By:

MIREYA ROBLES

The woman with Carthaginian eyes was looking towards the sea, and her gaze extended through many centuries. It was a ritual. It was a rite. A rite. To meet with the past in the silent vastness, in the vague murmur of briny foam. The morning, fresh, and the silence profiling her contours. She knew that she had lived many re-incarnations and the past, without file-cards in its fingers, did away with data. But there she was, the weight of millenary tensions, and the sea. And above all, that sensation of destiny: a certain place and a date. Like a tryst, concerted prior to birth. It was just a matter of meeting. It was a matter of converting the daily death into expectancy. It was a matter of visualizing the silhouette of that other being, at the other end of the tenseness of time, plowing through breath and space, or immobile, overcoming the wounds of a stagnant yearning, re-tracing the veins of the skin to rest in the warmth of the hands. The meeting. It was a matter of meeting. And beyond, on the shore, the moist sand seemed to contain all the atoms of the echo. Resonance, voice: reply. The woman, untouched by common hands that roll pennies and coins, let herself be caressed by the air, by a breeze that penetrated her deep silence. Behind had remained the house that once in other centuries had been inhabited by slaves. Rites to the African deities. Possessions of spirits that spoke through the voice of the medium. Intermittent messages from other epochs that persisted in flowing together with the present. But the north-star voice that should indicate the meeting place never materialized nor was ever heard amid the messages hurled by those who fell into a trance.

Once again facing the sea, open to the suggestions of those echoes which contained her past. The waves, like docile workers, deposited in the slowness of their gestures, pieces of timber, strips of algae, bottle caps, flasks. A flask. A flask of perfume. The woman's hand gathered the flask and hugging it with her soft firmness, brought it to her closest silence. Her glance fell upon the strange facets, the atomizer, on that fluid, wounded by the sun's rays, that had the consistency of oils and ointments. She let the aroma touch her flesh and she felt, as in other ages, already prepared to quit a precinct, this time, an open precinct, towards the search. With a movement out of long habit, she placed the perfume upon the skin of sand which served as her dressing table. And she directed her glance towards the timber. Towards that piece of timber which lay there, patiently, as it were waiting for her. She felt between her hands the dampness of the thick sheet of long and she tried to decipher the strange letters which formed a message in a language which was now unknown to her. She noticed that the plaque was meticulously halved in two, and she drew to her bosom the humid letters, as if embracing them. Without knowing exactly what was happening, she thought she understood. She raised herself slowly and with a firm step she went overtaking the remoteness of the beach. In the distance, the station. And in the isolation of the rails, the lonely trains. A ticket. The conductor with his visor cap. The rapid movement of successive images. And over the loudspeakers, a name, a town. And over the loudspeakers, a name, a town.

She waited for the train's definitive stop. She felt herself go down the ramp, and suddenly, on the railway platform. The expanding group of passengers went scattering, space inside, taking their luggage, greetings, embraces. In the vacated space of the platform, the silhouette of a woman. Her glance intense, her contour engraved in the silence. Immobile, and in her hands, the half of a sheet of timber, and strange letters.

A brief pause. Yearned-for peace. The breath gasping and deep. They advanced so as to shorten the distance. They looked into each other's eyes, and they recognized one another.

(Translated by Angela de Hoyos)

OLGA CASANOVA-SANCHEZ

Olga Casanova-Sánchez was born in Ciales, Puerto Rico in 1947. She moved to New York with her family in 1956 where she has lived ever since. She started writing at an early age, and in 1972 Las Americas Publishing Company published her first book of poetry - *Raíz al aire* [*Root in the Air*]. Two currents run through the book: one nostalgic; the other existentialist. Diana Ramírez de Arellano, the Puerto Rican poet and critic, says of Olga's poetry: "Hay algo de magia al eco de su aire, mucho de alba, de promesa y de rocíos juveniles"["There is a magical quality in the echoing of its air; a lot of dawn, promise and youthful dew"].

Her poetry has been published in several journals, including *La Revista del Instituto de Cultura Puertorriqueña* [*The Journal of the Institute of Puerto Rican Culture*]. Her book on Puerto Rican Literature - *La crítica social en la obra novelesca de Enrique A. Laguerre* [*Social Criticism in the Novels of Enrique A. Laguerre*] - is being published by Editorial Cultural of Puerto Rico.

Olga received her Masters degree from Hunter College, and is now finishing her doctoral degree at the Graduate Center of the City University of New York. She taught at Hunter College for two years, and has been teaching at Baruch College of C.U.N.Y. since 1972.

A two page biography of Olga appears in *Enciclopedia de la mujer puertorriqueña* [*The Encyclopedia of the Puerto Rican Woman*] (San Juan, Puerto Rico: Leo International Publishers, 1975-1976).

NI DE ANTES NI DE NUNCA

¡Qué día sería que morí sin darme cuenta!
Ni absurdas

tristezas
ni absorventes
alegrías
robaron mi
ambiente.

Vida ni de antes ni de nunca.
Vivir sabiendo que me he muerto.

Olga Casanova-Sánchez

NEITHER FROM BEFORE NOR EVER

It must have been some day for me to die unaware!
Neither absurd
sadness
nor absorbent
joy
stole my
ambient.

Life neither from before nor ever.
Living knowing I have died.

(English version by Robert Lima)

NIÑA QUE SIEMPRE VA CONMIGO

Yo no sé si ésta que está aquí escribiendo
soy yo la mujer, o es aquella niña
pálida, callada y triste que jamás habló.

Yo no sé si soy la madre de aquella
niña que siempre va conmigo.

Quizás la mujer nunca ha nacido
y esté ahora naciendo de mi mano.

Olga Casanova-Sánchez

THE GIRL WHO IS ALWAYS WITH ME

I don't know if the one who is writing here
is me the woman, or that girl
pale, silent, and sad who never spoke.

I don't know if I am the mother of that
girl who is always with me.

Perhaps the woman has not been born
and is undergoing birth now at my hands.

(English version by Robert Lima)

GLADYS ZALDIVAR

Gladys Zaldívar (Cuba) received the Ed.D from the University of Havana where she also completed most of the credits towards a doctorate in Philosophy and Letters. She received a B.A. from the Institute of Secondary Education in Camagüey, Cuba. She has been a lecturer of Spanish and Spanish Literature at the Secondary Basic School ''Manuel Bisbé'' (Cuba), the University of Maryland, and Western Maryland College in the United States. Spain was her place of residence during 1967 and 1968. Gladys Zaldívar's literary works can be found in the *Colección de Poetas de la Ciudad de Camagüey,* (Anthology of Poets from the City of Camaguey) edited by Samuel Feijóo in 1958; *Lunes de Revolución* edited by Guillermo Cabrera Infante in 1960-1961; ''Página Dos'' [''Page Two''] *Prensa Libre* (Cuba); *Exilio* (N.Y.); *Cormorán y Delfín* (Buenos Aires); *Vertical* (Bolivia); *Círculo Poético* (Troy, N.Y.); *Envíos* (N.J.), etc. In 1963 she obtained the Poetry Prize granted by the National Council for the Culture of Cuba; in 1971, *El Visitante [The Visitor],* her first published book of poems, was edited in Valencia, Spain. She received her M.A. from the University of Maryland and now she is writing her doctoral thesis for the same university in the field of Spanish American literature. Dr. Zaldívar has been co-author and editor of *Julián del Casal; estudios críticos sobre su obra* (1974) [*Julián del Casal; Critical Studies of His Works*] ; (*Cinco aproximaciones a la narrativa hispanoamericana contemporánea*) [*Five Approaches to Contemporary Hispanic American Literature*] (in press) and a collection of essays on the Cuban novel. She is now finishing for publication a second book of poems, *Fabulación de Eneas* [*Fable of Eneas*] and critical essays on La Avellaneda (in press), Lezama Lima and Reynaldo Arenas. She has delivered lectures at the University of Maryland, Western Maryland College, Sarduy Gallery (N.Y.), Miami-Dade Public Library System (Fla.), Ada Merritt Community School (Fla.), Instituto de Cultura Hispánica (Fla.), etc. She belongs to the International Association of Hispanists, Sigma Delta Pi, Phi Kappa Phi, and many others.

VAGAMUNDO EN LA TORRE

Concéntrico recuerdo en la mudanza del pájaro
que regresa de ruinas
                ah templos de infancia
con su noticia su angélica fotografía que punza
como un juego enterrado en el humo
del antifaz solemne de los vasos en punto ciudadanos
y otra vez desde aquí el viaje con dos tres ángulos azules en fuga
porque pronto vendrá el número avanzando en el miedo
con su mapa de nichos su música de caballero inexorable
a enajenarnos del retorno no a la imagen de aúrea muerte
sino a la mariposa de madera donde alzamos el vuelo de
                mentiras que es tan cierto miserables tan verdad
concéntrica esperanza del vagamundo en la torre
vagamundo nutriéndose de espejos
en la inútil repetición del mismo gesto
vámonos alto cogidos del ala hasta donde el número sea ciego
alto hasta el reino del nadiemuere en que seremos un solo
                nombre único
uno solo como quieta llama descubriéndonos realizándonos
ya estoy de vuelta camaradas
sangre a sangre desciendo estos peldaños
con mi bolsa cargada de fantasmas cargada en suma de caminos
y sé que soy pez de ceniza buceador de sombra incorregible
y no me importa porque ahora soy también vértice de todos mis relojes

VAGABOND IN THE TOWER *

Concentric reminiscences in the movement of the bird
that returns from the ruins
                Oh, the infants realm
with its remembrance its angelic photograph that stings
like a game buried in the smoke
of the solemn mask of the staccato steps which are caring for us
and once again the trip form here is one or two or three
                angles of blue that fly away
because soon the number will advance in fear

with its map of niches its music from an inexorable gentleman
who comes to drive us away from a return not to the image of golden death
not to the image that always flies with foam
but to the wooden butterfly where we rise high in a flight
       of lies so certain so true you wretches
concentric wish of the vagabond in the tower
a vagabond who lives in the mirrors
in the useless repetition of the same gesture
let's go on up grabbing on the wing up to where numbers cannot see
high up to the kingdom where no one dies where we will be but one single name
one alone like a quiet flame that discovers us and makes
us whole but now I have come back comrades
drop by drop I am descending the stairway
my bag is filled with phantoms filled that is to say with regal roads
and I know that I am a fish of ashes diving incorregible into the shadows
but now it matters not because I also am the highest point
       far above all my clocks.

HECTOR FLOTANDO EN LA NOCHE

somos al margen de la muerte en ella nos nombramos
cruz de sombras y seguimos aullando la sangre del recuerdo
nos bautiza la muerte y cenamos presencias increíbles
(la sangre del recuerdo derrumba sobre mí sus muros)
los jazmines levantan pequeñas banderas en la noche
las baldosas heridas acuden con su queja de musgo
un golpe de azafrán reconstruye la sonrisa del ángel de mí
todos acuden a la evanescencia del orden para venir al polvo
y soy la casa ardiendo en el oculto espejo de lo cotidiano
el amoroso afán roto en la estrella como un río deshojándose
el aroma del suelo escondido en la palabra que no nombra su nombre
el pecho de la arena abierto sobre tanto viaje en los ejes de la búsqueda
soy el incierto número de la turquesa que derrama sobre mí su lluvia despiadada
y azul es cada acto en el costado de la esfera donde mi corazón anuncia su ruptura
soy el duelo del aire camaradas la imagen de un fondo oscuro

descorro sombras infinitas mientras veo jugar los dioses en la cuerda
descorro sombras manipulo el olvido como una negra baraja
que ha de quemarse junto al árbol que ha de sepultarse en la lengua del árbol
que ha de resucitar en los pétalos de fuego que pronuncian los muertos
el olvido camaradas es un pájaro que ha de traer la noticia del jade a nuestros
huesos
buscad la tierra que sostenga el párpado del áscua
que veo jugar los dioses en la cuerda
buscad el templo de la espuma el altar de sonidos
que veo jugar los dioses en la cuerda
buscad la hostia de recuerdos donde el penate eche anclas
en la recóndita flor de nuestro espejo

HECTOR FLOATING IN THE NIGHT*

We exist on the edge of death death gives us our names
a shadowy cross and we go on trailing the blood of memory
death baptizes us and we dine upon incredible presences
(the blood of memory topples its walls upon me)
jazmines raise tiny flags in the night
the cobblestones when struck respond in mossy protest
a touch of saffron rebuilds the angel smiling at me
everyone responds to the evanescence of order by coming to dust
and I am the house burning in the secret mirror of dailiness
the loving desire broken upon the star like a river losing its petals
the fragrance of soil hidden in the word that names not its name
the breast of sand open to endless voyages along the lines of search
I am the vague number of the turquoise that sheds upon me its heartless rain
and blue is every act in the side of the sphere where my heart predicts its
rupture
I am the lament of the air comrades the image of a dark depth
I pull open infinite shadows as I see the gods playing on tightrope
I pull open shadows I shuffle forgetfulness like a black deck of cards
which will burn up close to the tree which will be buried in the tree's tongue
which will rise again in the fire petals pronounced by the dead
forgetfulness comrades is a bird that will bring news of jade into our bones
look for earth to sustain the flickering glow of the coals
for I see the gods playing on the tightrope
look for the temple of foam the altar of sounds
for I see the gods playing on the tightrope

look for the wafer of memories in which Penates can be anchored
in the secret flower of our mirror

*Translations are by Arthur A. Natella and Elias L. Rivers.

IRIS ZAVALA

Iris M. Zavala was born in Ponce, Puerto Rico under the sign of Capricorn a dark night of December, 1936. Ponce is one of the most important towns of the island, in the geographical extreme of the great triangle. Thirteen dusty streets, inhabited by black eyes and grave gestures.

After a few years, she went to San Juan, the capital city, where she studied at the Academia Católica. With adolescence came the university, readings, writing. A B.A. in Río Piedras was followed by a trip to Spain; in 1962 she finished her Ph.D. at the University of Salamanca. Her childhood and adolescent hero, Miguel de Unamuno, came to life in her first book— *Unamuno y su teatro de conciencia* (1963) [*Unamuno's Theater of Conscience*].

Scholarship and creation have been her goals since childhood. Scholarly books and articles on XVIII to XXth century literature and history of ideas, as well as poetry. Both concepts are to her, the same creative process and she tries to merge them. Therefore the reader (if any) will find that her three books of poetry— *Barrio doliente* (1965) [*Scarred Clay*], *Poemas prescindibles* (1971) [*Prescindable Poems*], *Escritura desatada* (1975) [*Untied Writing*]— make wide use of history, philosophy, art, literature and foreign languages (French, Italian, German, Latin). Many friends helped her in writing her books, most of them are dead and illustrious: Dante, Cervantes, Erasmus, Goethe, Marx. Their peculiar erudition will save her, she hopes, from lamentable blunders. Indefatigable research in archives and libraries has given her whatever understanding she has of memories, expectations and disappointments.

Ms. Zavala is in the process of finishing a *novella, Speciosa miracula* [*Fanciful Dreams*], in which she tries to recreate the turn of the century in Ponce in a fanciful way, liberated from the restraints of time. She invokes obscure people, forgotten builders from the depths of the past, hesitating whether to bring them up to the screen of the present. Suggestions are accepted.

Since in the capitalist age a human being must dutifully put on layers of makeup and dress, Ms. Zavala is a professor of Hispanic Languages at SUNY at Stony Brook. She has published various scholarly books on Peninsular and Latin American Literature and she earnestly hopes that she has been able to slip out of each new fashion, reappraising to her students the nature of literature, bedfellow of truth.

The first two poems presented here, and their translations, are taken from *The Puerto Rican Poets*, and the last poem is from *Escritura desatada*.

El gran mamut...

El gran mamut sueña quijotes
de enormes ojos de neón
monstruosa luciérnaga que enfoca
un continente desolado
o será una isla sola
protegida por el dios de los ejércitos
el que Moisés llevaba
y traía
humo viento fetiche
hágase la luz
ya hecha de metal
no usado por enormes
fábricas higiénicas lustrosas
donde un hombre o será un esclavo
amarillo negro y blanco
ya casi sin color
produce su artefacto
que en 1943 extermina
ángel de luz
satanás histórico
ya olvidado
que se reproduce y se transporta
en largos y admirables
retadores de sonido y tiempo
dirigidos por quijotes
vestidos de western
con cabellos largos

Sonrisa mentira cohetes...

Sonrisa mentira cohetes
abre sus brazos de animal
acuático
o anaconda atrapado
el soldado
de Minnesota Filipinas San Juan
negro criollo all american
irracional
ernorme gato amaestrado
que hunde sus uñas
perfumadas y sinuosas
en tibia carne
de otro hombre
voz incomprensible
en este mundo cuadriculado.

Smile Lie Rockets...

Smile lie rockets
opens his arms of an aquatic
animal
or a trapped anaconda
the soldier
from Minnesota Philippines San Juan
Black creole *all american*
irrational
enormous trained cat
that sinks his perfumed and
sensuous nails
into the warm flesh
of another man
incomprehensible voice
in this squared world.

(Translated by Digna Sánchez-Méndez)

y pequeños mensajes
llama de amor viva
para Ho Twyn Li y Ernesto Pérez
carbonizados.

The Great Mammoth...

The great mammoth dreams quixotes
of enormous neon eyes
monstrous fireflies that focus
on a desolate continent
or is it a lone island
protected by the God of armies
the one Moses brought
and took back
smoke wind fetish
let there be light
already made of metal
not used by enormous
lustrous hygienic factories
where a man or is it a slave
yellow black and white
almost without color
produces his artifact
that in 1943 exterminates
angel of light
historical satans
already forgotten
who are reproduced and transported
in long and wonderful
challengers of sound and time
led by quixotes
in western dress
with long hair
and small messages
flame of living love
for Ho Twyn Li and Ernesto Pérez
charred.

(Translated by Digna Sánchez-Méndez)